KITCHEN PLANNING
MONOCHROME

WITH PERSPECTIVE DRAWING ESSENTIALS

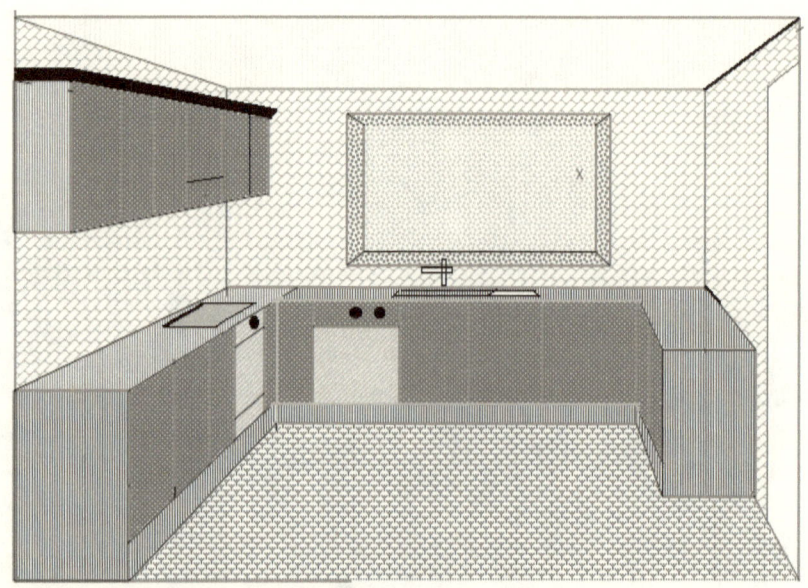

1

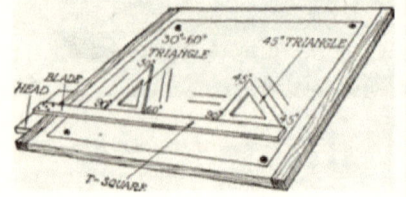

INTRODUCTION TO PERSPECTIVE

This is a new look at perspective especially for the paperback format which has a limited number of pages. This publication is all about perspectives and not about planning. We have already published various planning guides and we will be publishing a kitchen planning and perspective and a bathroom version. Please note this is a MONOCHROME version which allows us to offer a really comprehensive guide with STEP BY STEP instructions, at a very keen price

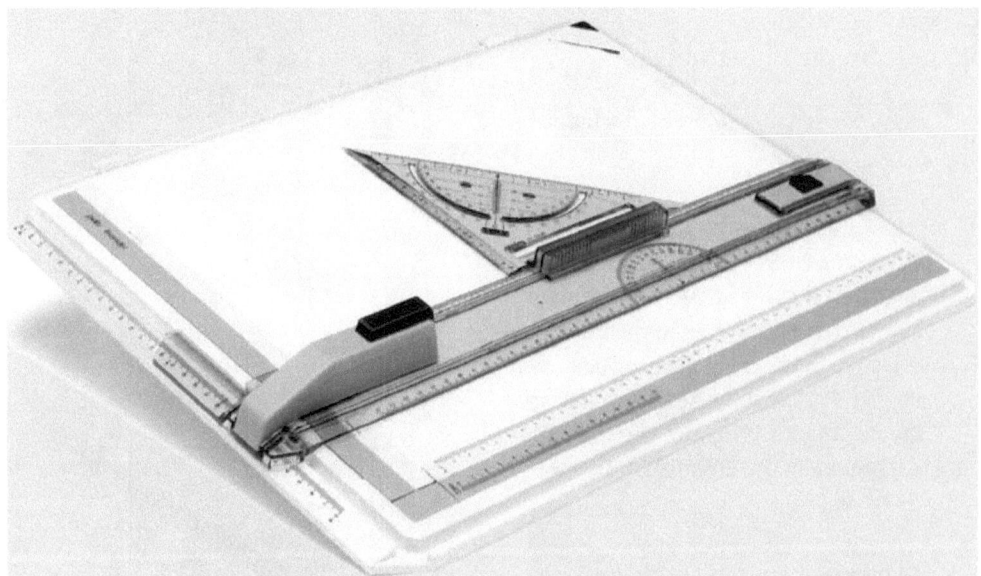

EQUIPMENT

It is best to start by familiarising yourself with the drawing instruments. Don't worry if you cannot follow the drawing to begin with. It will soon fall into place and you will start to see the perspective earlier and earlier at each attempt. When you handle the pens or pencils don't make too hard an impression. In fact a light stroke is the best technique but you may need to start a bit heavier just to follow the process Lets start with the drawing board, clearly many professionals will be using a full size drawing board but the A4 board is perfectly adequate for most purposes, Easy to carry around and simple to use.

You should find information supplied with the board but most of them are similar. There is a fixed horizontal ruler which slides up and down the board and has a lock (shown in red in this case) You should not draw any lines unless the ruler is locked. There are some big, famous German brands such as Rotring, offering products at competitive prices. Walk into any major stationers and you should find a selection.

The boards have a track around the edges so it can be used in portrait or landscape mode. Horizontal lines are drawn with the main sliding ruler. Vertical and angle lines are drawn using the set square. You can see the 45° set square in the illustration below.

To become proficient in all the basic techniques you will need a scale rule, a 45° and a 30° set square.

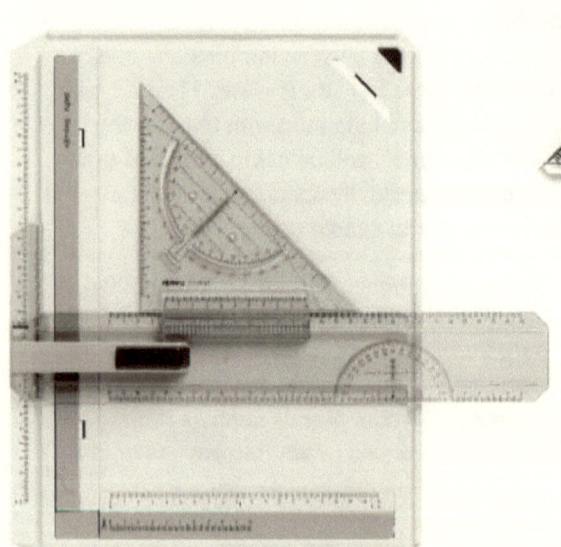

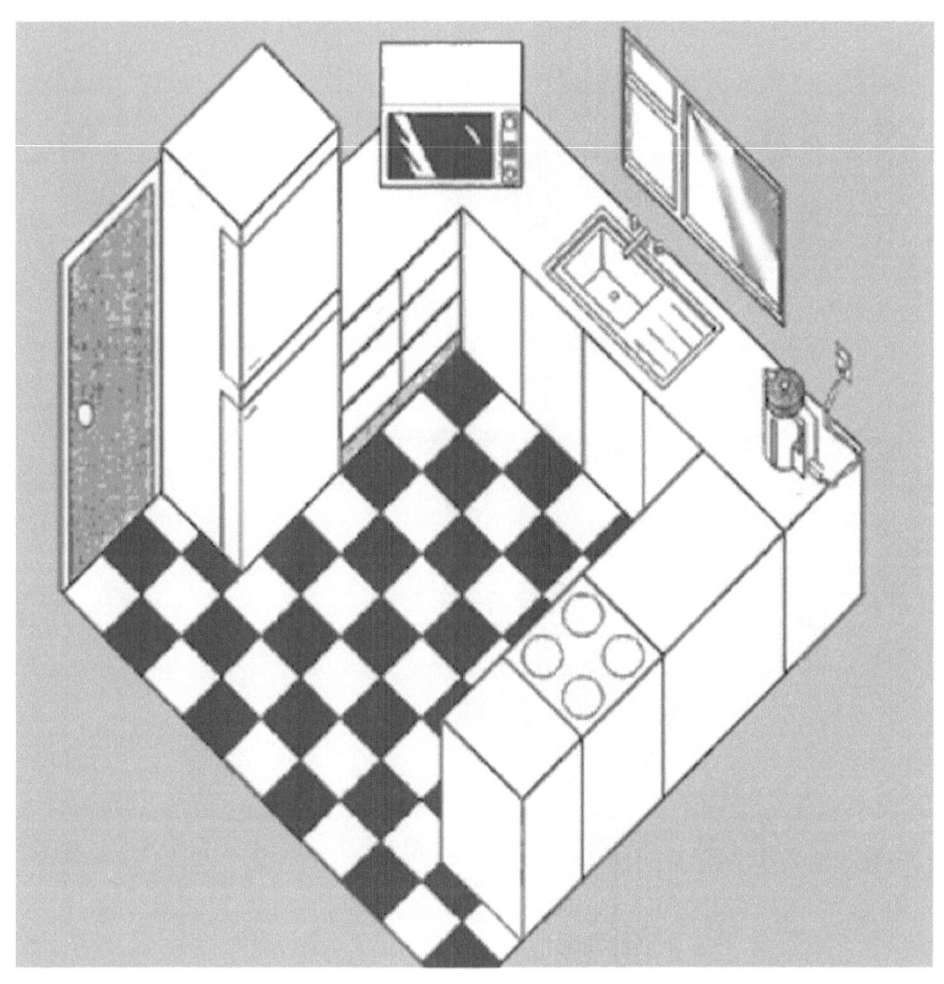

VARIATIONS of 3D DRAWING

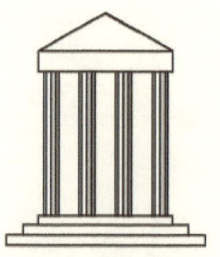

Front elevation

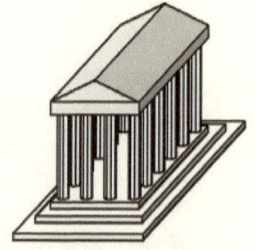

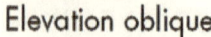

Elevation oblique

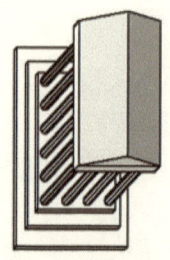

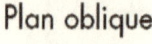

Plan oblique

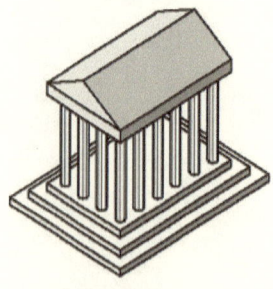

Isometric

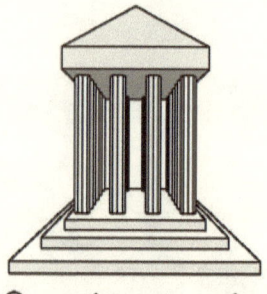

One-point perspective

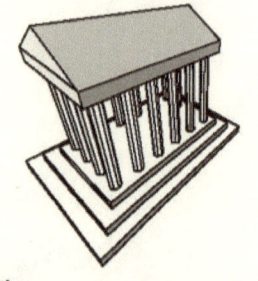

Three-point perspective

TYPES OF 3D DRAWING TECHNIQUES

There are a large number of techniques but the main ones we will be considering here are AXONOMET-RIC, ISOMETRIC, 1 POINT PERSPECTIVE, 2 POINT PERSPECTIVE AND BIRD'S EYE PERSPECTIVE. Axonometric and Isometric are similar techniques but using 45° and 30° set squares respectively. These are both in scale whatever you draw. they are sometimes referred to as parallel perspective or planametric.

The other techniques are true perspectives using one vanishing point or two vanishing points. Only part of the drawing is in an actual scale. The rest of the dimensions - the projected dimensions - need to be calculated or found with the perspective ruler. We will discuss the perspective measurements later but first we need to look at the very quick, and simple techniques of Isometric and Axonometric.

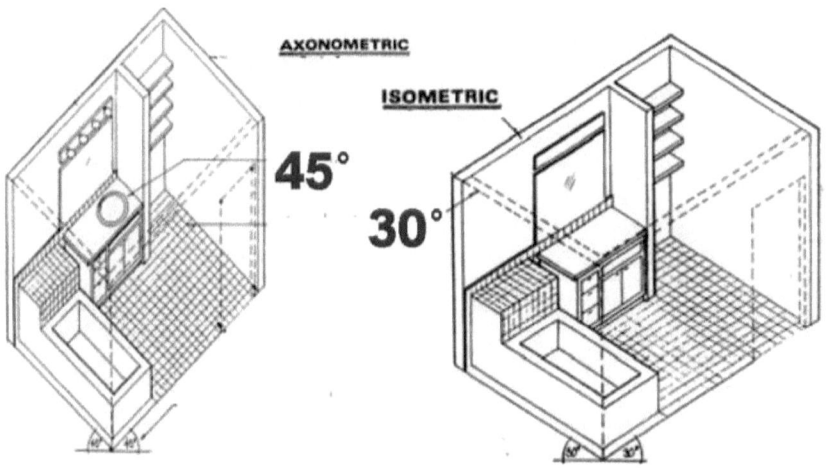

As you can see, the Axonometric method uses 90° vertical lines and 45° projection lines. the Isometric is virtually the same techniques but uses 30° projection lines.

Although both drawings above show bathrooms we have found that the Axonometric is easiest for bathrooms and the Isometric best for kitchens.

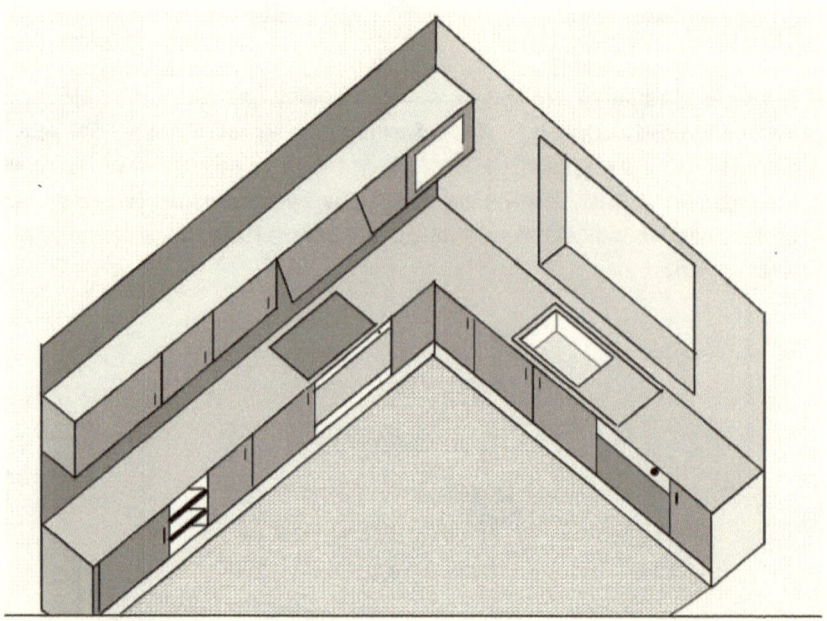

3

AXONOMETRIC & ISOMETRIC

Ok let's start drawing. Clearly we prefer to use a drawing board but you can use a simple drawing programme on a computer such as Adobe Illustrator or similar types which are often very cheap or even free. the choice is yours but if you have the dexterity for hand drawing you can produce a superior presentation - that's what it is all about

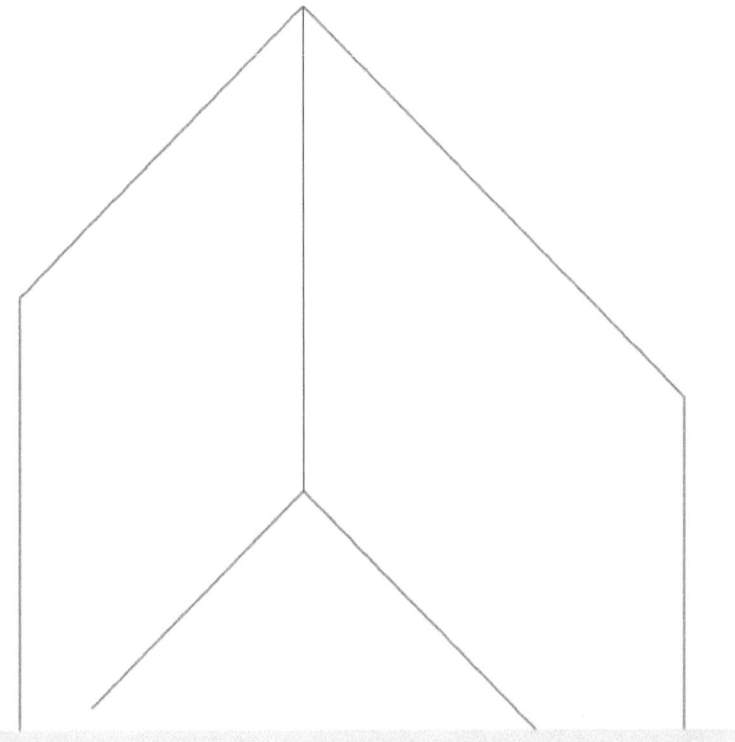

AXONOMETRIC
KITCHEN
STEP 1

SIMPLE BASICS

Start with a vertical line to show the corner of the room you wish to highlight. Use a standard 2.4m high in a 1:20 scale. For larger rooms you can use a 1:25 scale. At the top and the bottom of this line use your 45° set square to project the floor and ceiling along both walls. Using yourr scale ruler measure the lenght of each wall as required by the plan and draw a vertical line at each end to complete the room outline. Keep the lines nice and light as you will need to erase hidden lines later.

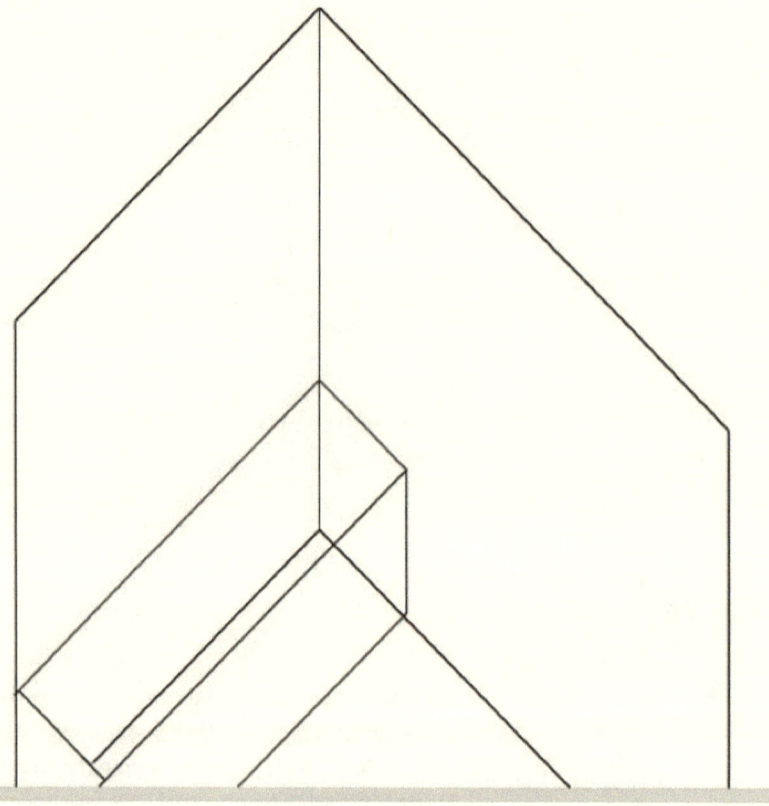

Now construct the
BASE LINE carcase
outine using the
same technique

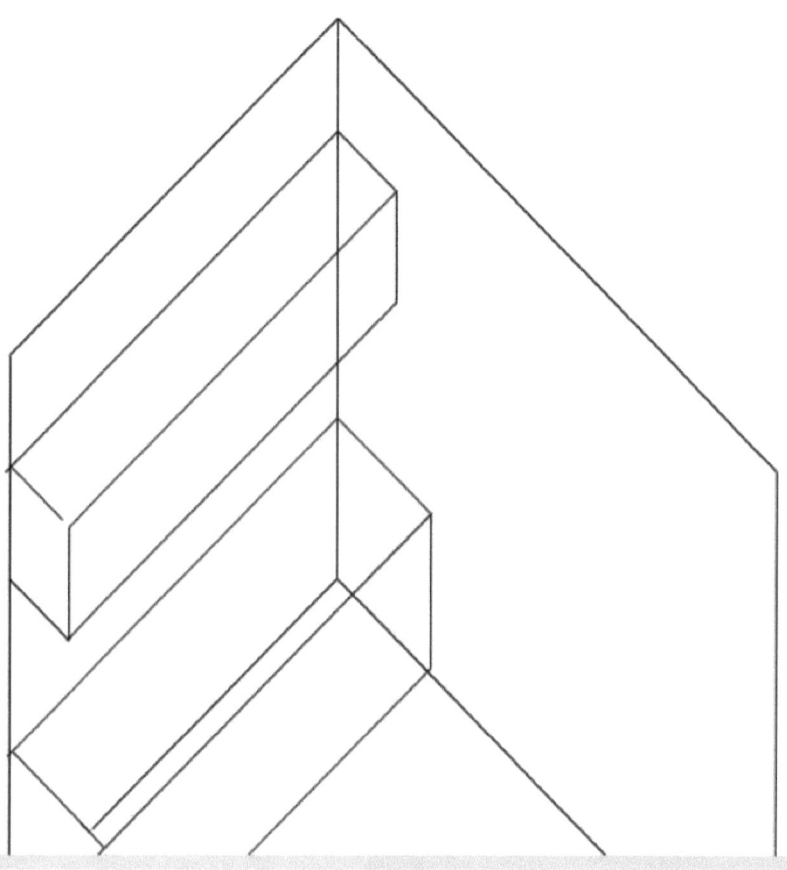

Now construct the
WALL UNIT
carcase outine
using the same
technique

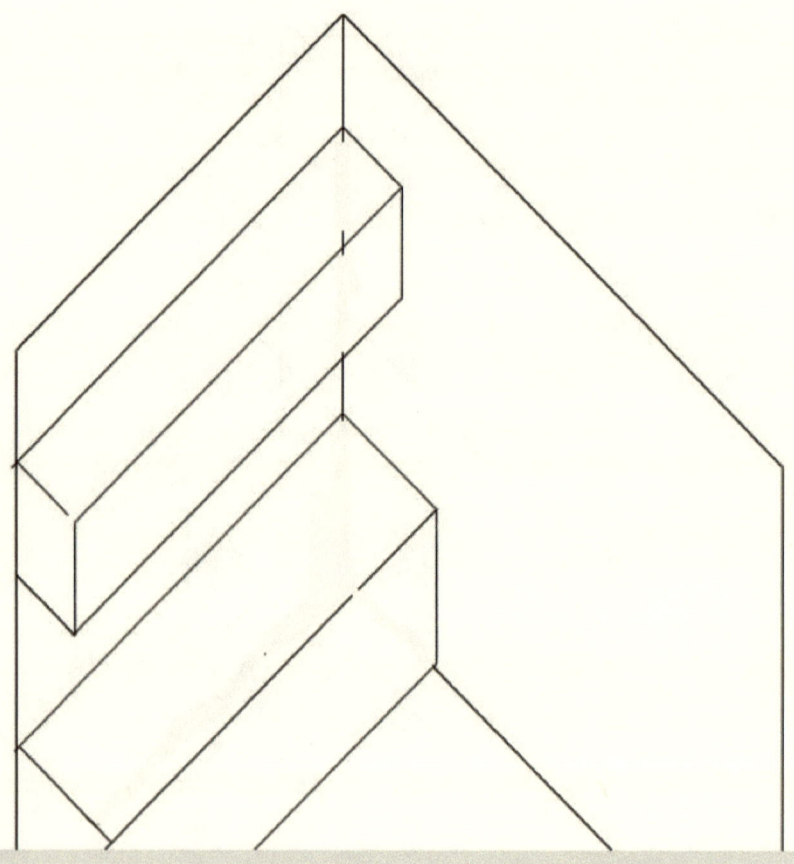

Now erase the
various floor lines
etc which are
hidden by the
carcassing

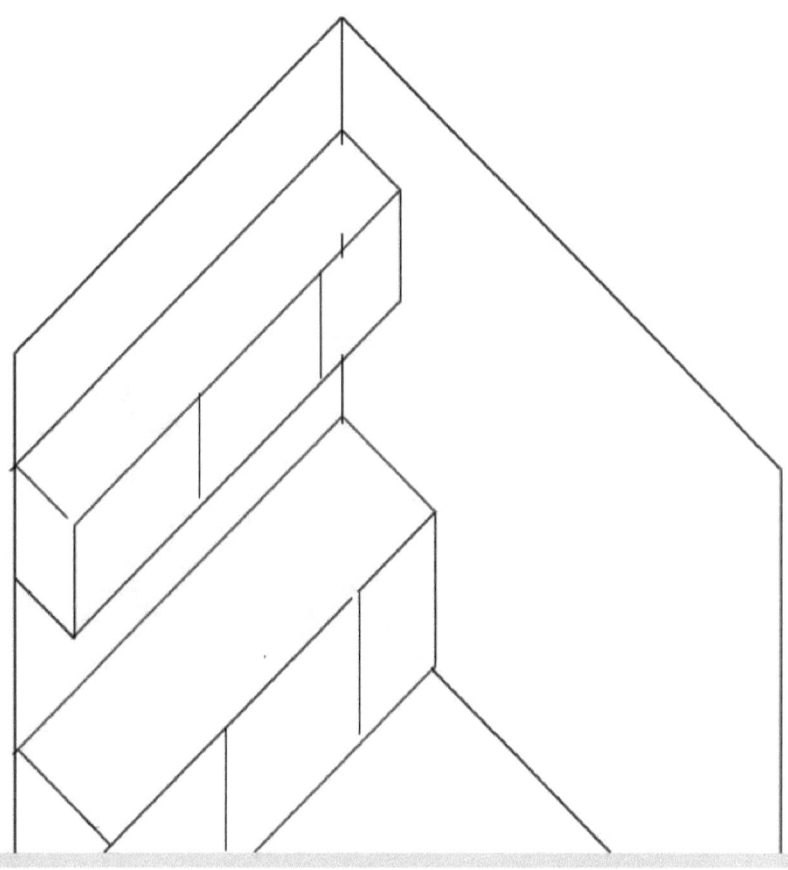

Using vertical lines
show the various
divisions on the
wall and base
units . Everything is
in scale

Finishing touches

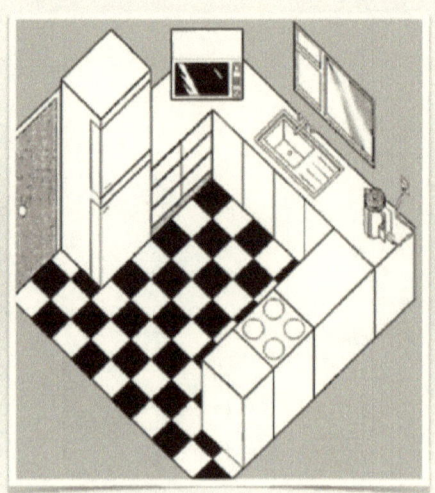

* add the appliance details (control panels etc.)

* add furniture details (cornice, light pelmet, gallery rails etc)

* add architectural and decorative features (doors, windows, jars, vases etc)

You may wish to leave this stage until you have practised more.

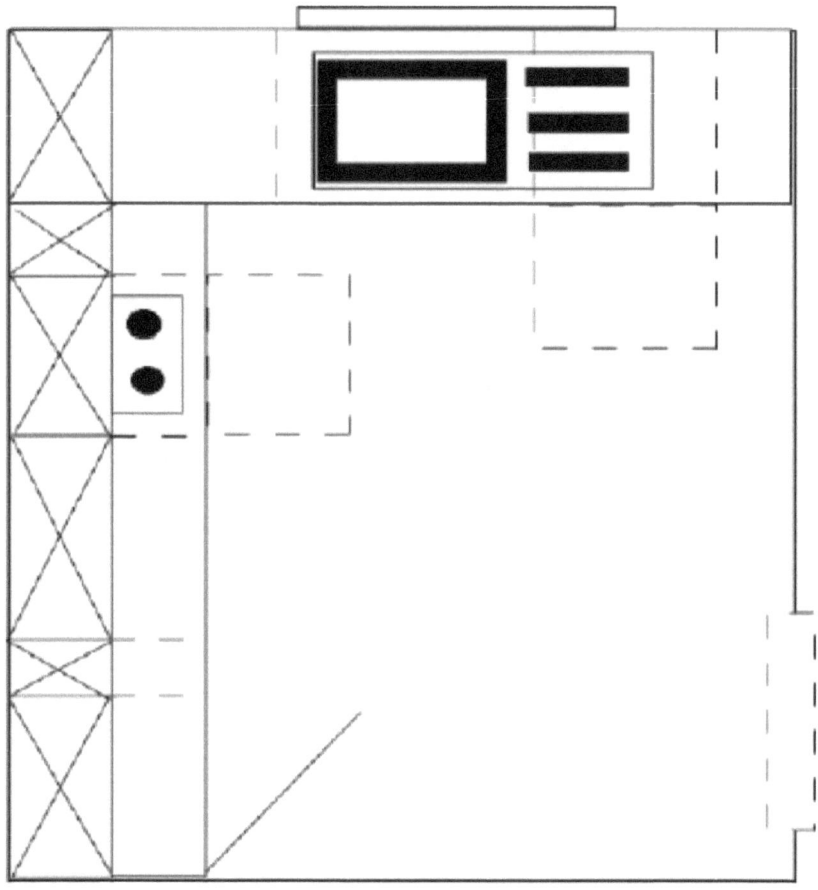

AXONOMETRIC KITCHEN DETAILED

We are now going to look at another Axonometric plan but with a bit more detail. The sizes are not shown and the plan will not be true to scale after printing but if you have any kitchen or bathroom experience it should be obvious.. For example you can see a cooker and a dishwasher with a drop down door these are obviously 600mm.

As before the
corner of the room
in scale

Mark off the height
of the room - either
the actual or the
default
measurement

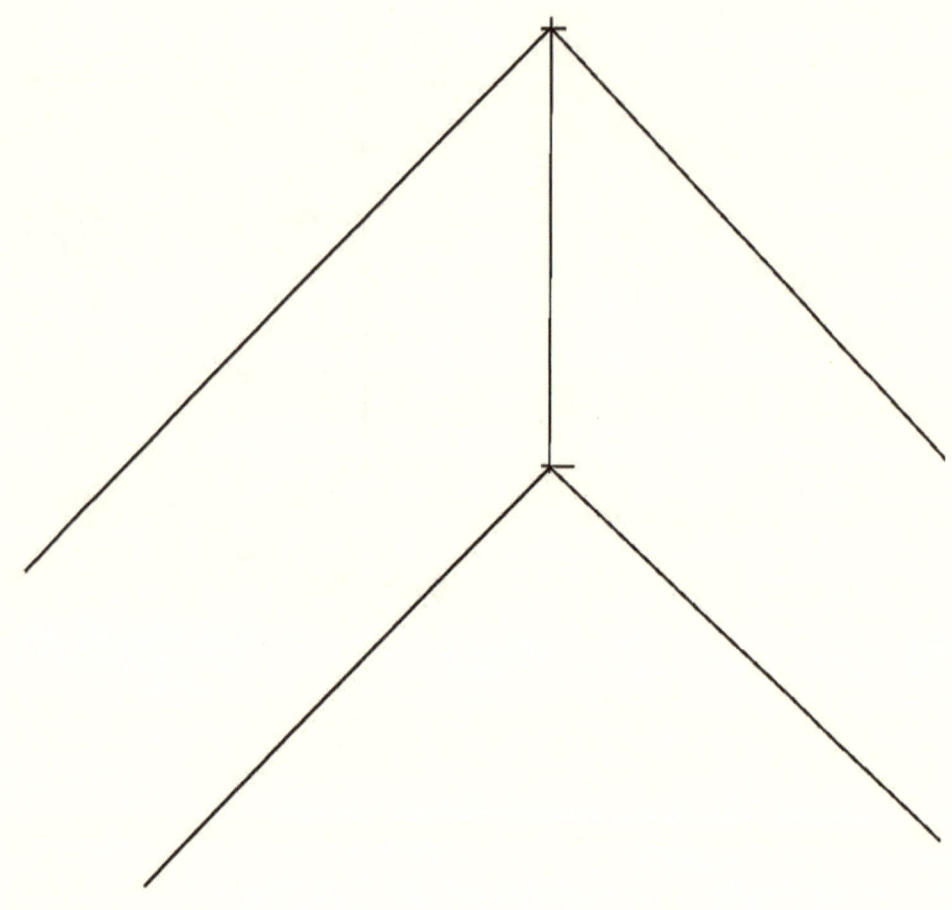

Project the two
walls from these
measurements

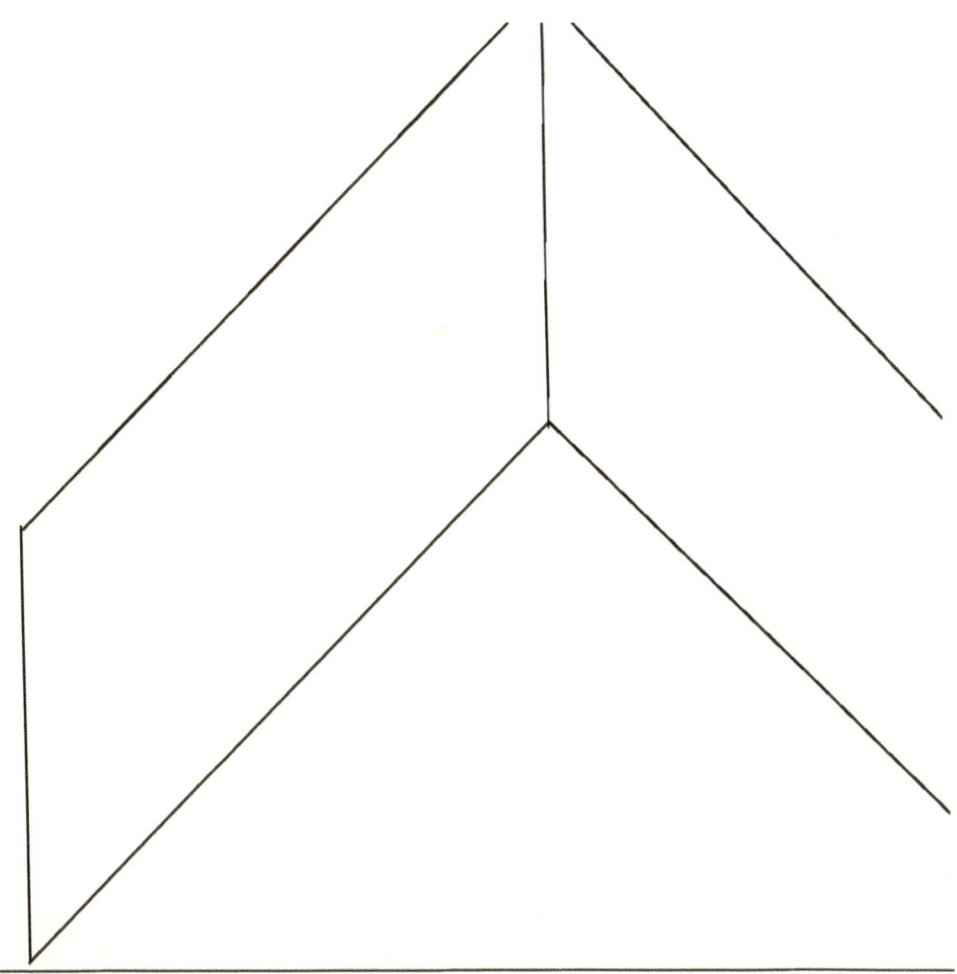

Measure the ends
of the walls as your
scale plan provides

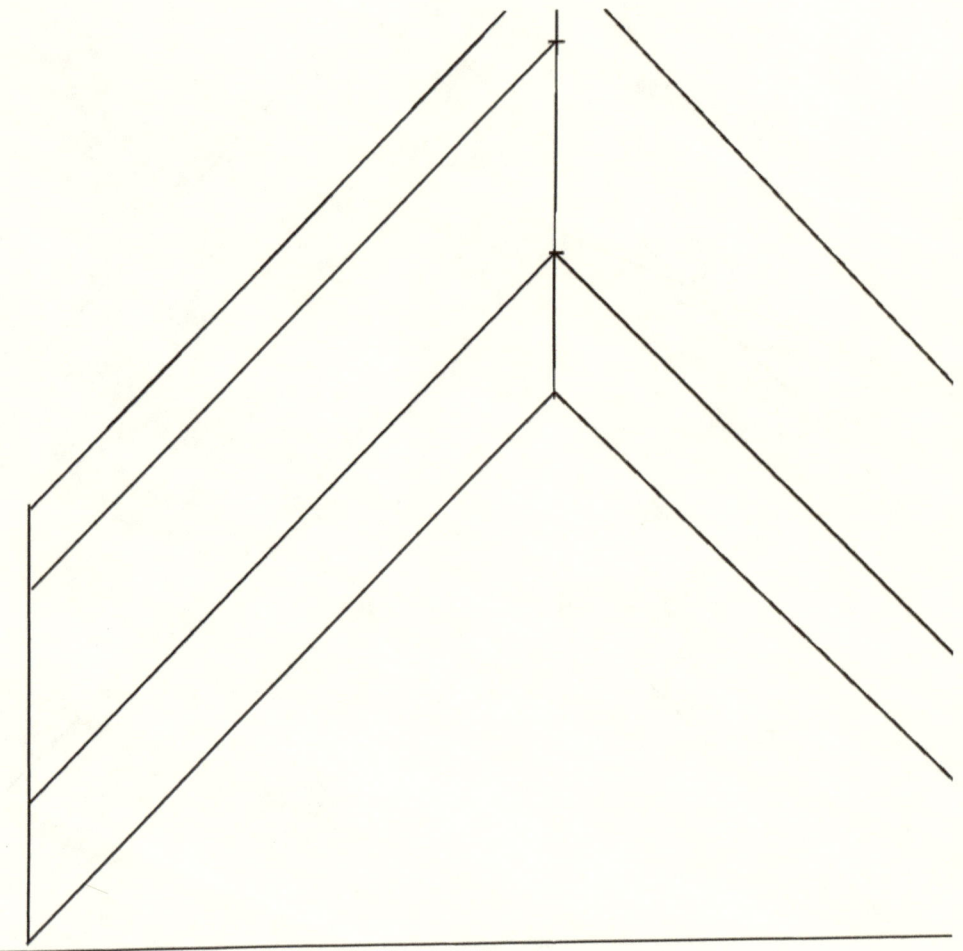

Proceed to show
the worktop height
and the wall unit
height in scale.
You can also leave
a wall unfinished
if , for example,
units do not run the
whole length

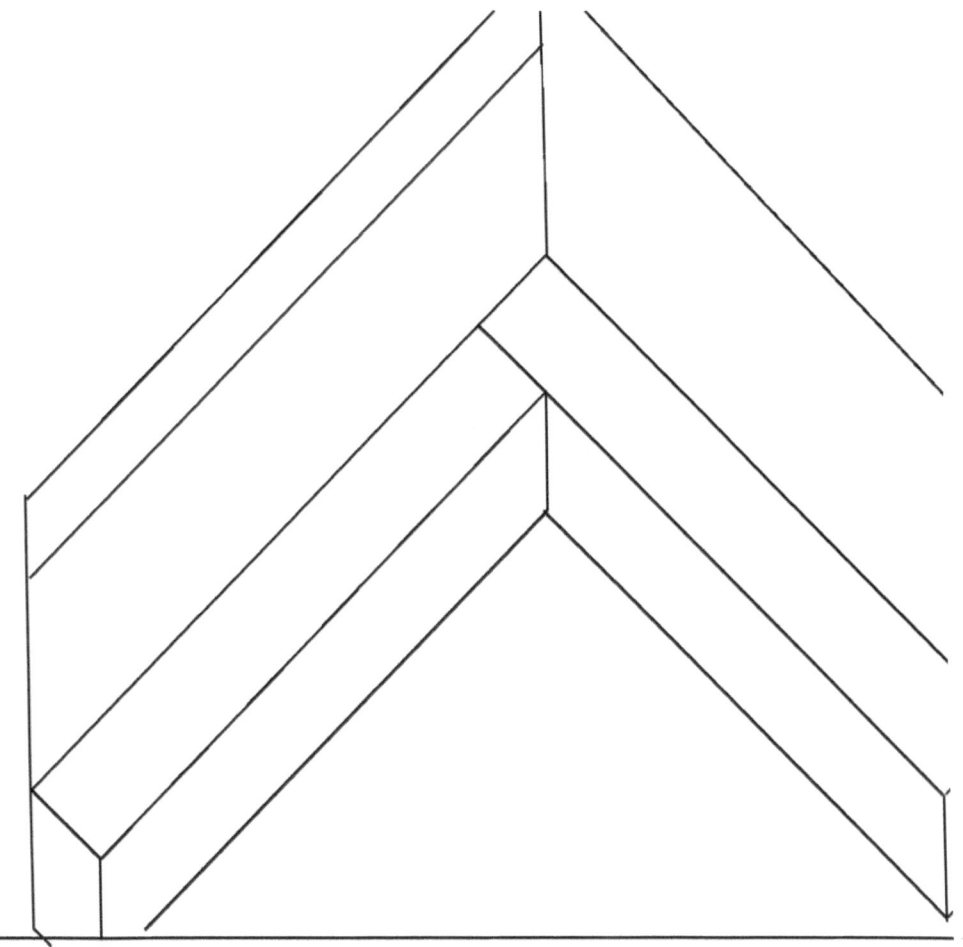

We are now
finishing the base
line carcassing

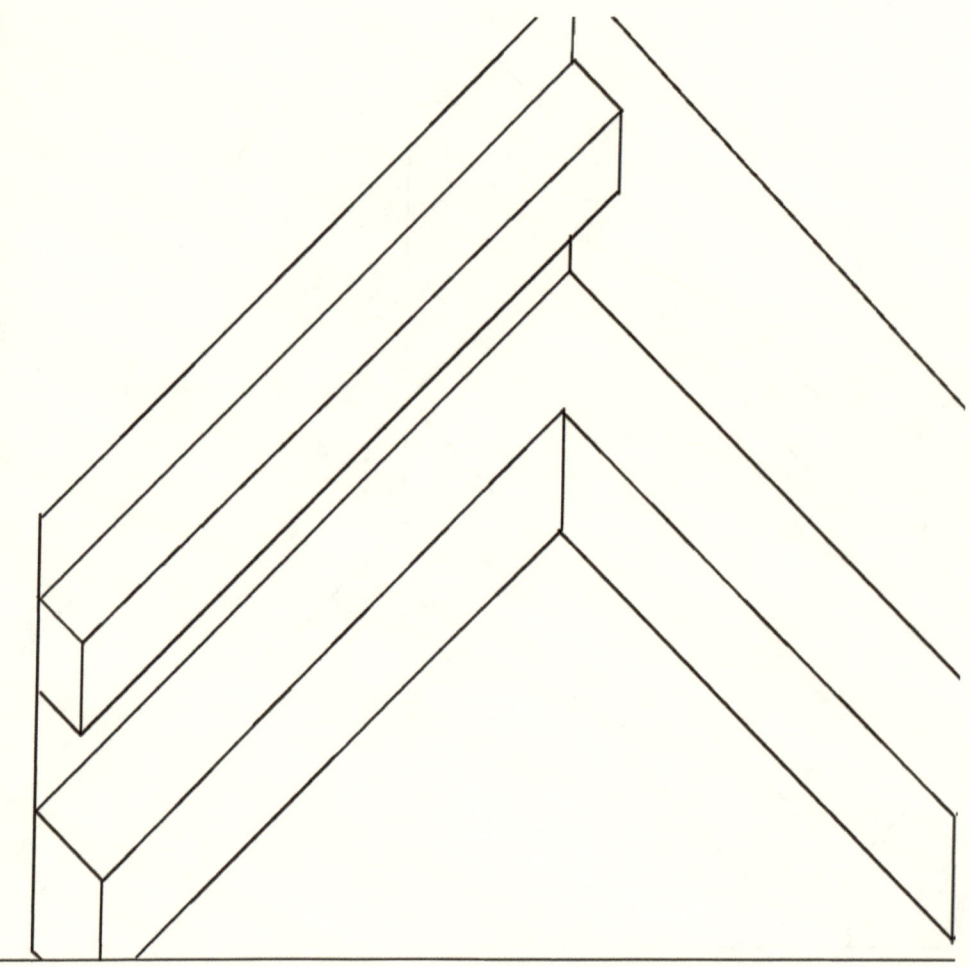

Proceeding to
complete the wall
carcassing and
remove the hidden
lines.

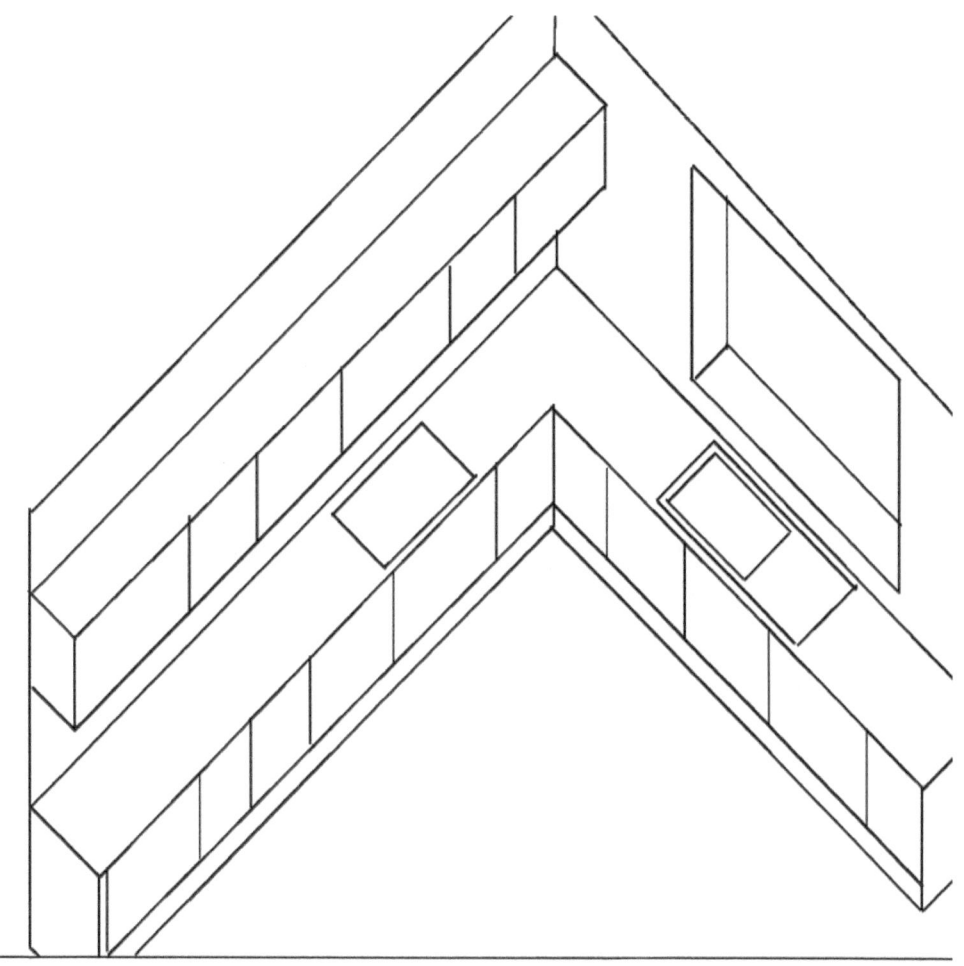

Now adding unit
sizes and various
details such as
windows sink , hob
etc.

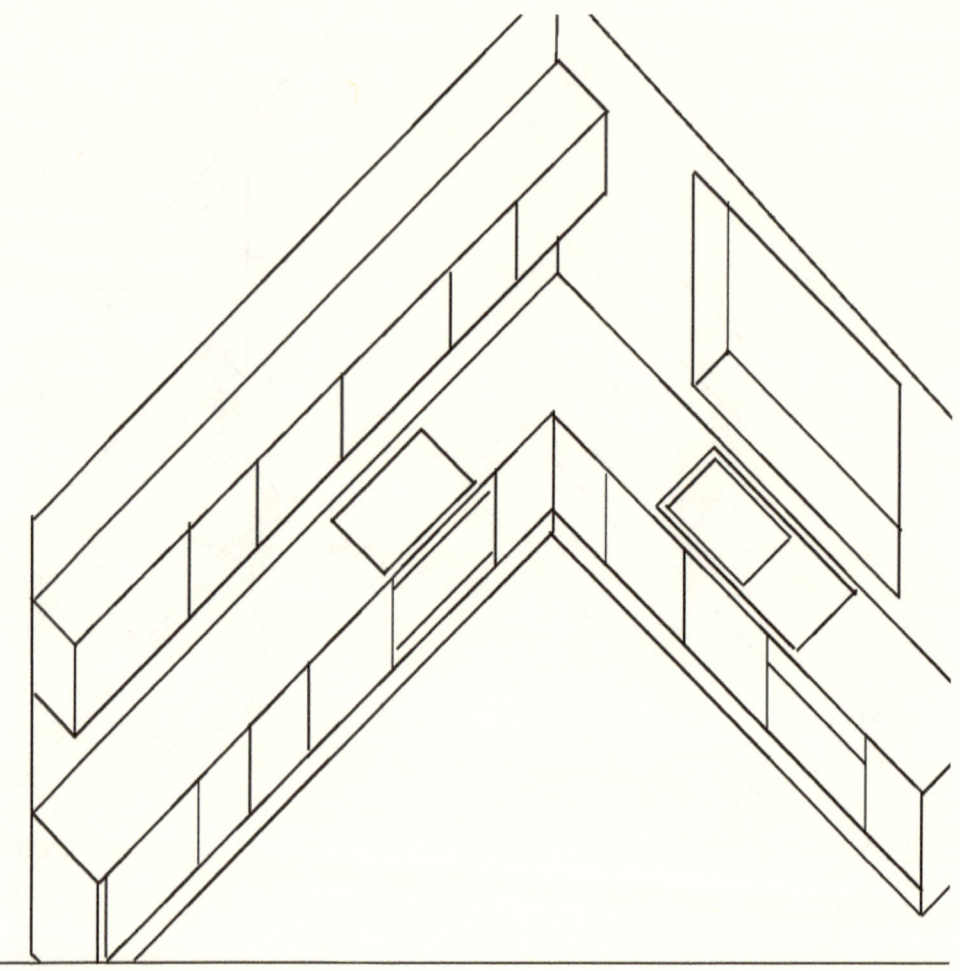

Continuing with
detail of appliances
plinths - you can
also add worktop
thickness and other
finer details if
desired.

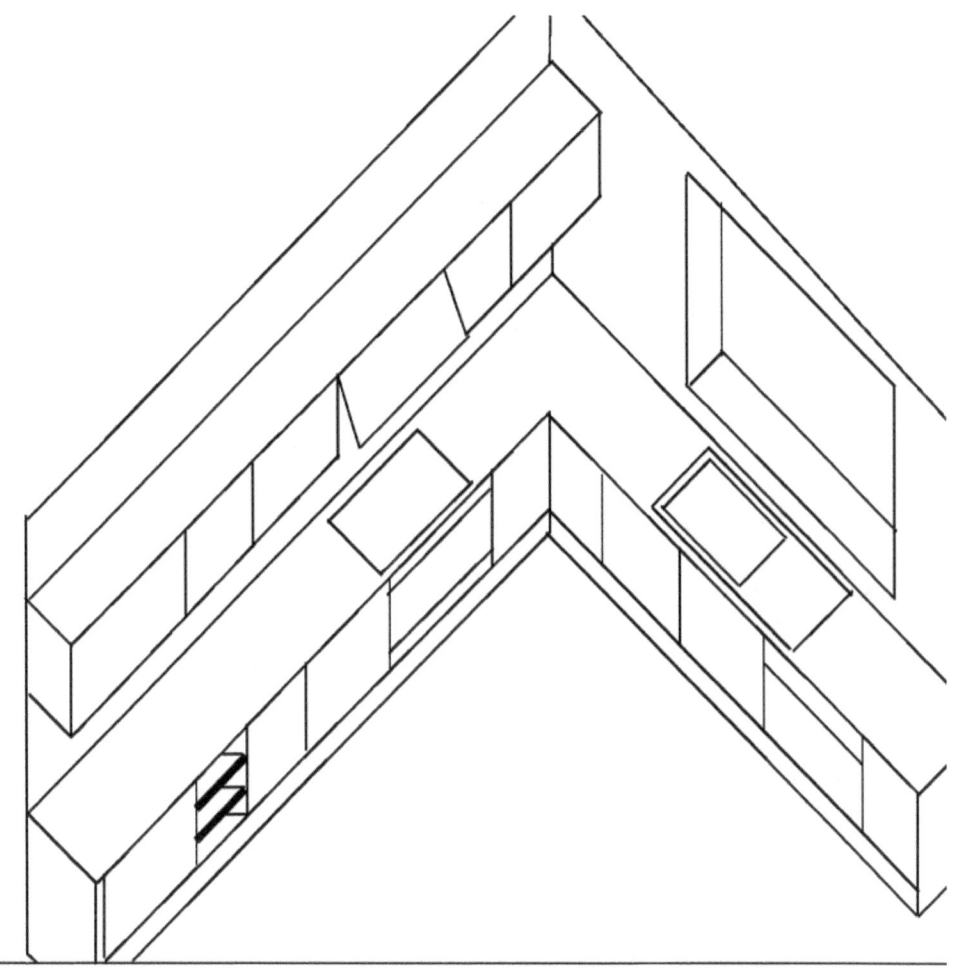

Adding other
features such as the
extended cooker
hood door and a
shelving unit

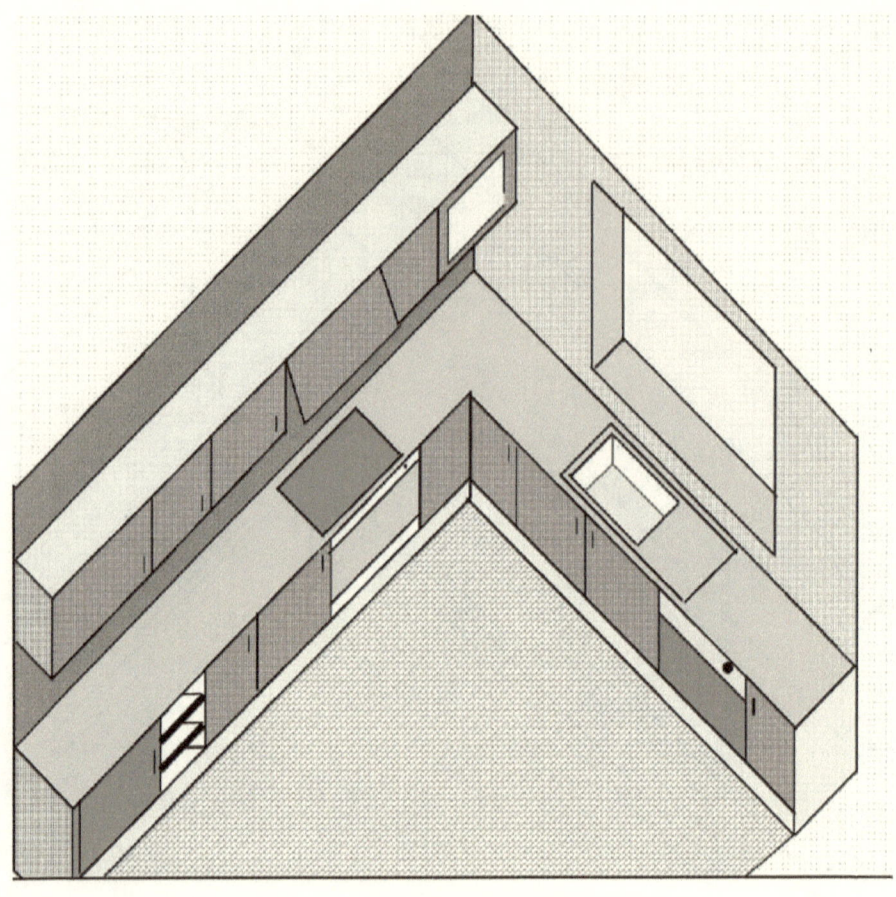

Final detail with
flooring and
rendering - very
effective in colour

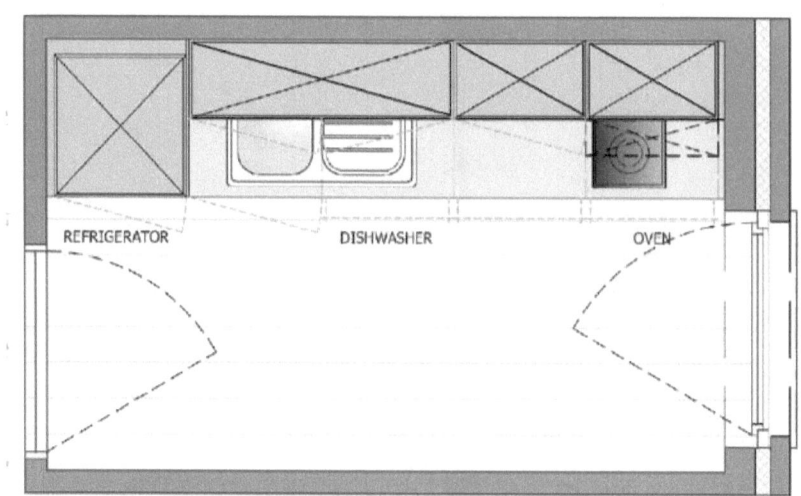

REFRIGERATOR DISHWASHER OVEN

ISOMETRIC KITCHEN METHOD

This is essentially the same as the Axonometric method but using the 30/60° set square. You will soon learn when to use the 60° set square but you will also find it useful for things like cooker hood doors coming out from the wall unit line.

Always remember to start with a SCALE PLAN and draw everything in ISOMETRIC to the same scale throughout

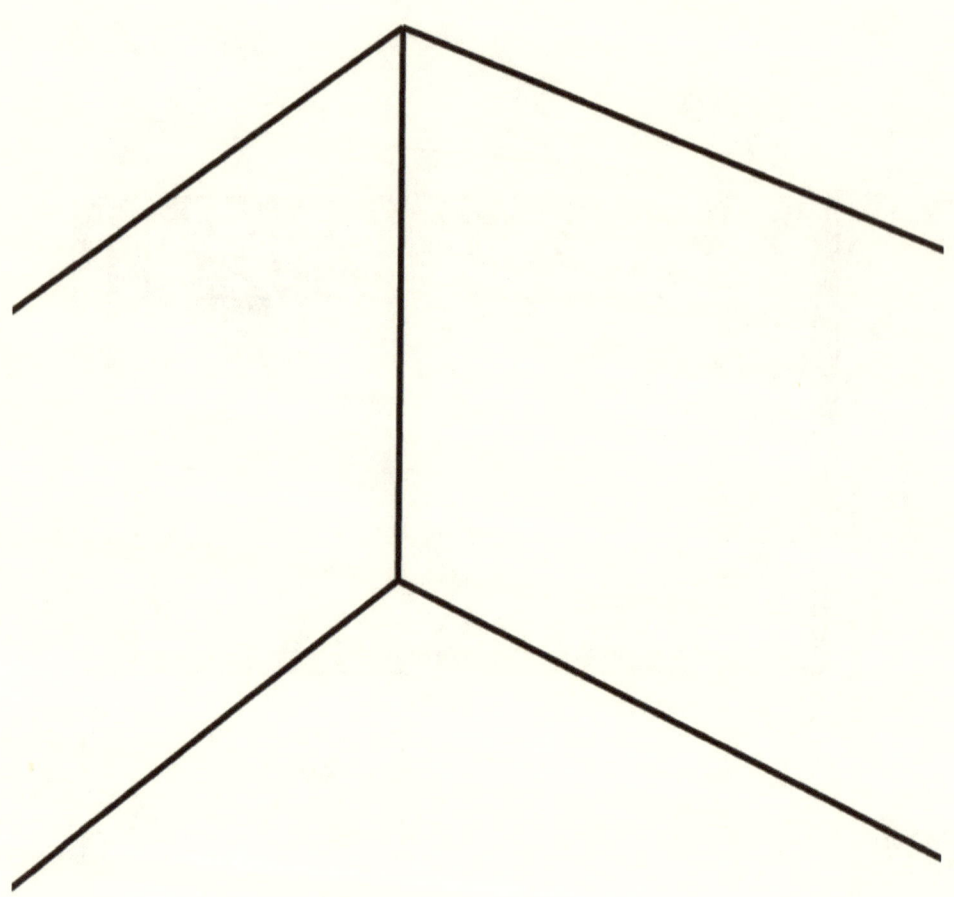

As with the
Axonometric
choose the corner
then draw the walls

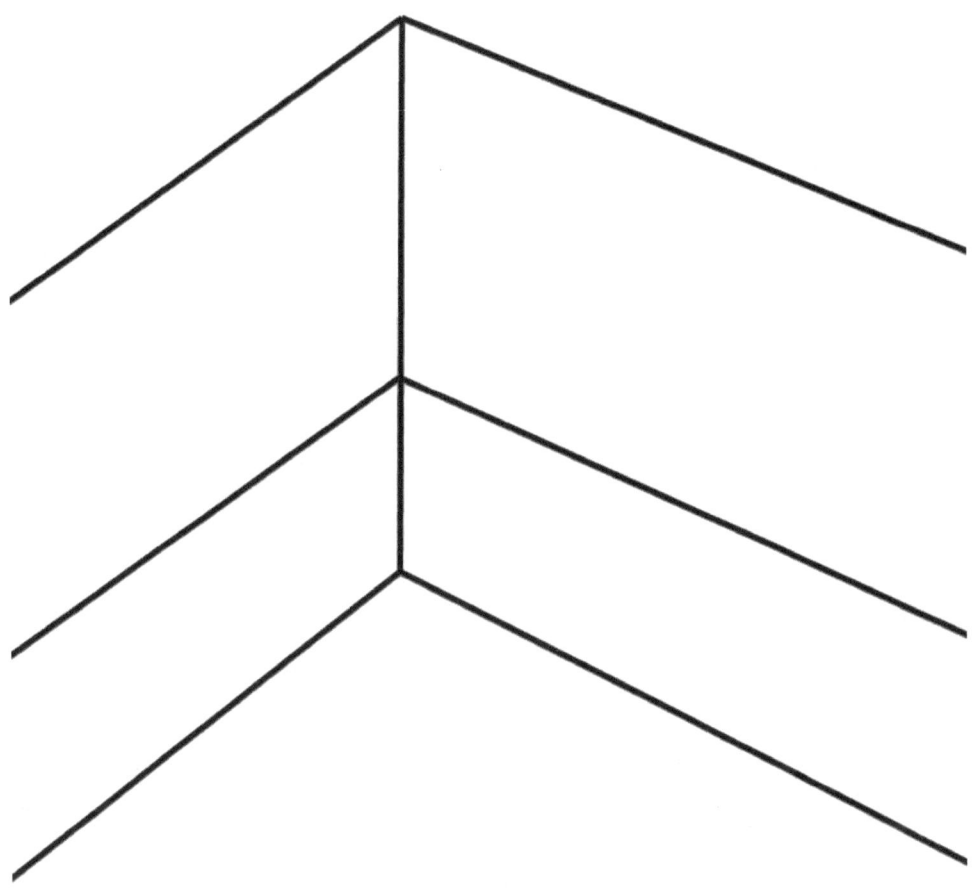

Then start laying
out the carcassing.

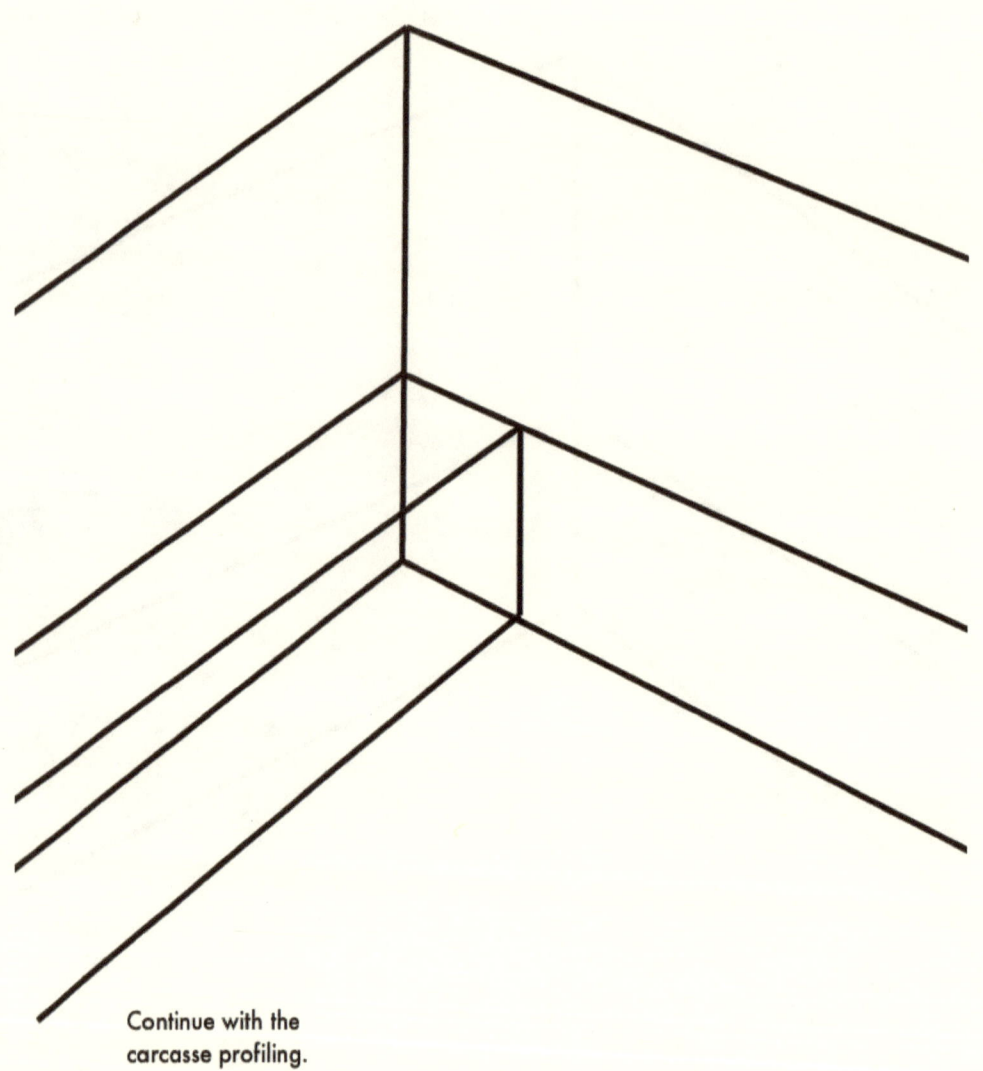

Continue with the
carcasse profiling.

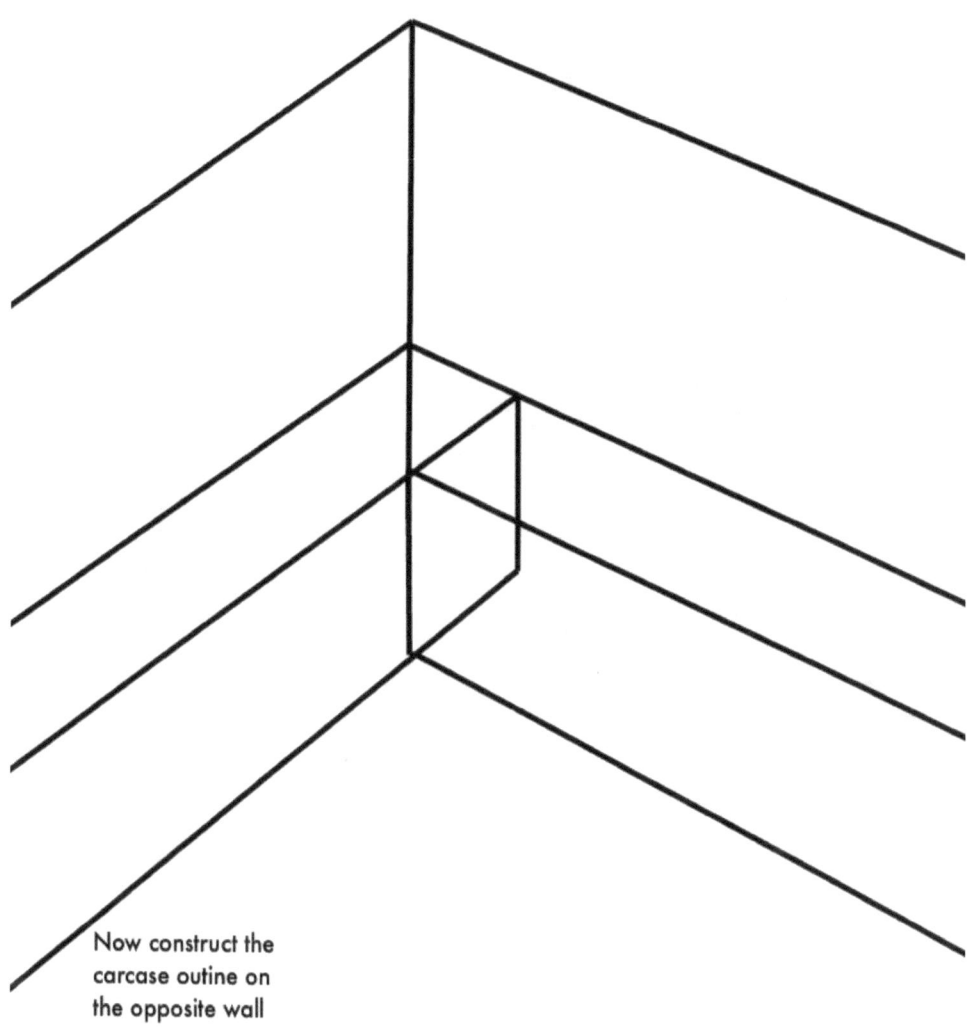

Now construct the
carcase outine on
the opposite wall

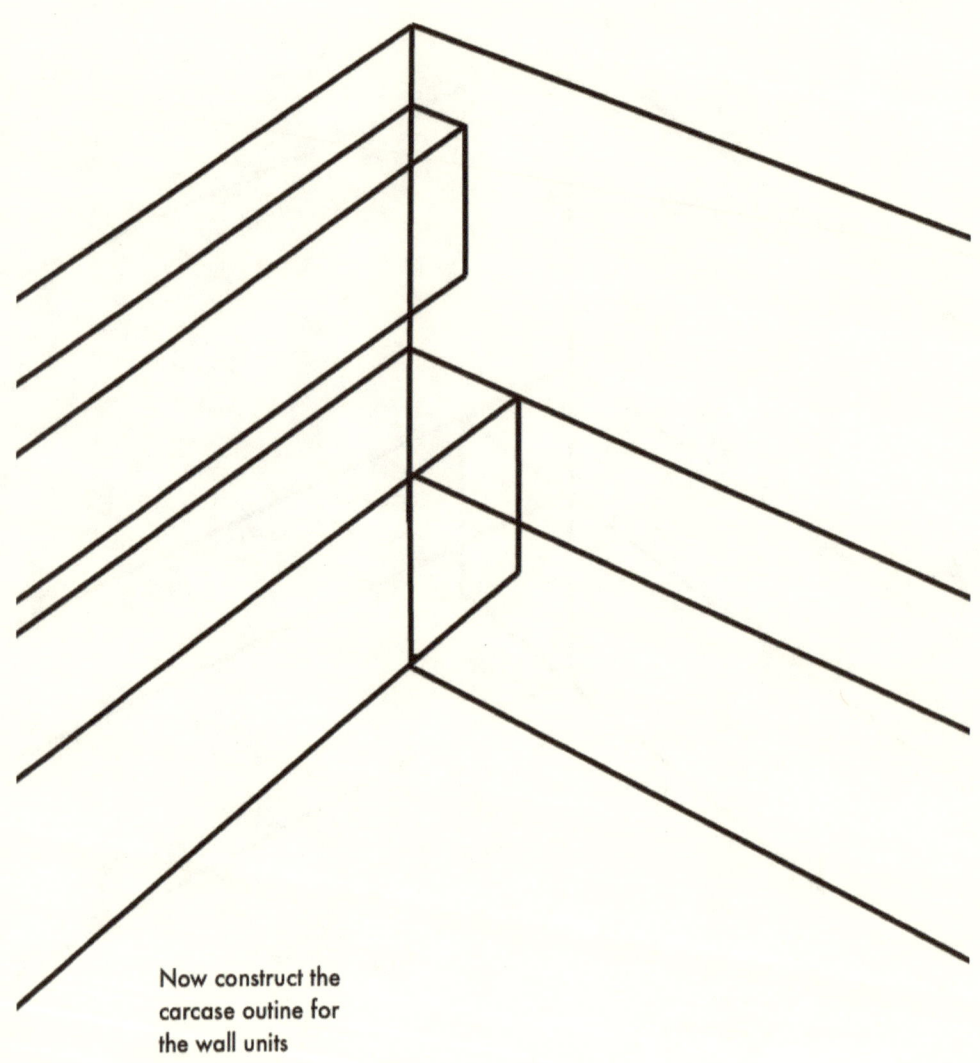

Now construct the
carcase outine for
the wall units

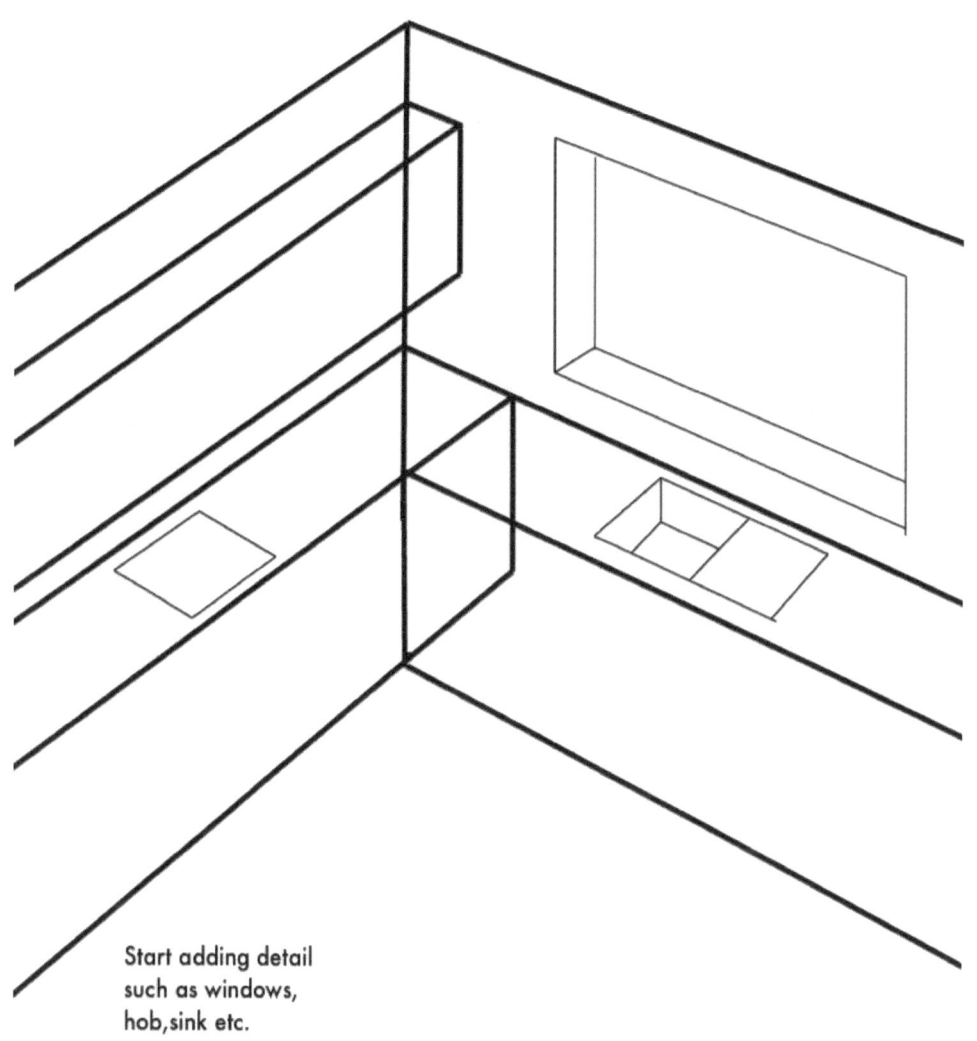

Start adding detail
such as windows,
hob, sink etc.

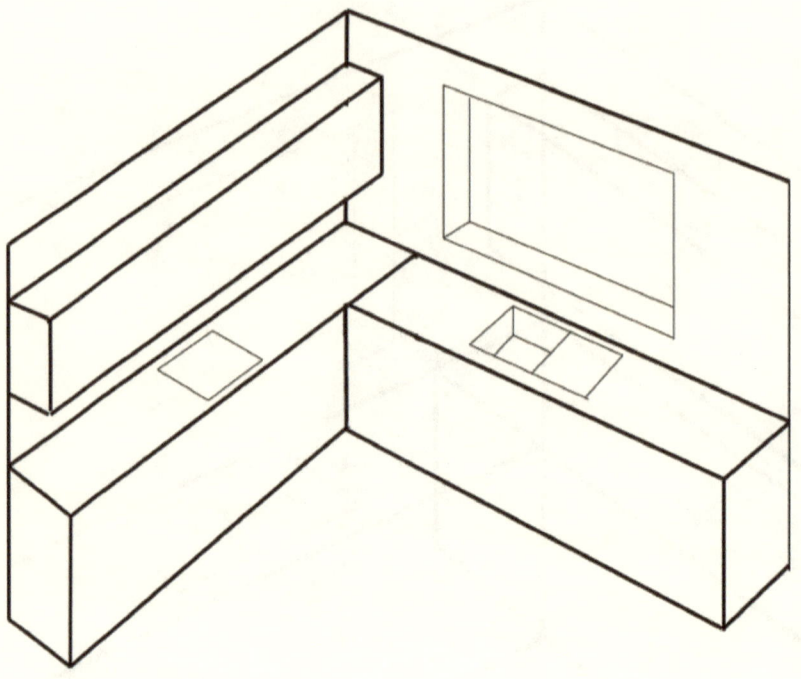

Tidy the drawing
removing hidden
lines, finish
carcasse profiling
etc.

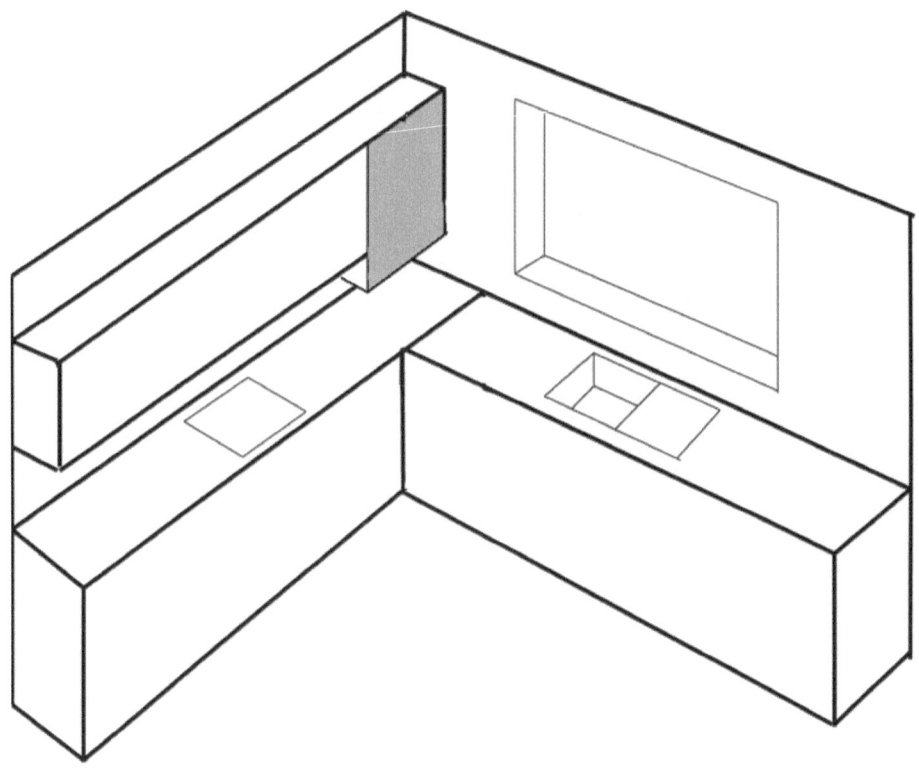

Add further details
as required

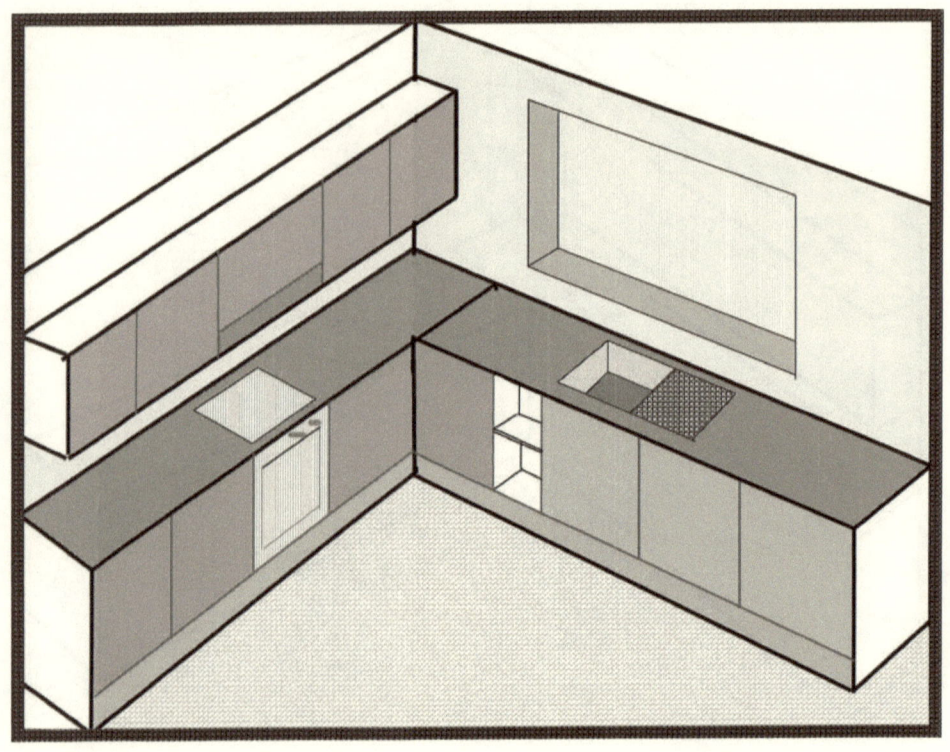

Finish the draswing and
detail of sink, shelves
etc. Remember you can
also add worktop
thickness and plinth
insets if required.

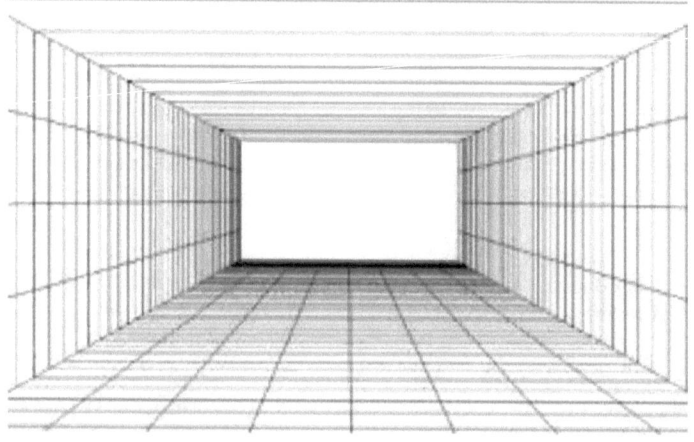

VANISHING POINT

4

The vanishing point is said to have been discovered, or should we say, introduced, in the 14th or 15th century. . I have to say that I am skeptical about this. The vanishing point is so obvious in drawings but more importantly in real life instances. Have a look at the railway line perspective. . OK there weren't any prehistoric railways but there surely were many instances that would have indicated the need and use of the vanishing point. It is perhaps well worth remembering that even Neanderthal man left some quite elaborate drawings the their dwelling caves??

In the past a lot of learners used to use the Perspective grid. We always found this very tedious, extremely restrictive and incredibly boring. It is, of course only usable for one discipline and unless you regularly use tracing paper it is a total waste of time. It is actually easier to draw properly, from scratch, and choose the view that suits the project and the drawing best.

You have probably guessed by now that 1 POINT PERSPECTIVE DRAWING uses one vanishing point. And, of course, 2 POINT PERSPECTIVE DRAWING uses two vanishing points.

You generally place your vanishing points on the horizon ine which is traditionally about eye level - around 1600 mm, but in reality you can choose anywhere but you need to choose the best place for your view. For interiors the standard placement is best. With a 1 point drawing you simply bias the vanishing point away from the longest wall so you can get the best view of that wall. With 2 point drawings you place the vanishing point as far away from the drawing as possible. Obviously with an A4 drawing board this doesn't give you much scope but a rule of thumb is to place it on the outside rim of the board.

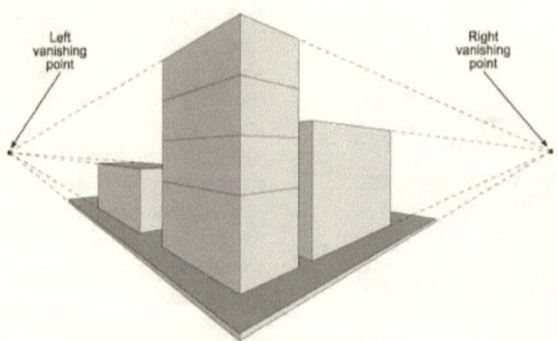

Left
vanishing
point

Right
vanishing
point

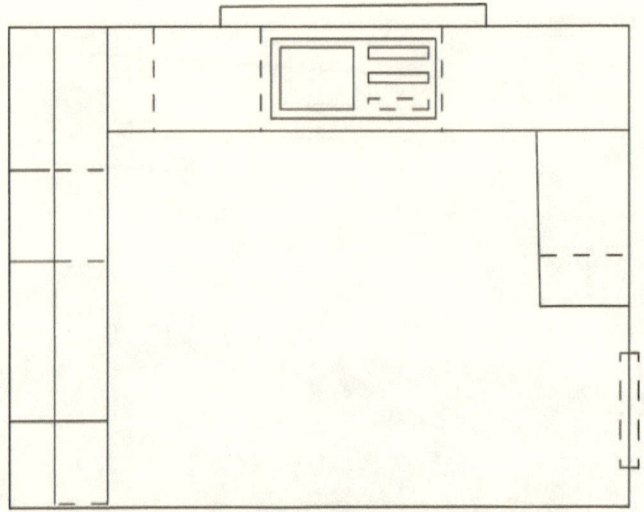

1 POINT PERSPECTIVE

AS BEFORE, START WITH A SCALE PLAN.
PART OF YOUR PERSPECTIVE DRAWING IS
IN SCALE BUT YOU ALSO NEED THE
MEASUREMENTS TO ENSURE THAT YOUR
PRESENTATION IS ACCURATE. A COMMON
ERROR IS TO TRY TO DRAW A PERSPECTIVE
WITHOUT FIRST DRAWING THE PLAN. DO
IT PROPERLY, IN THE END IT IS QUICKER
AND MORE EFFICIENT.

The first step is to
draw the back wall
in SCALE

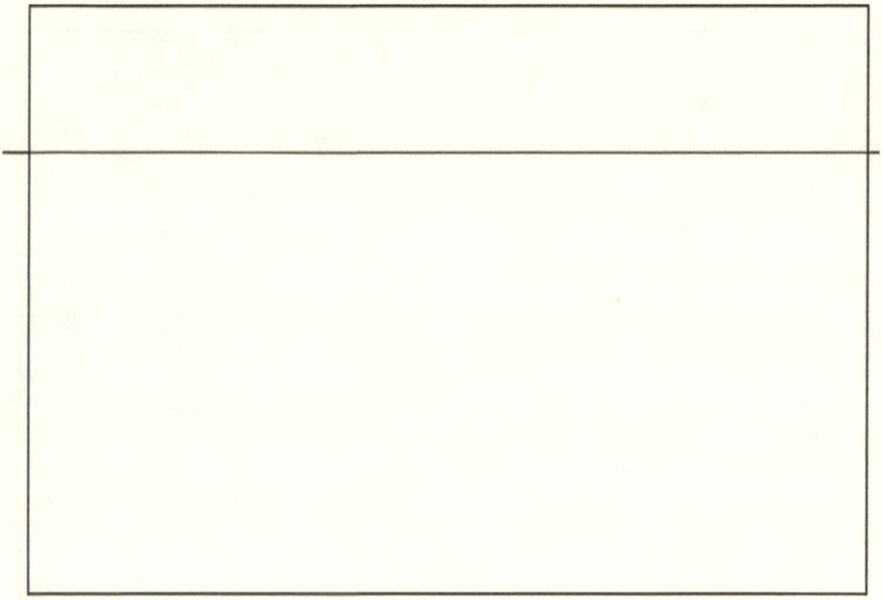

Next - locate the
horizon line -
default is 1600mm

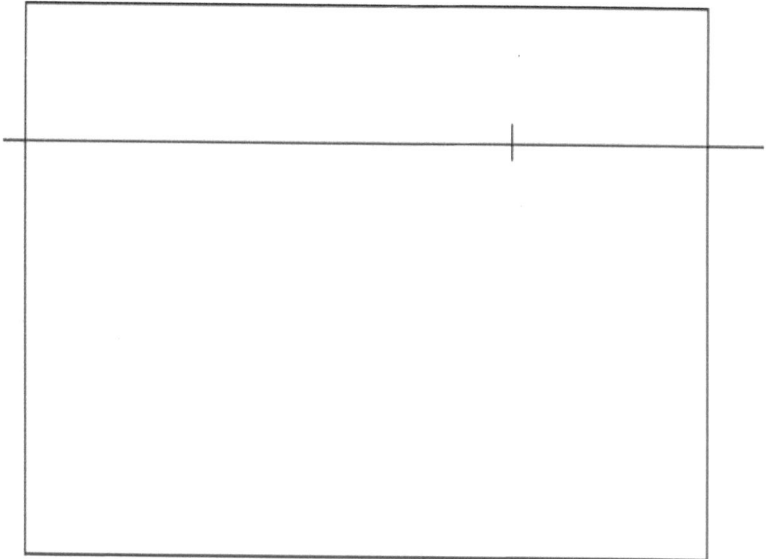

Now Place the
vanishing point on
the horizon line.

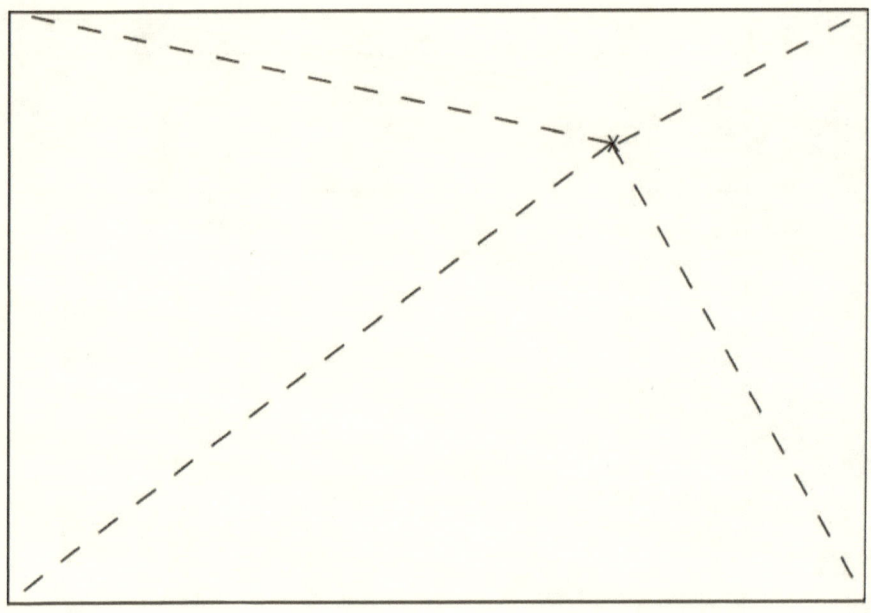

Then line up the
vanishing point with
all four corners of
the wall - this is the
start of projecting
the walls

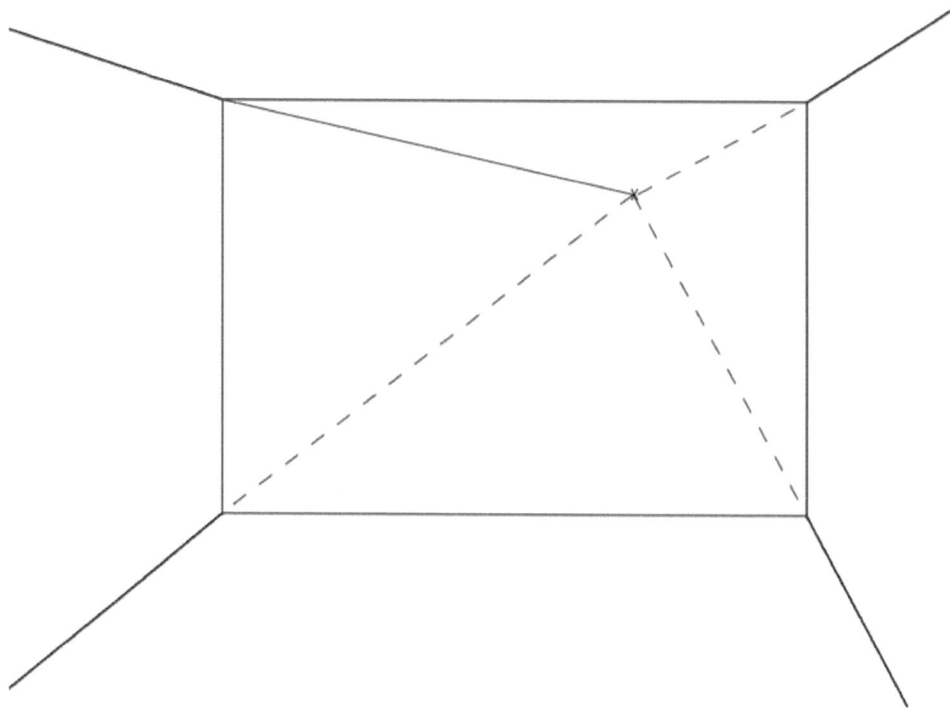

Next project the
lines to outline the
walls, floor and
ceiling

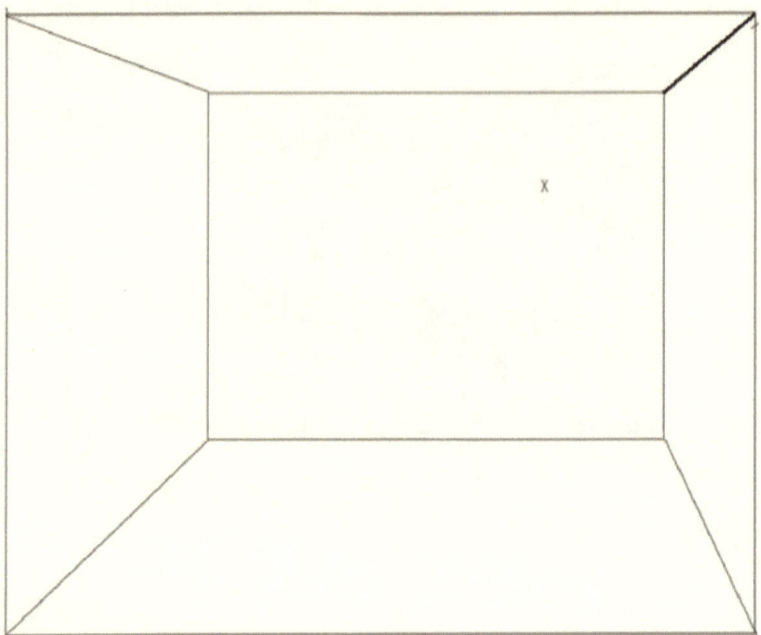

X

Next locate the
ends of the walls
and square the
front of the room so
you can now see
an enclosed room -
this is not always
practical with
larger rooms

The perspective measurements can be
found using a measuring device (see
return measurements) or quite simply
using the perspective ruler - you will find
an example later in this book - to use
copy the ruler and paste onto a piece of
stiff card.

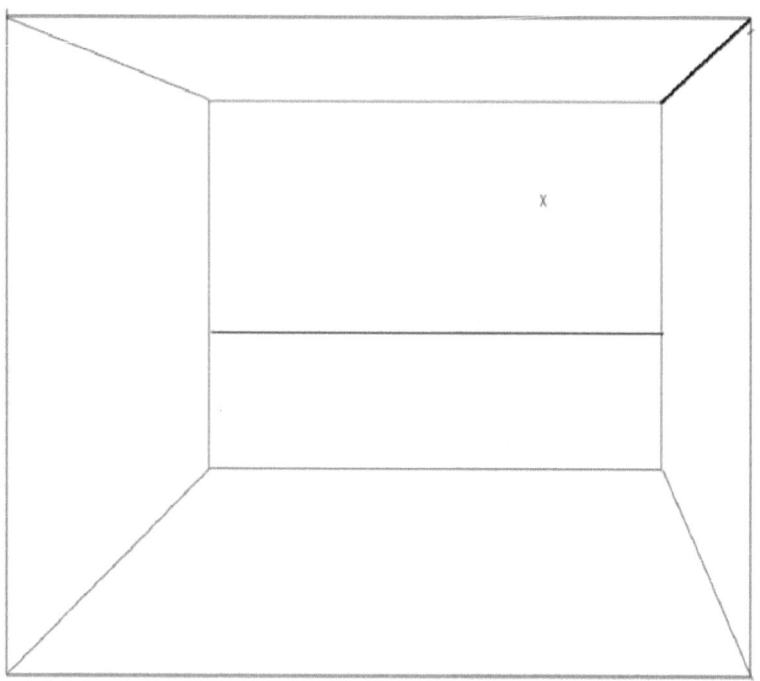

Next locate the
carcassing on the
back wall -
Remember this is in
Scale

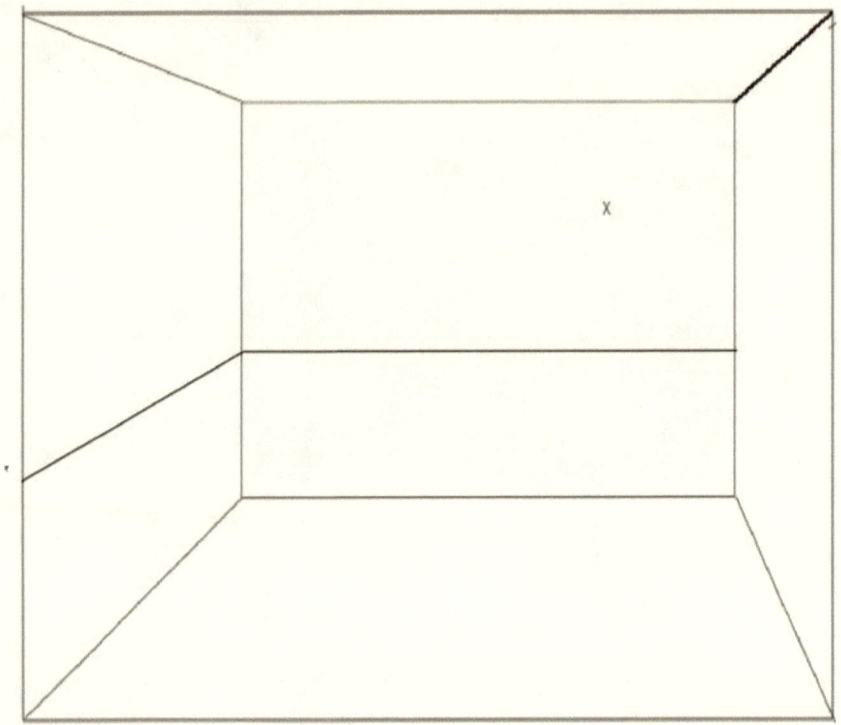

X

Then using the
vanishing point
project the
carcassing along
the return wall

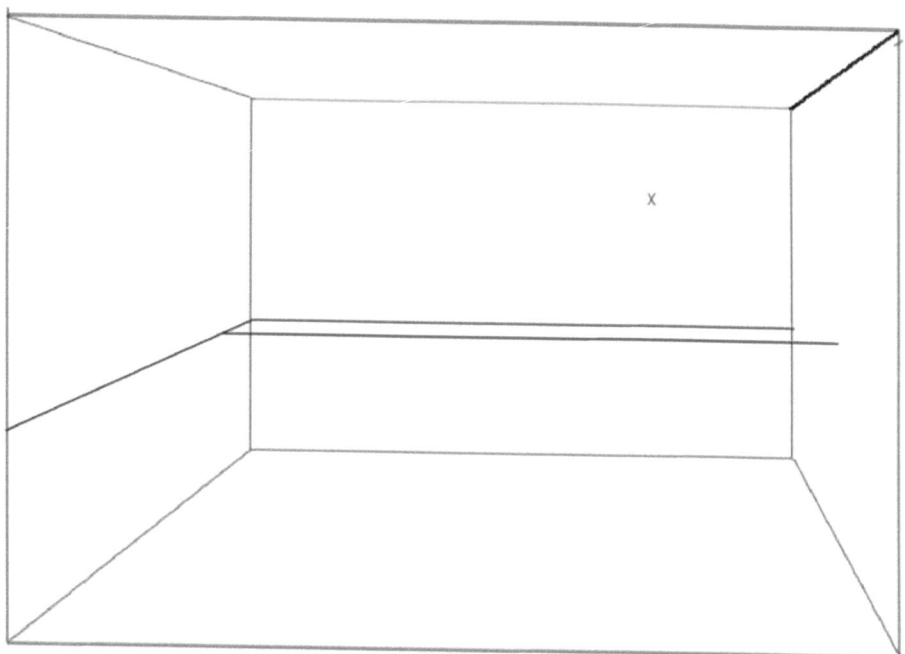

Now find the depth
of the units on the
back wall using the
perspective ruler

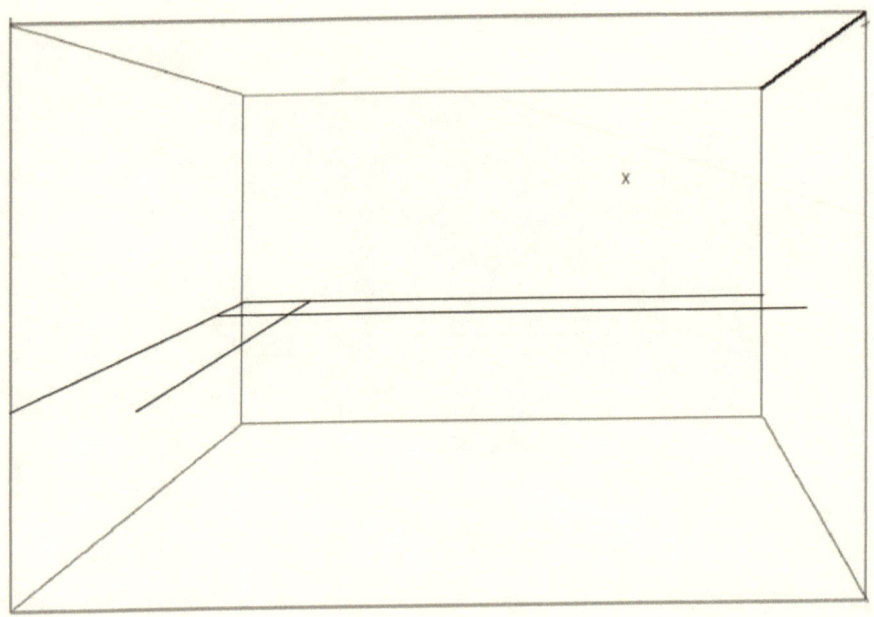

Now project the
front of the return
wall arcassing

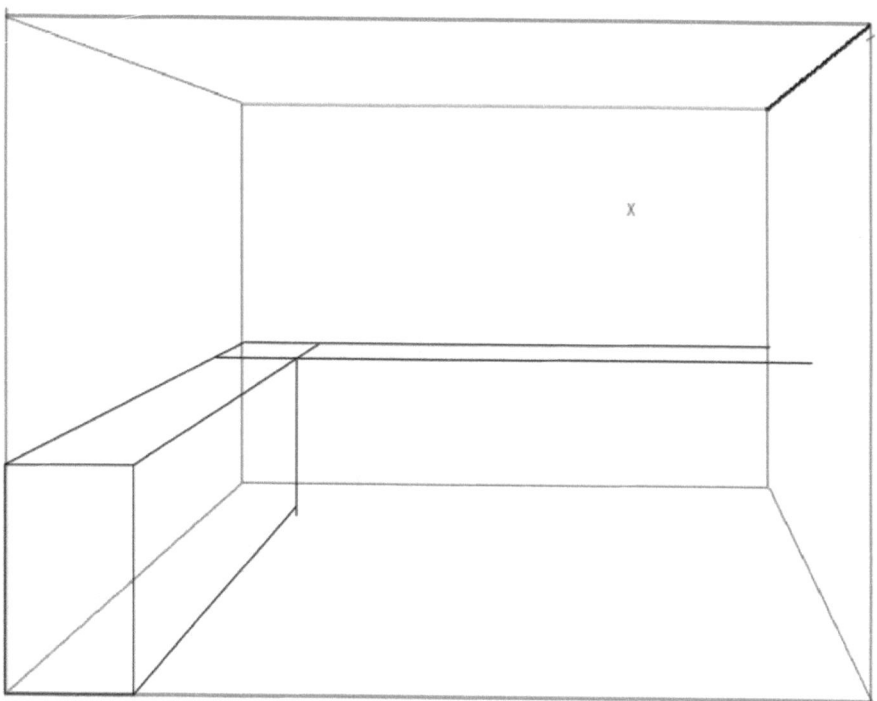

X

Then using the
vanishing point
square the
carcassing on the
return wall -
REMEMBER all
vertical lines are
90°

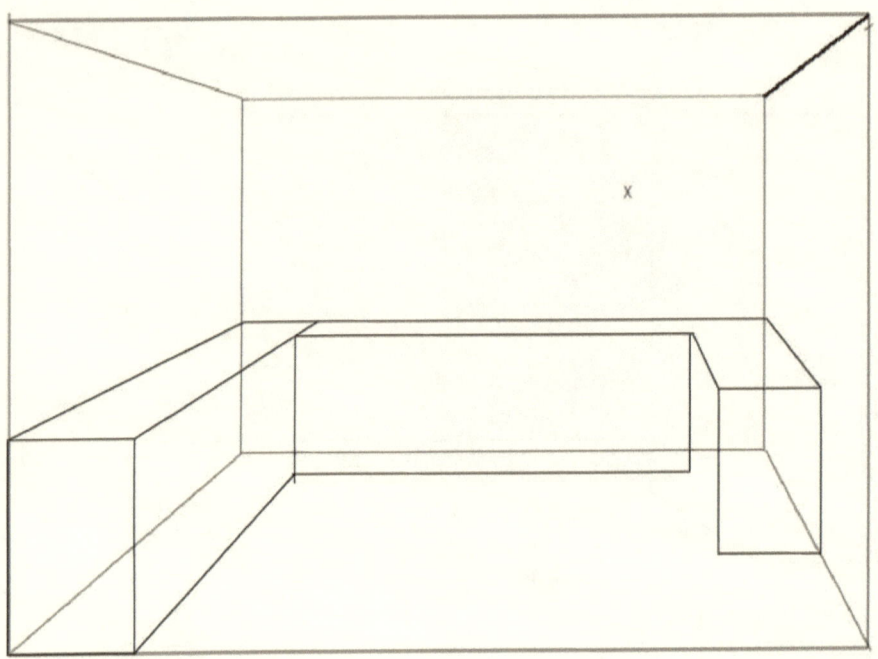

X

Now complete the
carcassing on the
back and right
hand return walls
with the vanishing
point and the
drawing board

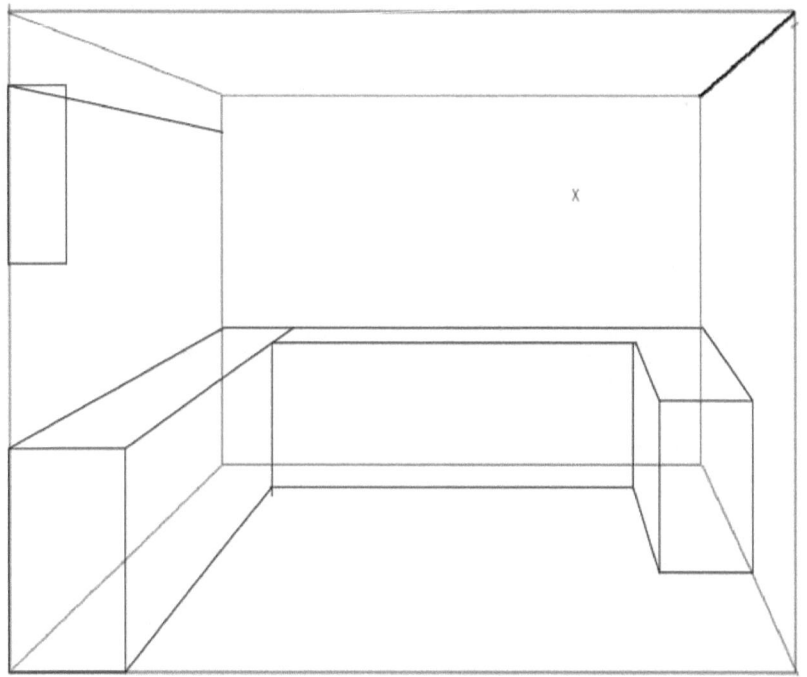

X

Next find the wall
line using the same
methods

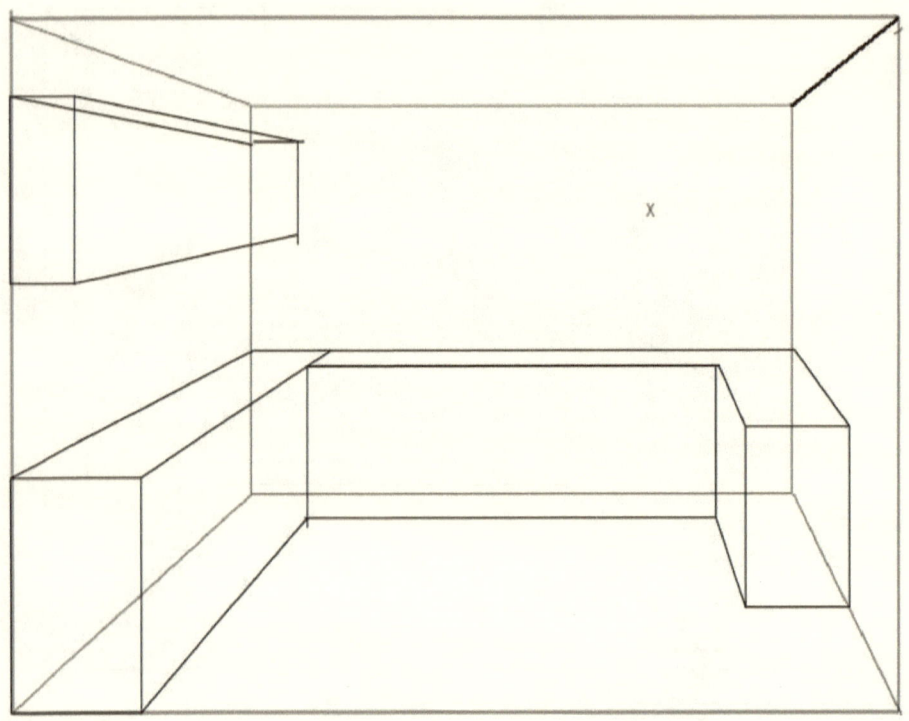

X

Complete the
carcassing outline

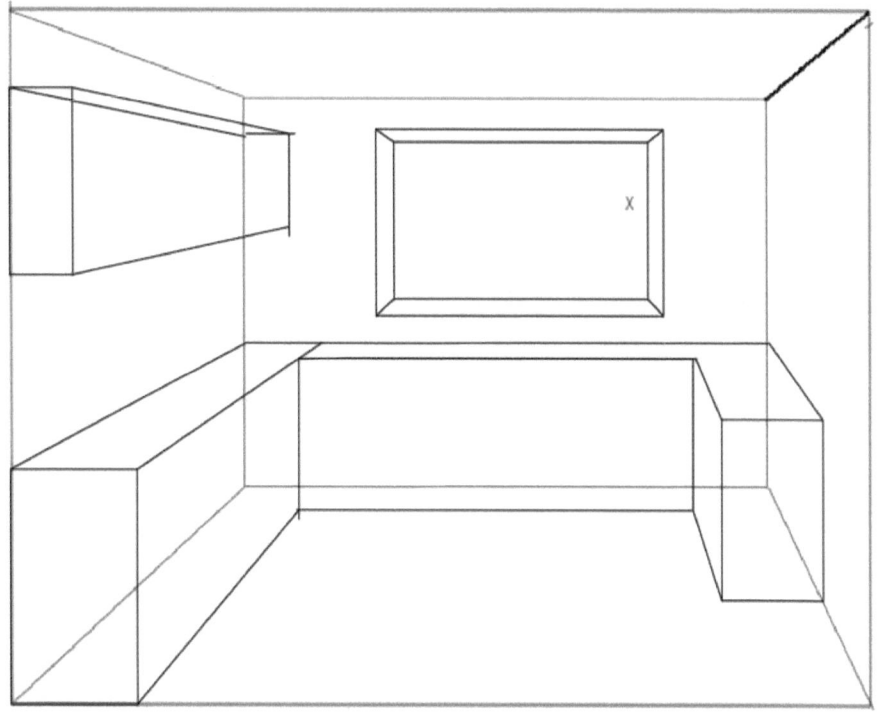

Start adding detail

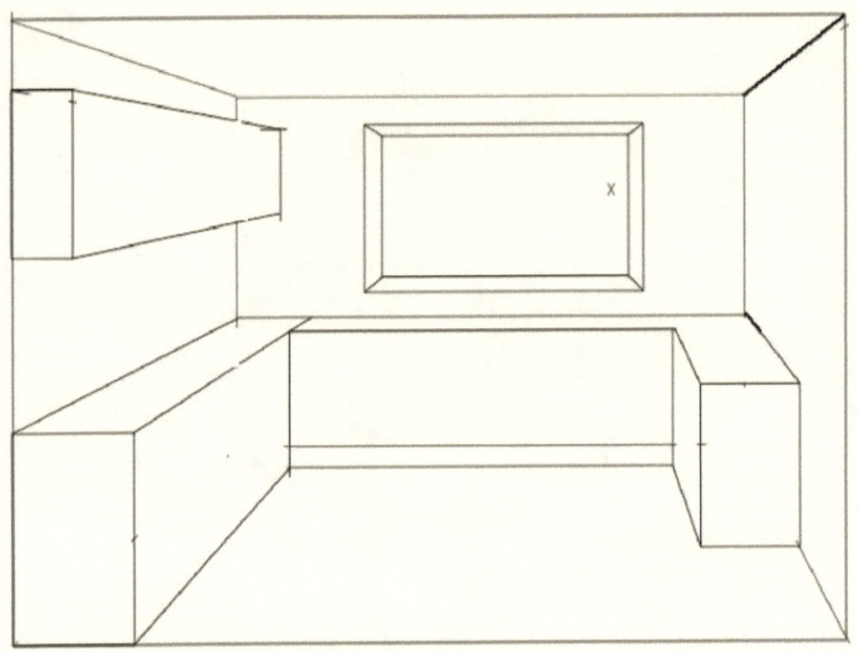

Continue with
detail such as plinth
etc.

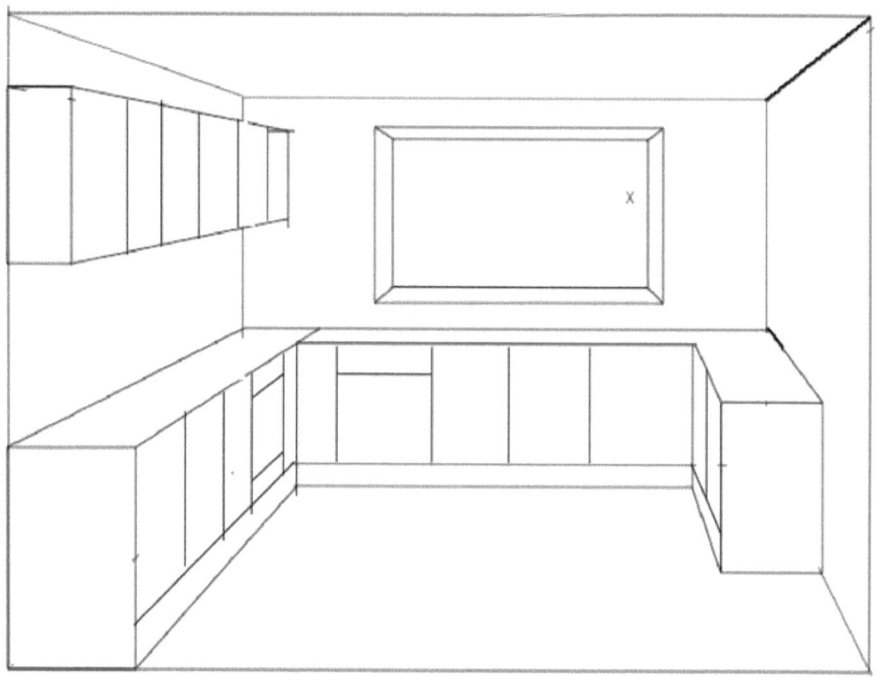

Carry on locating
individual unit and
door sizes. On the
back wall you can
measure on the
wall in scale then
project forward.
On the return wall
us the prspective
ruler.

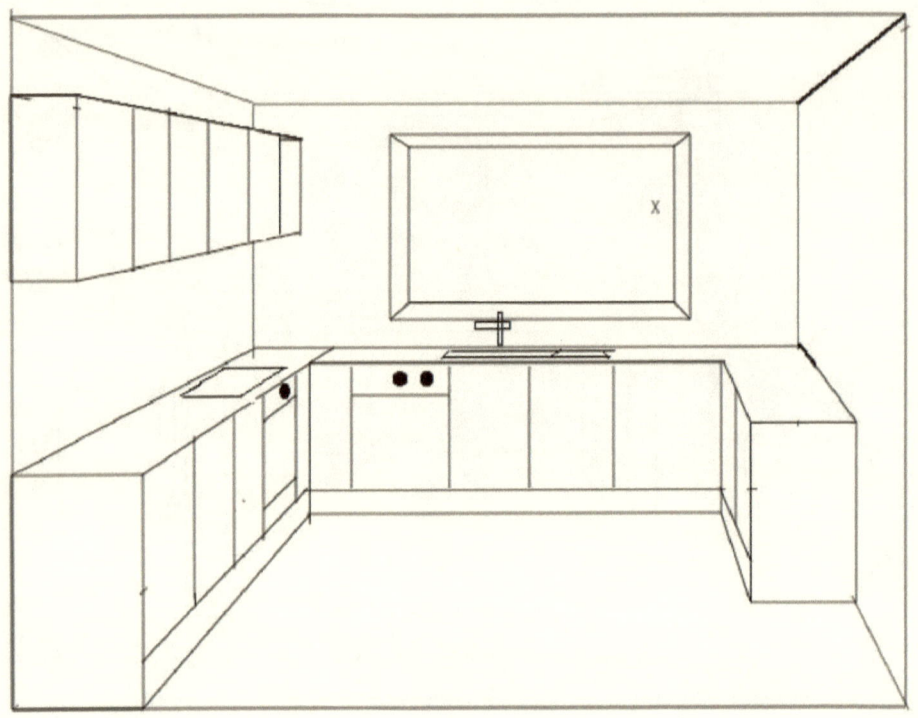

Now finish the
outline and detail.

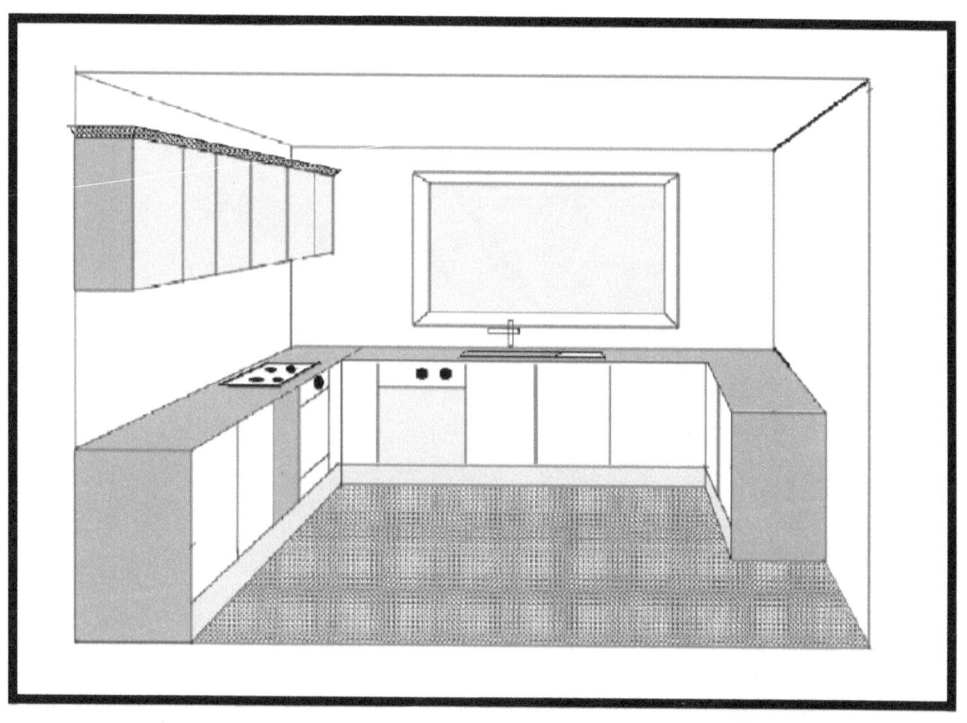

Finish with a splash
of rendering for a
very effective
presentation

The
Perspective
Ruler©

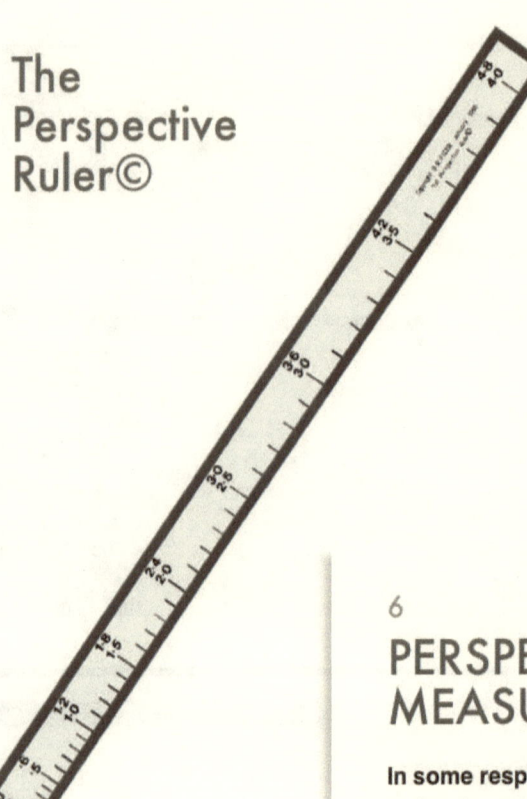

6

PERSPECTIVE MEASUREMENTS

In some respects this is the most diffi-cult aspect of perspective, but mainly 1 point and 2 point perspectives. The method is more or less the same for both so we shall just elaborate on the basic principles.

One of the things that our Designers found was that they could not teach their delegates how to judge the dimensions. We had developed the scale ruler as shown earlier. This was simple, effective and allowed the delegates to relax and get on with the more important drawing skills. In fact, it isn't really necessary but it is a big help in distance learning and for speed of the drawing. We shall show over the next few pages how to interpret the return measurements in a variety of different ways.

For simplicity for at least the first few drawings we strongly recommend using the Perspective Ruler©. All you have to do is to plot the measurements - cumulatively. Don't use it like an ordinary ruler measuring 600mm then another 600mm then say 500mm you must measure 600mm then 1200mm then 1700mm which you can do without moving the ruler.

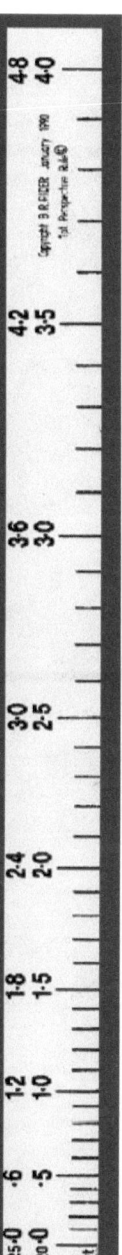

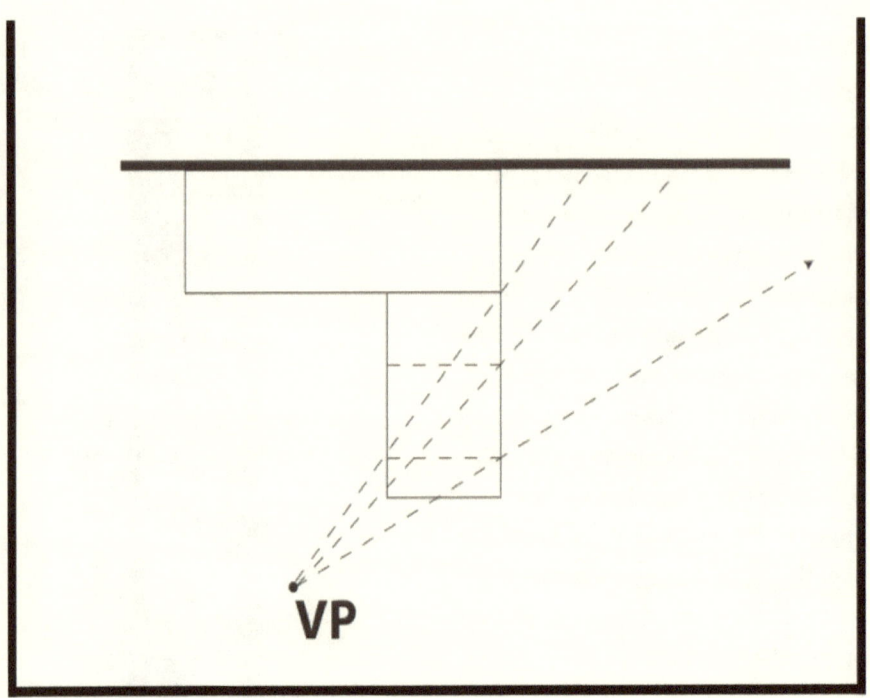

VP

PERSPECTIVE MEASUREMENTS THE FORMAL METHOD

This is the proper method to achieve accurate and consistent return measurements. Please note the VP shown is in fact the viewing point although it is in effect, an additional vanishing point. If you start with your original scale plan you should then transfer the return wall to your perspective drawing (we have shown it here as a group of kitchen units. You then choose your VP - it is not critical except the view that it provides. The VP should be as far away as possible on your drawing board or even off the board. Using the VP just like a vanishing point you line up the VP with the measurements of the individual units and project them to the wall shown as a solid line. For a more compact image you would project the floor line in perspective and then transfer the measurements to this line instead of the back wall line - the choice is yours. You then draw in perspective from your drawing vanishing points.

Point to note

Locate the viewing point as far away as practical - the further away the more condensed the return measurements

Always start with the ends of the wall - this then sets your final scale from your original scale plan

It is possible to transfer the return wall measurements directly on your perspective but to begin with use your scale plan and then transfer only the measuring points

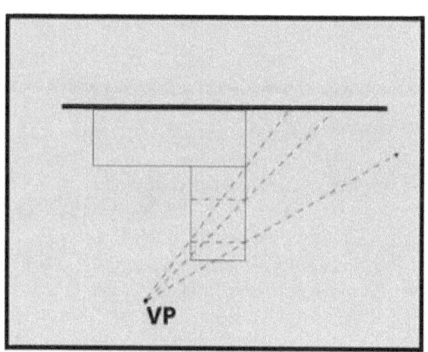

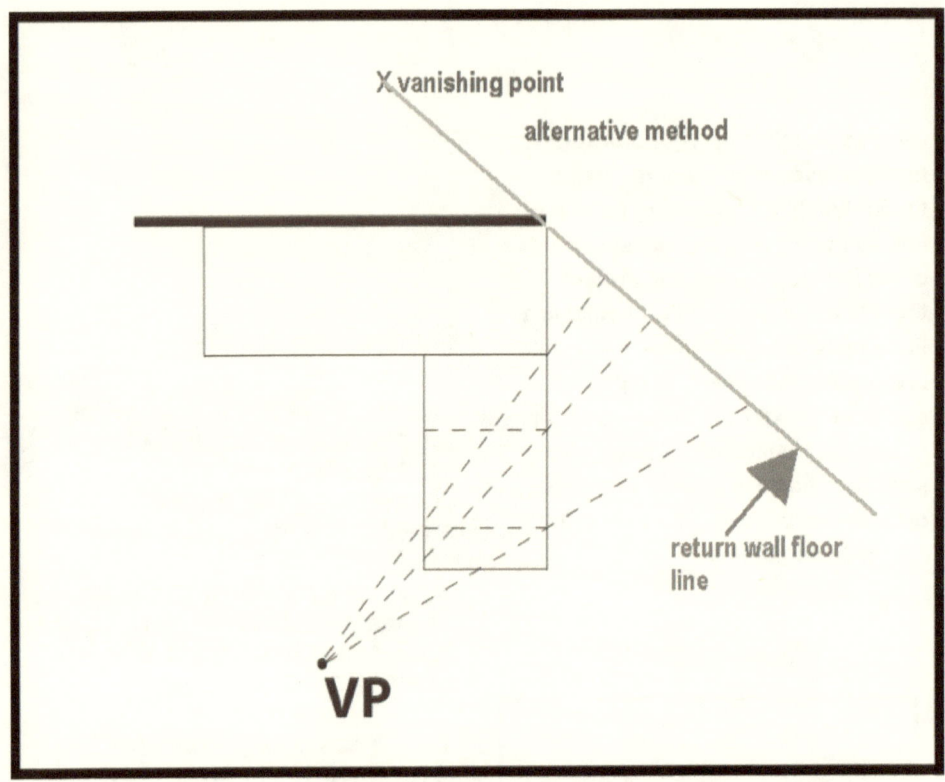

X vanishing point

alternative method

return wall floor line

VP

Using the same initial steps project the return wall floor line from your chosen vanishing point, Then from your chosen viewing point transfer the individual unit divisions to the return wall line rather than the floor line. This then provides a slightly more compact drawing especially if the room is larger than average. Try it a few times until you get the hang of it. Use a simple scale plan with method one and then practice with the alternative method. Once you get the hang of the return wall you will, in fact, either use the copied perspective ruler or simply judge the room. As you can automatically find the end of the room or the section of the room you wish to draw judging the intermediate steps is quite a simple progression so all you really need is the end of the room and a few intermediate measurements and judge the rest - you will soon get the hang of it.

Alternative method using a perspective return wall

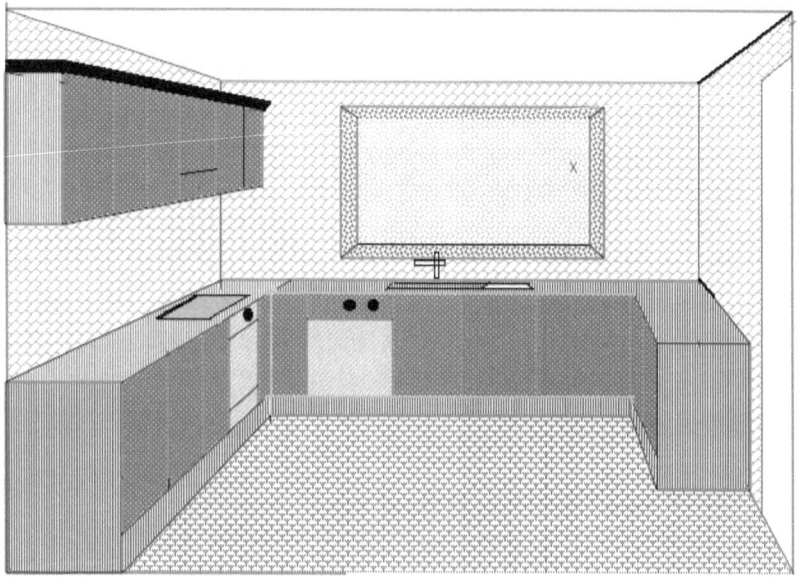

7

2 POINT PERSPECTIVE

The 2 point is more demanding and time consuming but generally gives the best balanced view in wide projects such as a kitchen. You can also expand this into a multipoint perspective but for most projects this is probably not necessary.

So on to the 2 point. For larger rooms you may find this useful but it should become obvious for each project. You simply use your judgment to get the best view for your project. Except for the fact you have two vanishing points and you draw from the vanishing point to one or the other walls depending upon whether you are projecting in or out, the steps are virtually the same as 1 point.

But be careful - many of the examples shown for 2 point are for buildings - not interiors. If you are drawing buildings this is the correct format but it is not suitable for interiors except possibly very large open internal spaces.

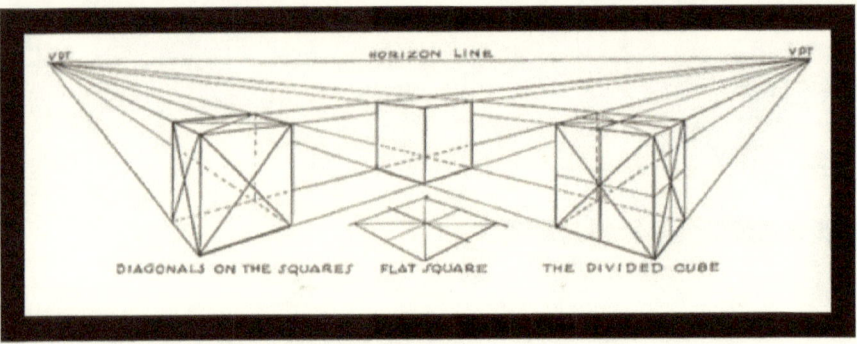

DIAGONALS ON THE SQUARES   FLAT SQUARE   THE DIVIDED CUBE

Two Point Perspective

65

This is the method to use for interiors

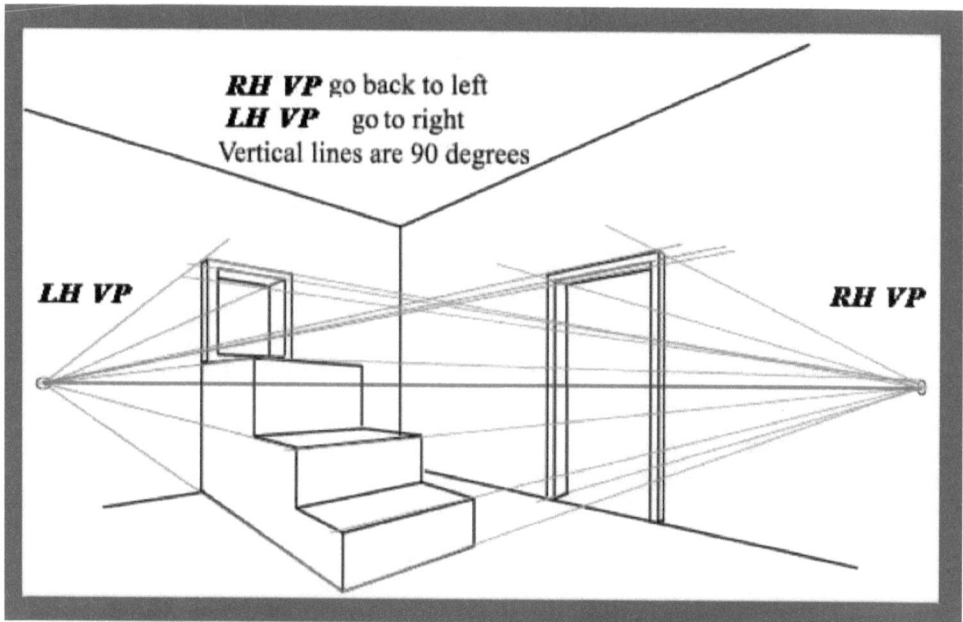

RH VP go back to left
LH VP go to right
Vertical lines are 90 degrees

LH VP

RH VP

66

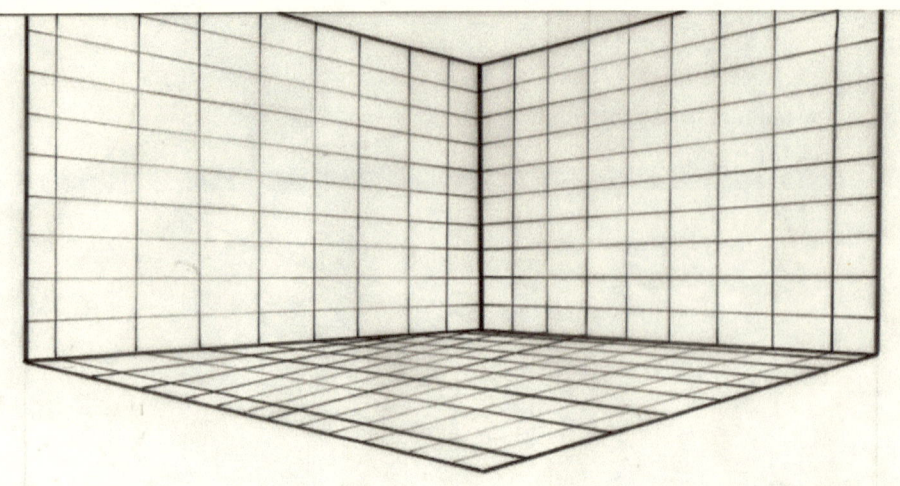

As before you can use a grid or construct a grid but it is very boring and quite tedious and does not provide the best view for all presentations. The time factor is actually better with the proper method each time. The drawing below shows a new interior start. Ignore the third point on the lower corner this is a measuring point.

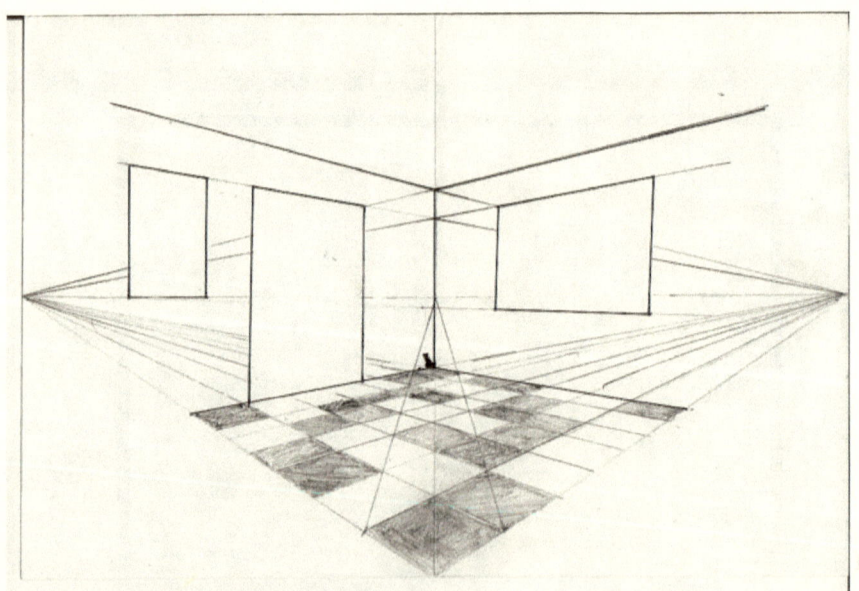

As before start with
the corner of the
room in scale and
refer to your scale
plan.

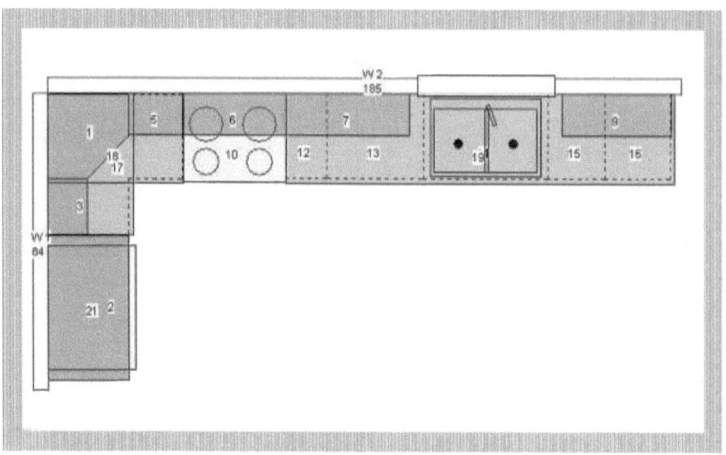

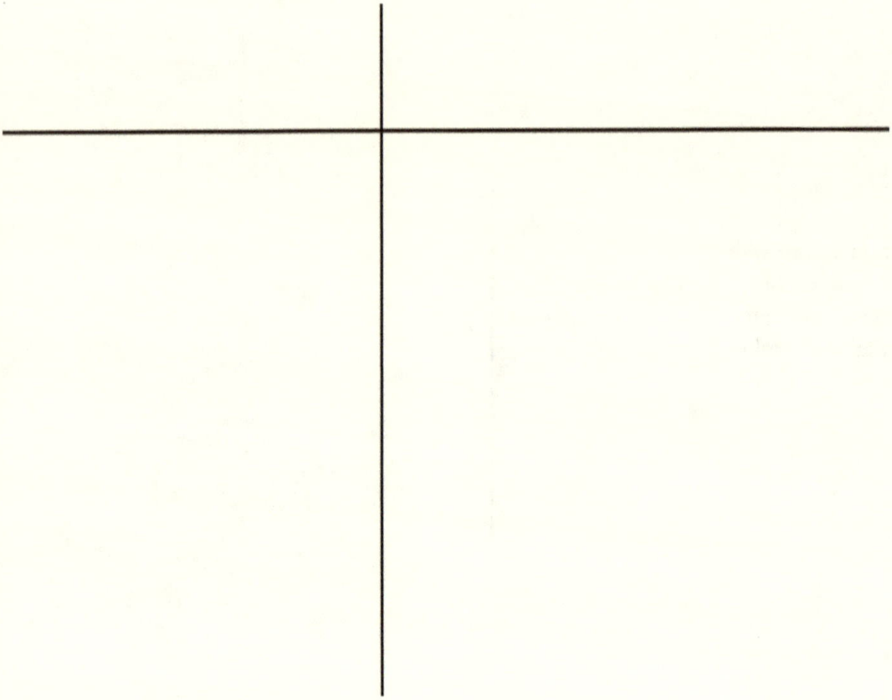

Now choose your
horizon line -
default is 1600mm

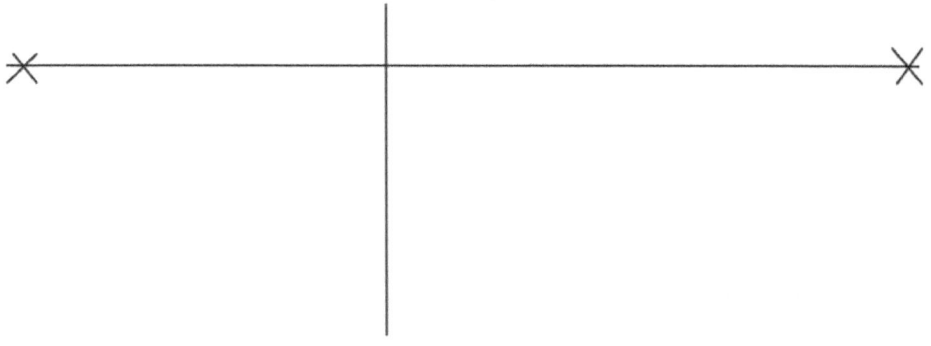

Now choose your
vanishing points -
as far as the board
allows

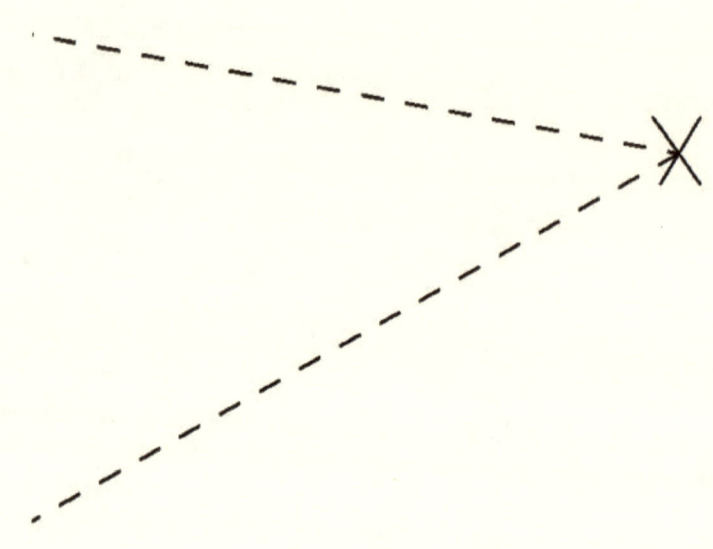

Next line up the VP
to project the walls

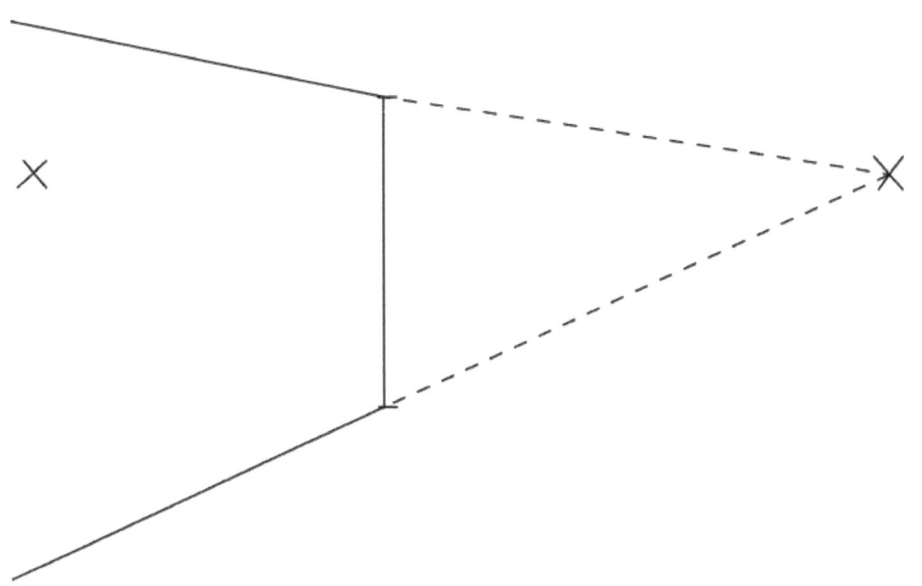

Continue with
projecting the walls

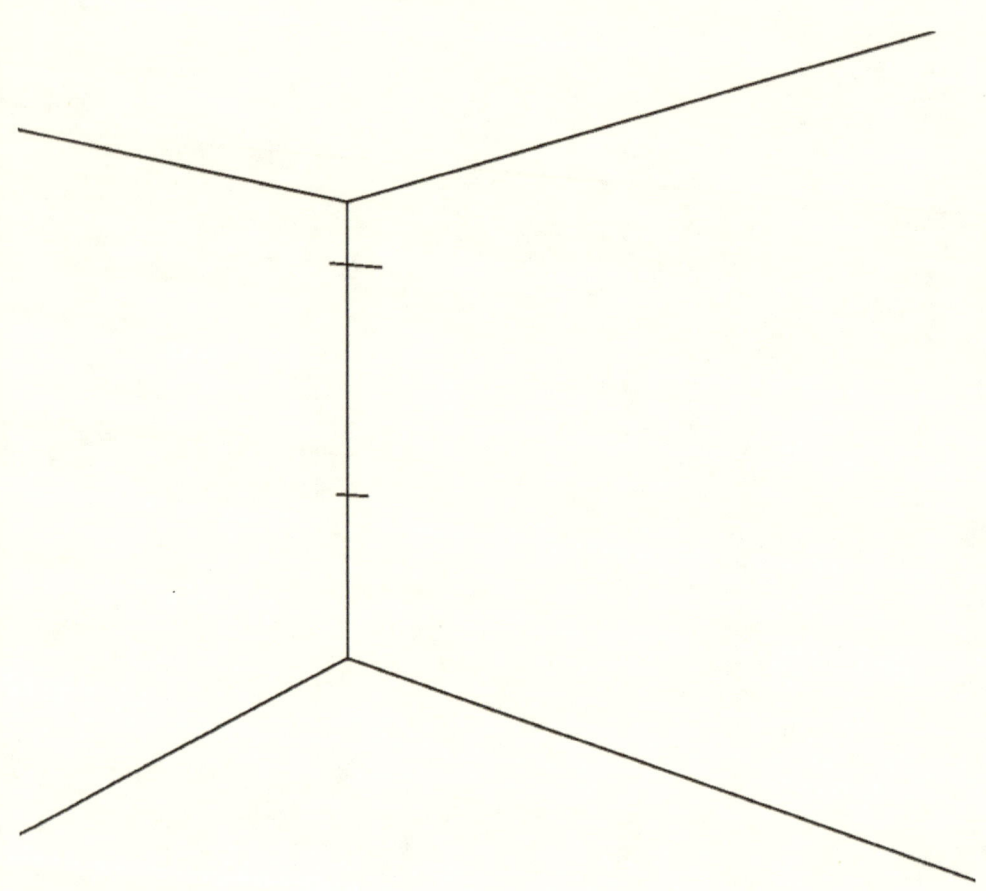

WE have now
completed the walls
but not found the
ends.

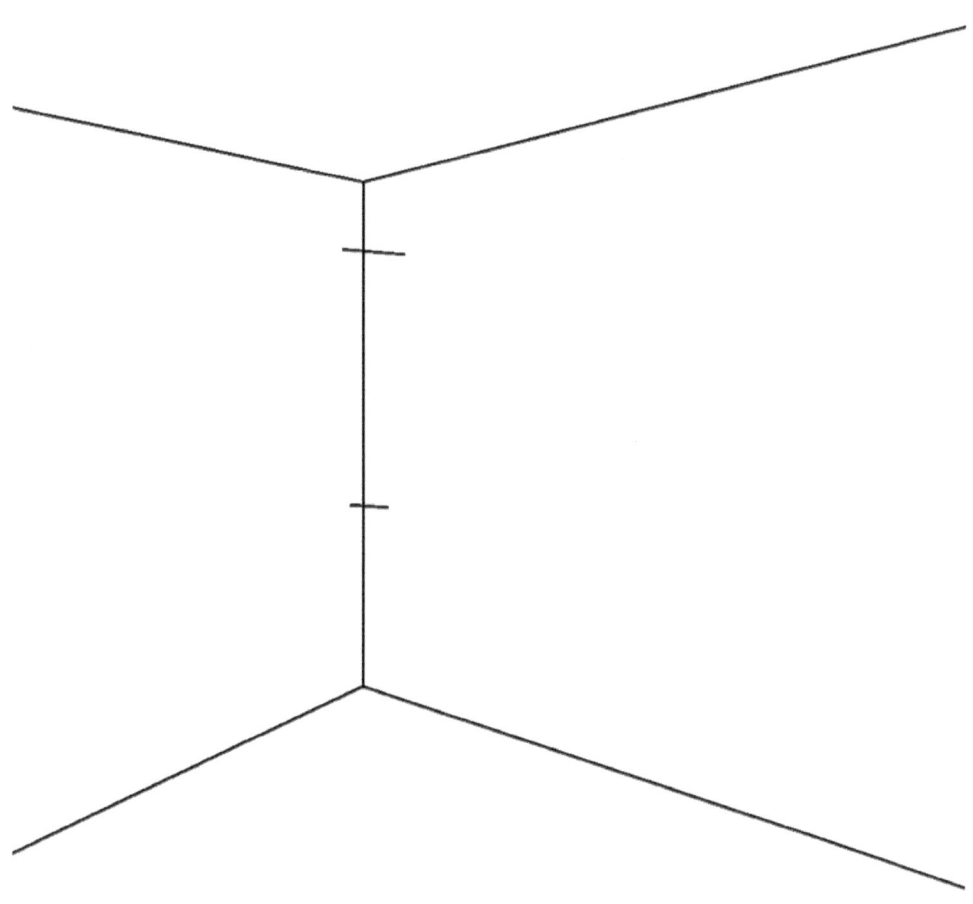

Set up the
carcassing outline

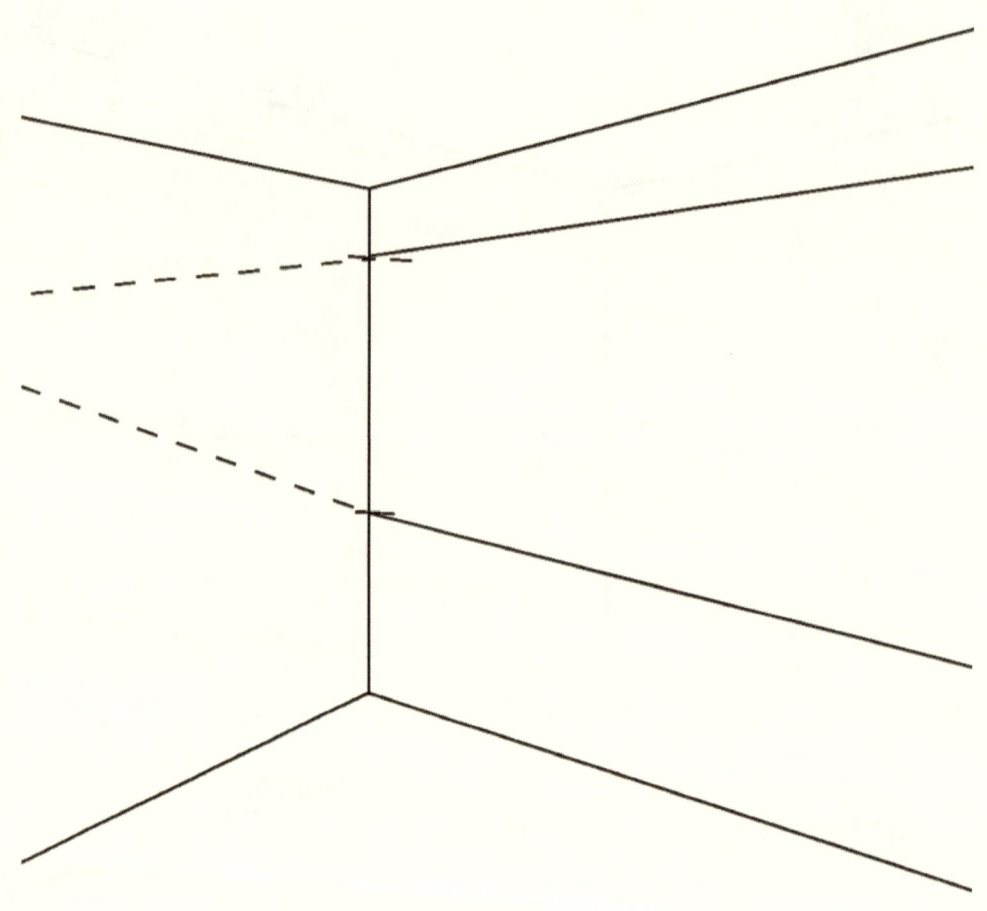

Continue with the
carcassing outline

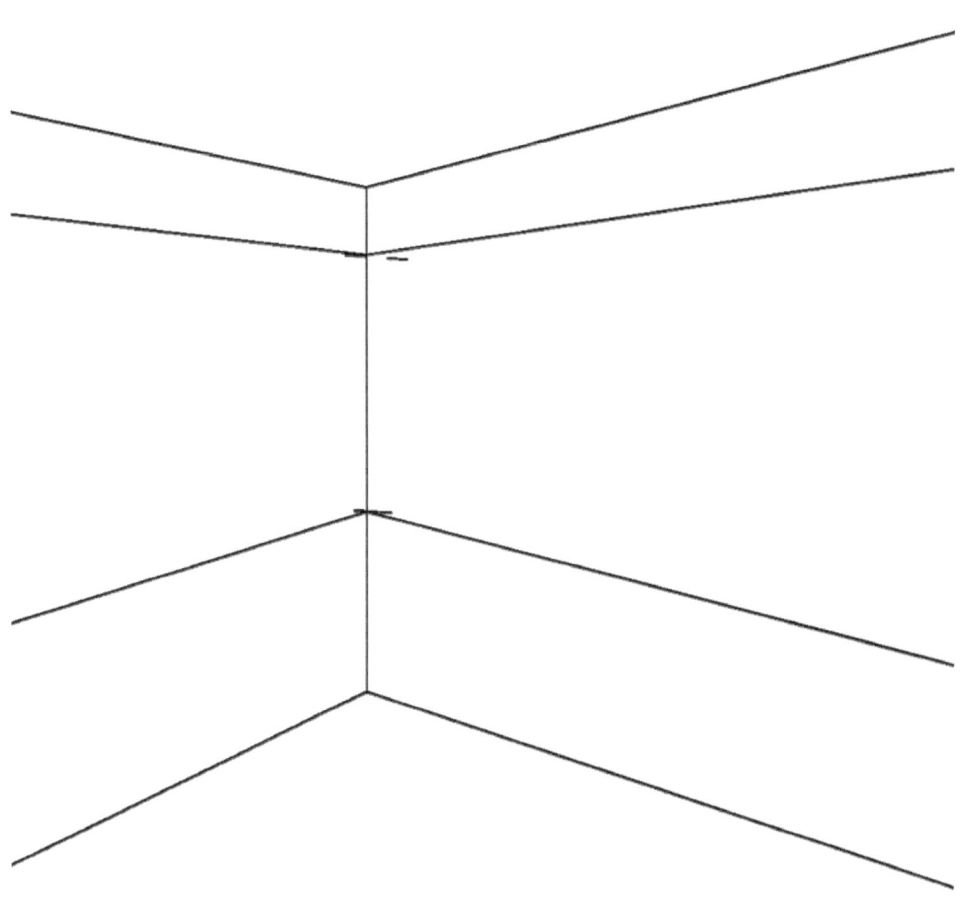

Carcassing outline
for the opposie
wall

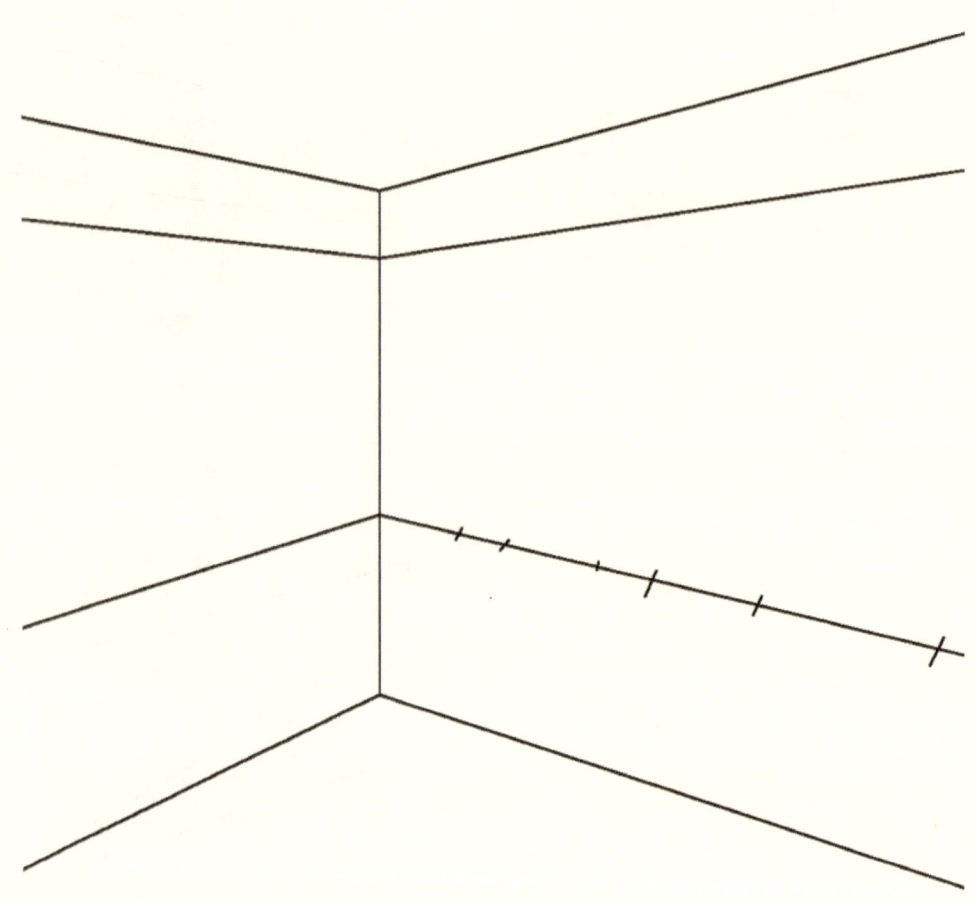

Using yuor
perspective ruler or
other measuring
system set out the
base carcasse
points.

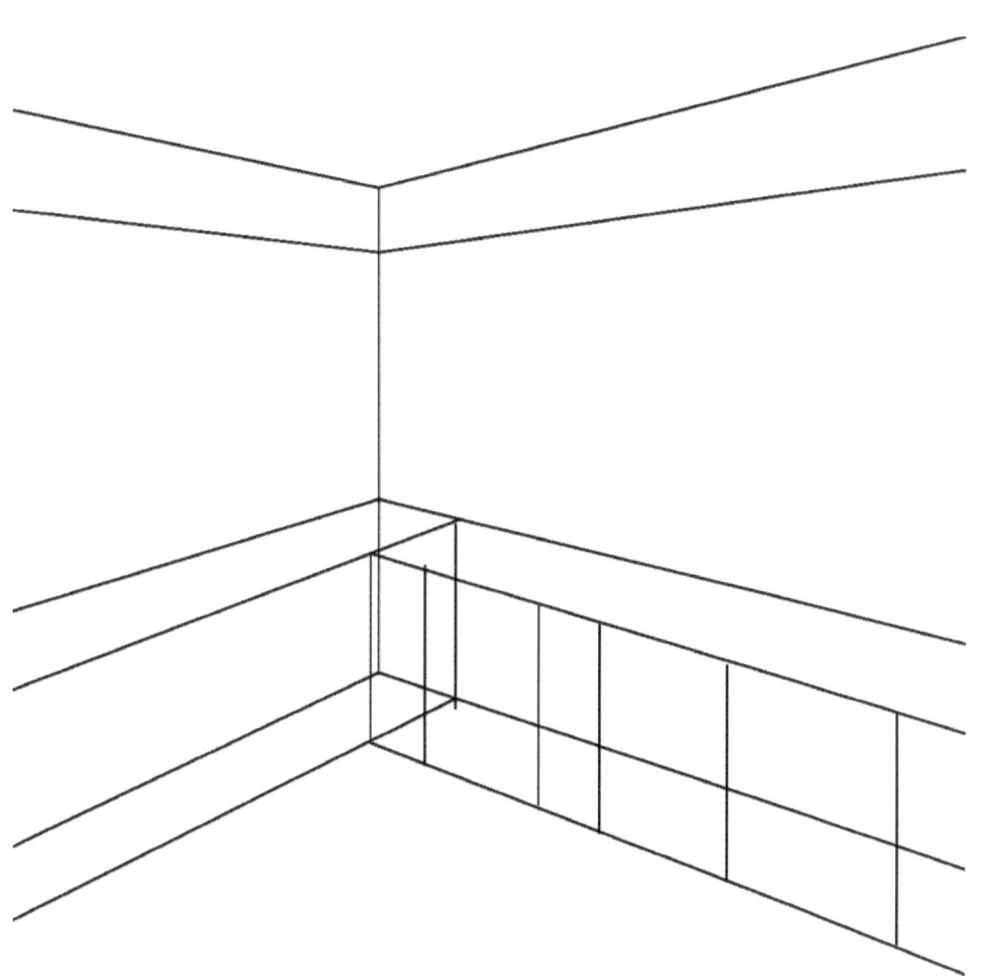

Using these
dimensions
complete the base
line carcassing

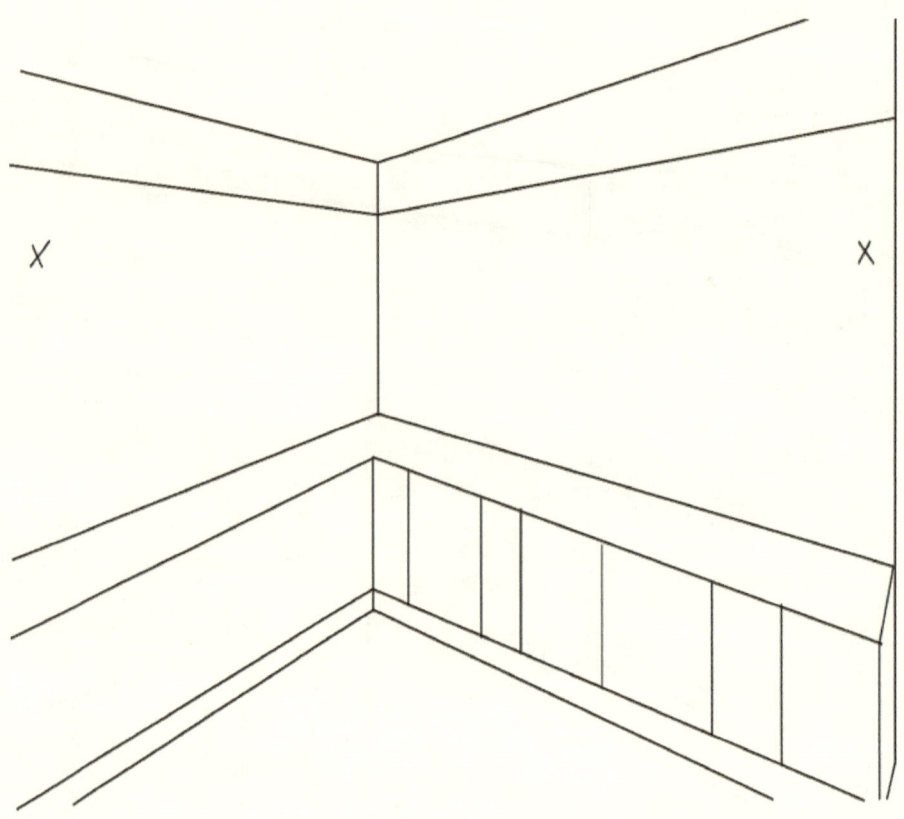

X X

Tidy the drawing
and complete the
outline as
dimensions allow

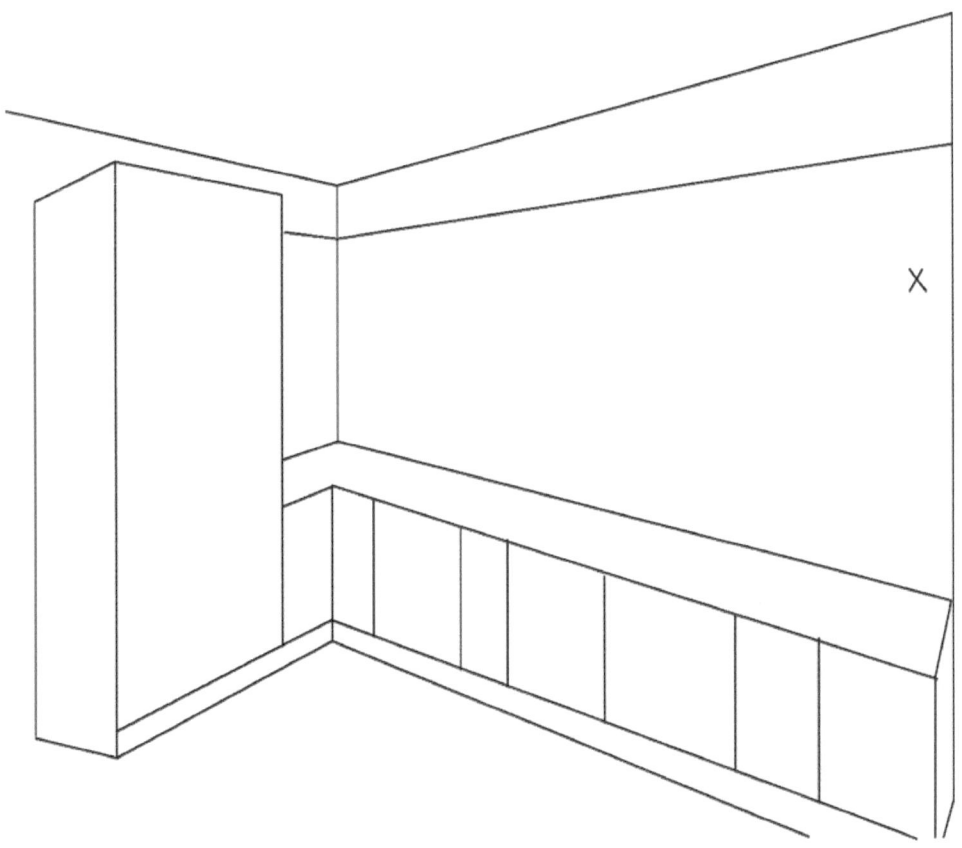

X

Next complete the
LH carcassing
including the tall
unit

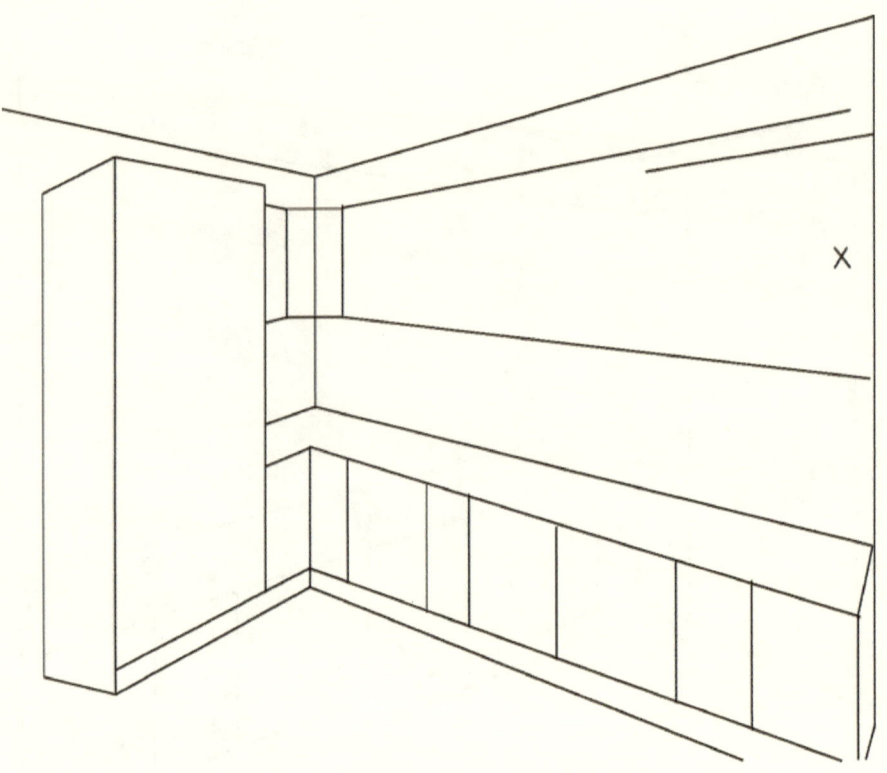

X

Next sart the wall
carcassing

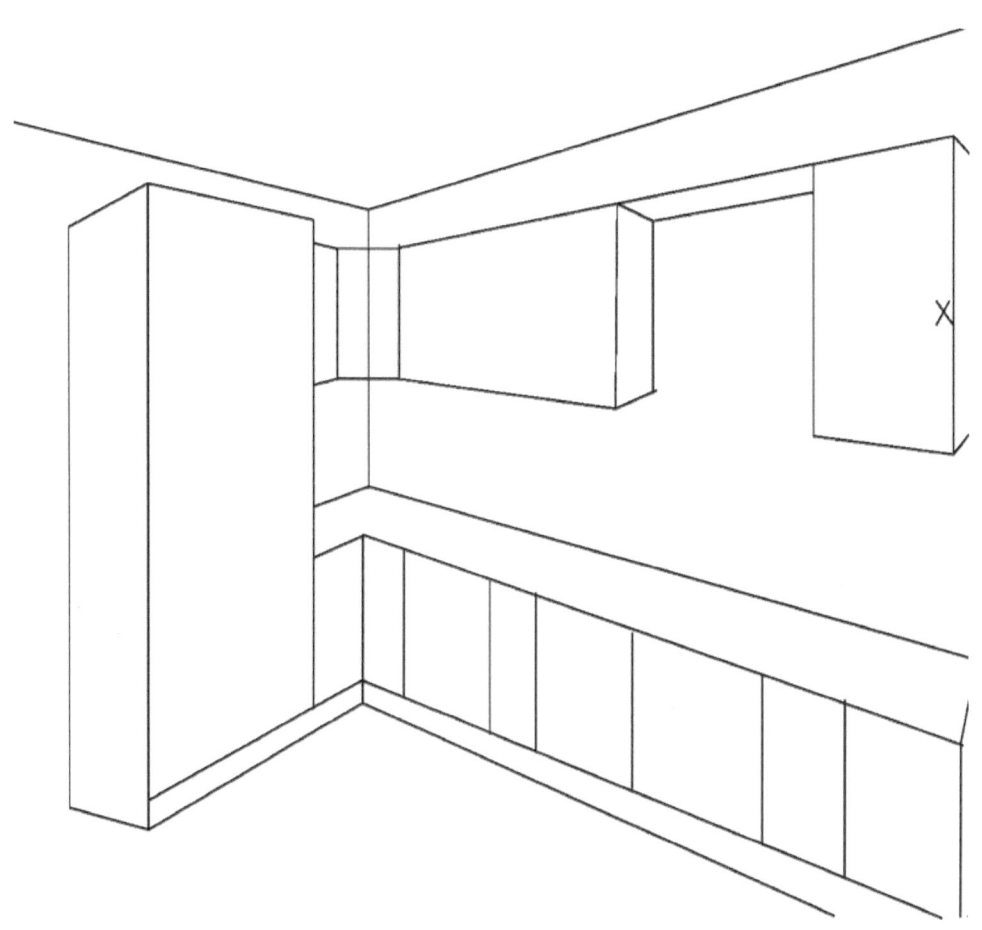

Complete the
carcassing
including a flyover
shelf over the
window

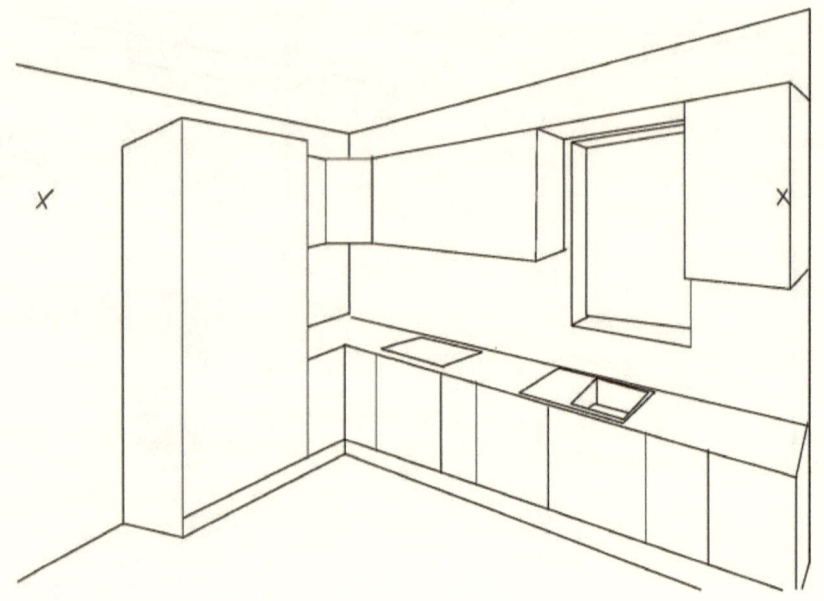

X

X

Finish detail
including windows,
sink, hob etc.

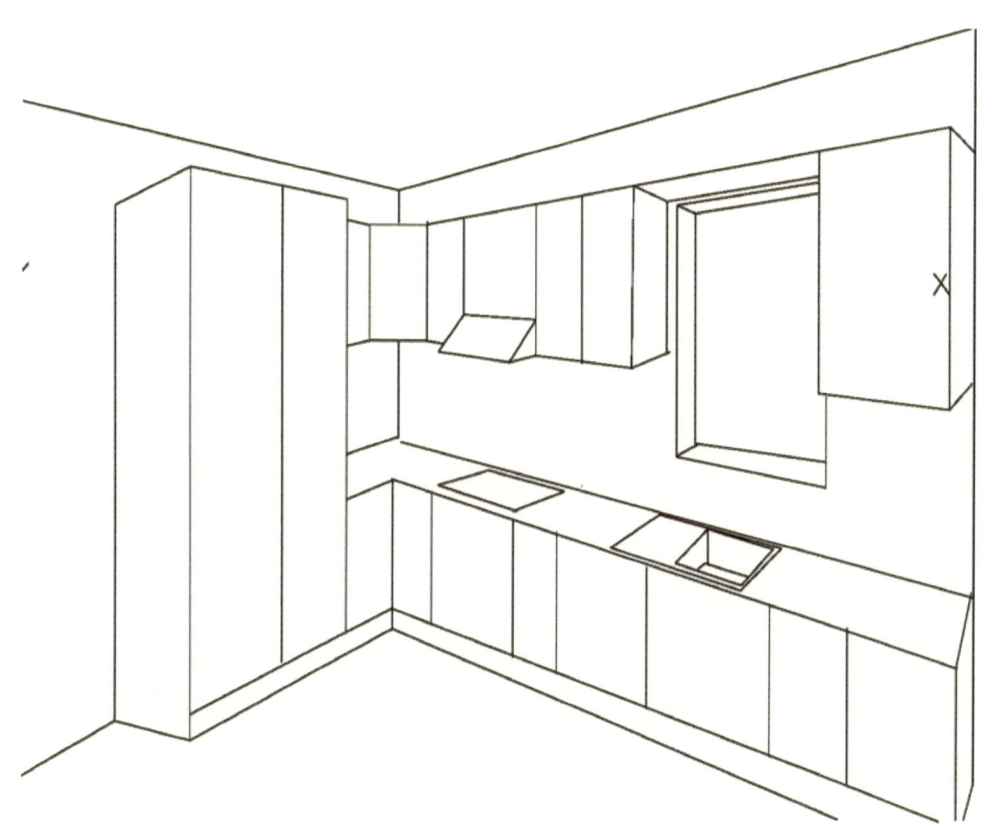

Continue with
detail such as
fridge doors,
cooker hood and if
you wish worktop
thickness etc.

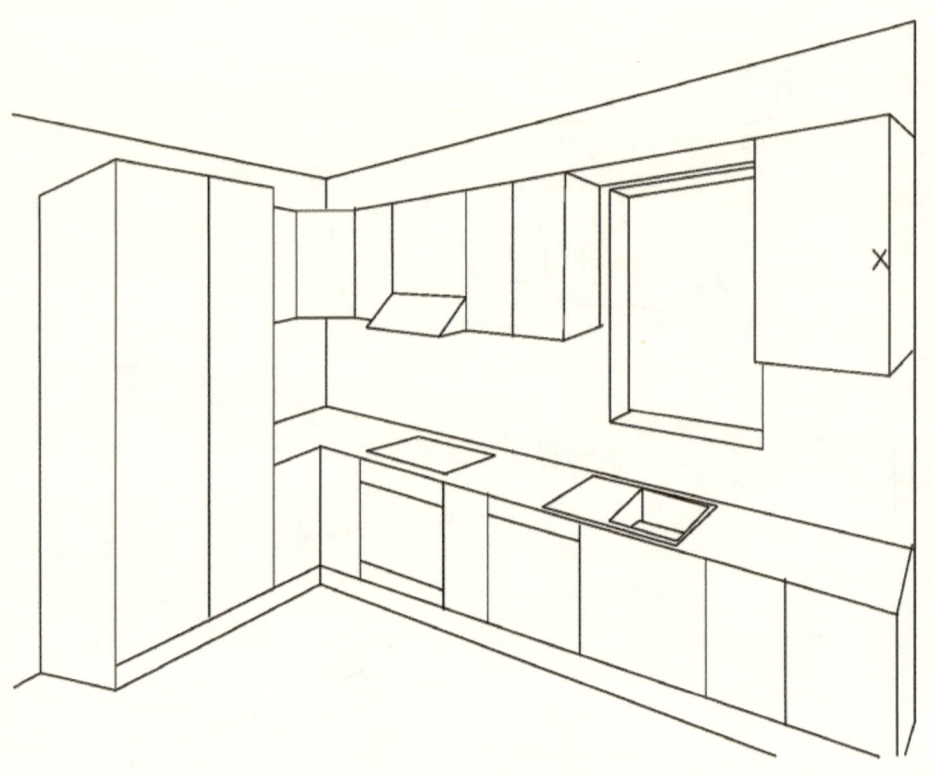

More detail

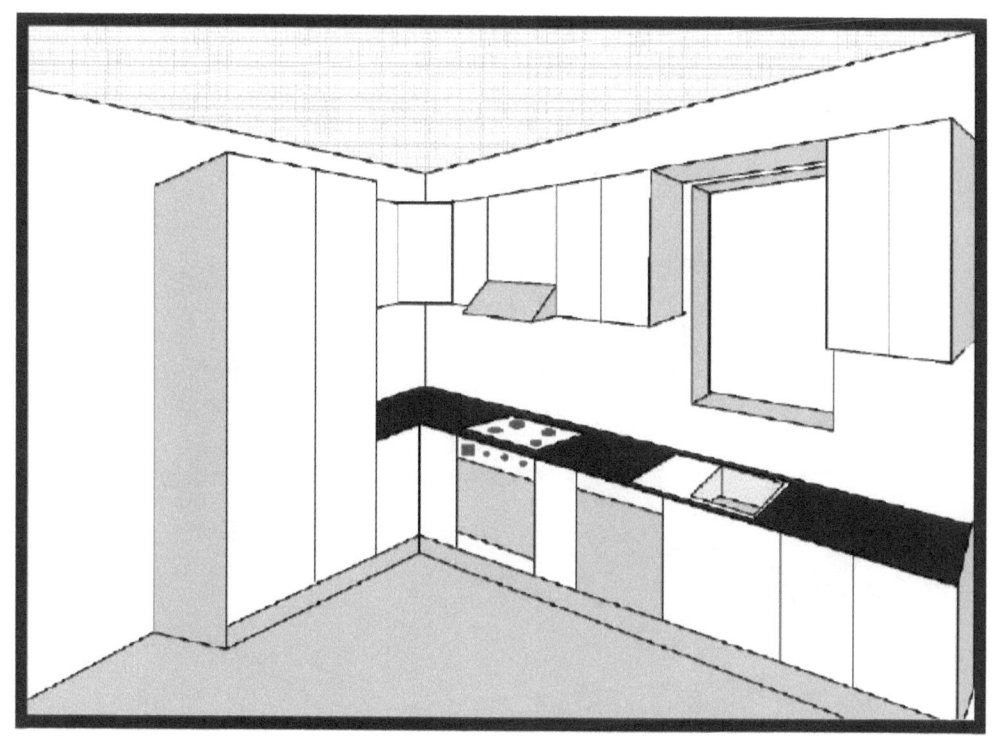

Final detail and
rendering as per
choice

ROOM
EXAMPLES

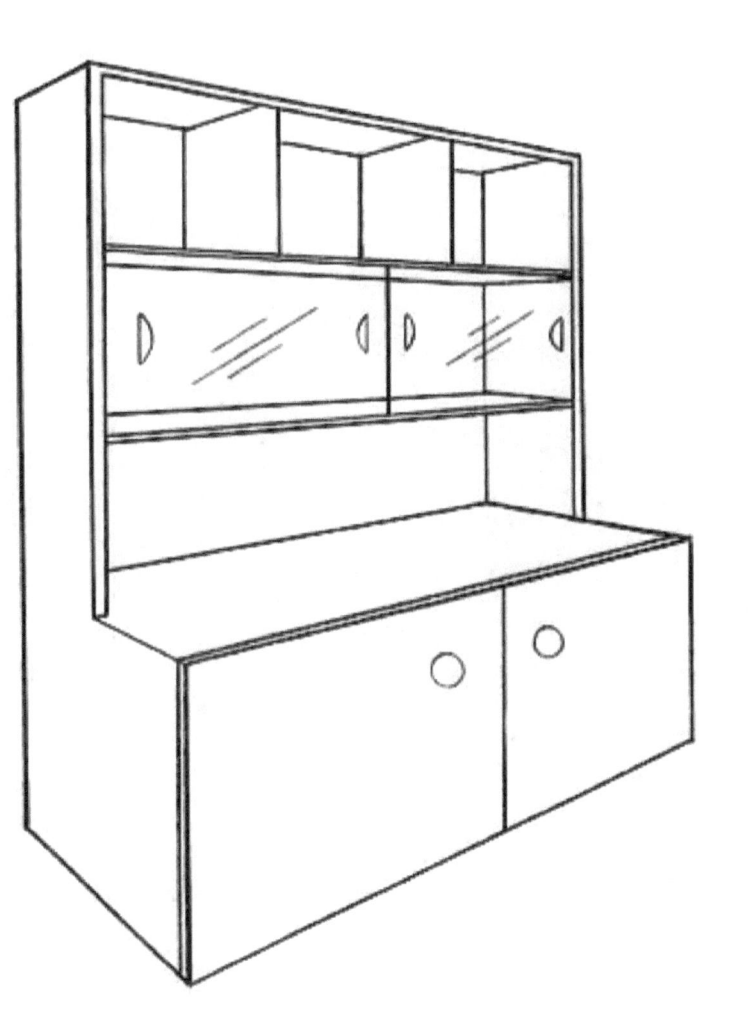

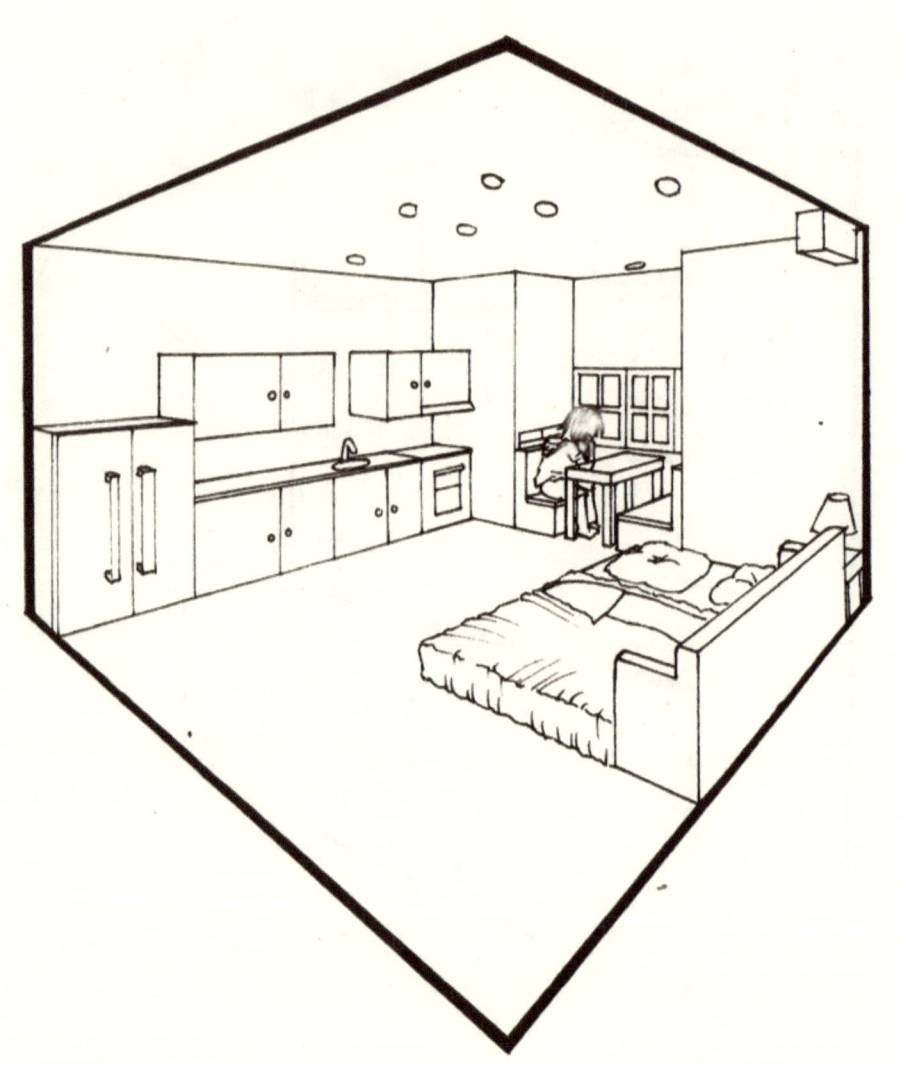

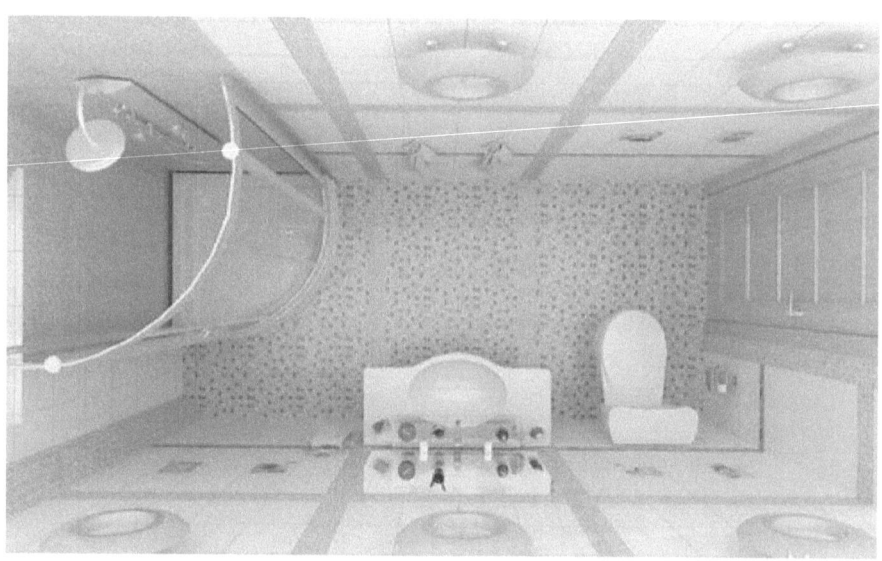

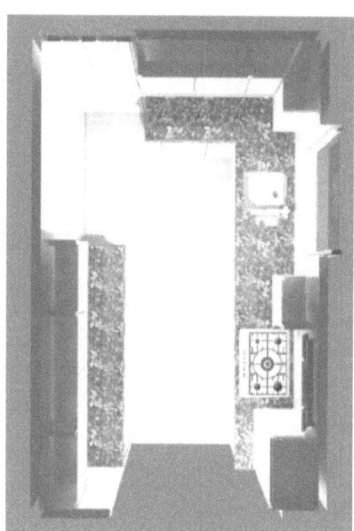

9

BIRD'S EYE PERSPECTIVE

This was always my favourite for kitchens as you can create the 3d drawing very quickly from your plan or a reduction thereof. The big advantage in presentation is that you can see the entire project even where it is an elaborate construction with Islands, Peninsula etc.

Birds Eyes are one of the simplest 3d drawings. All you need is your original scale plan and, using tracing paper, simply select your vanishing point somewhere on the floor to project the walls units etc. in birds eye.

This is especially useful for showing really complex shapes and the beauty is you don't need to worry about perspective measurements just use an ordinary scale rule and measure along the vertical lines you are drawing. Works fine.

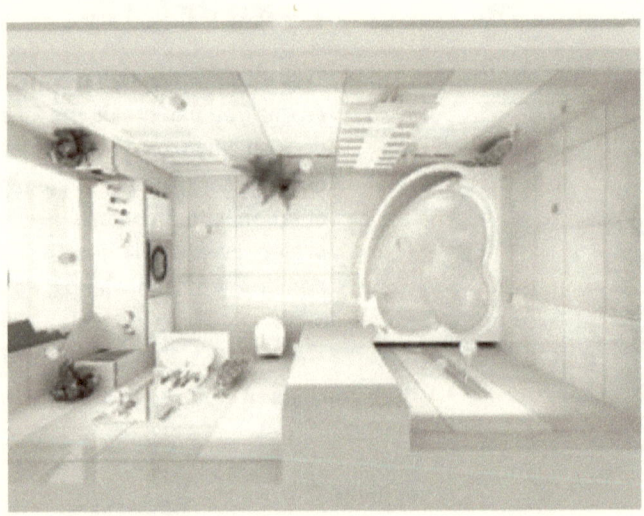

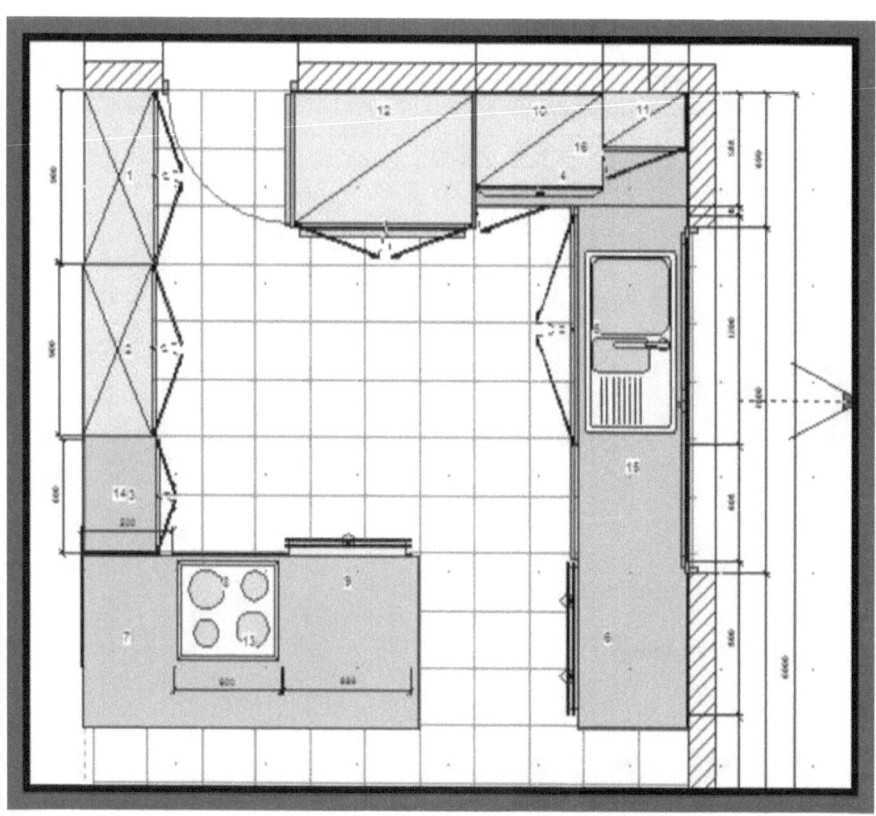

BIRD'S EYE TRANSFORMATION

You can see on this plan that it has been projected in some areas to create a birds eye effect. With just a little more work you could achieve an effective birds eye throughout the entire plan. Just choose the position of the vanishing point so you can "see" the units you want in greater detail

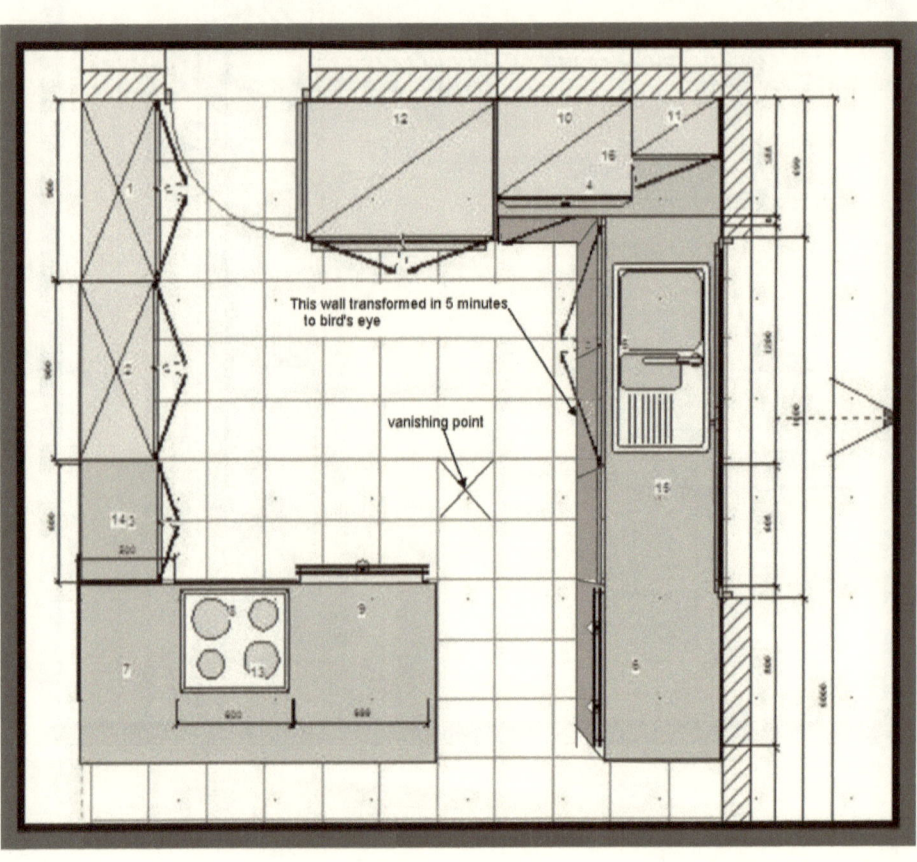

This wall transformed in 5 minutes to bird's eye

vanishing point

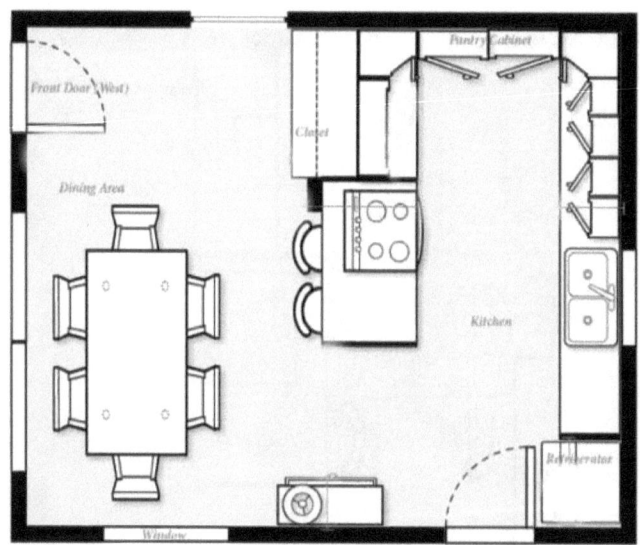

Front Door (West)

Dining Area

Closet

Pantry Cabinet

Kitchen

Refrigerator

Window

South (Car Port / Garage)

10

BIRD'S EYE TRANSFORMATION

Lorem ipsum dolor sit amet, ligula suspendisse nulla pretium, rhoncus tempor placerat fermentum, enim integer ad vestibulum volutpat. Nisl rhoncus turpis est, vel elit, congue wisi enim nunc ultricies sit, magna tincidunt. Maecenas aliquam maecenas ligula nostra, accumsan taciti. Sociis mauris in integer, a dolor netus non dui aliquet, sagittis felis sodales, dolor sociis mauris, vel eu libero cras. Interdum at. Eget habitasse elementum est, ipsum purus pede porttitor class, ut.

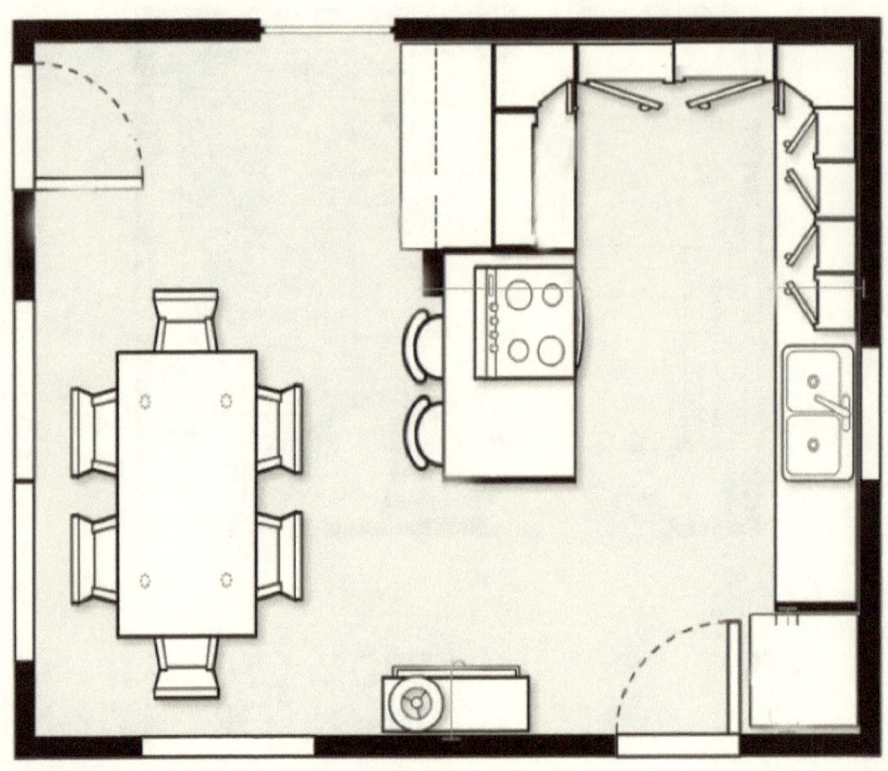

You can draw
directly from the
plan but you will
find it easier to
reduce the plan to
basics

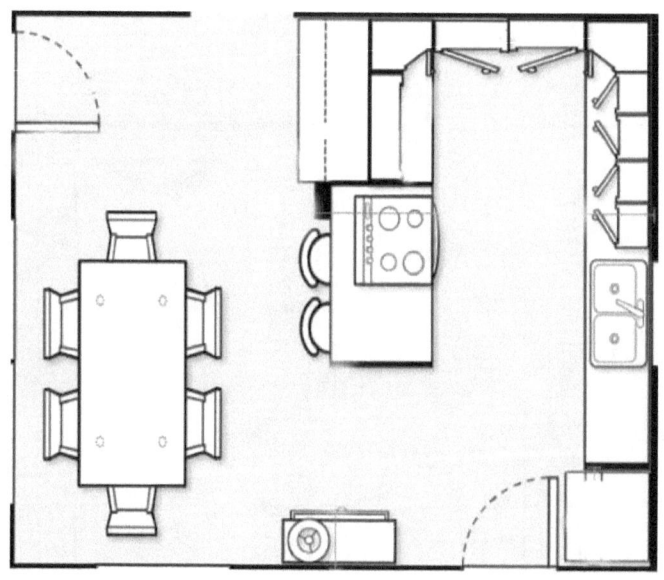

we have deleted
much of the
unwanted detail

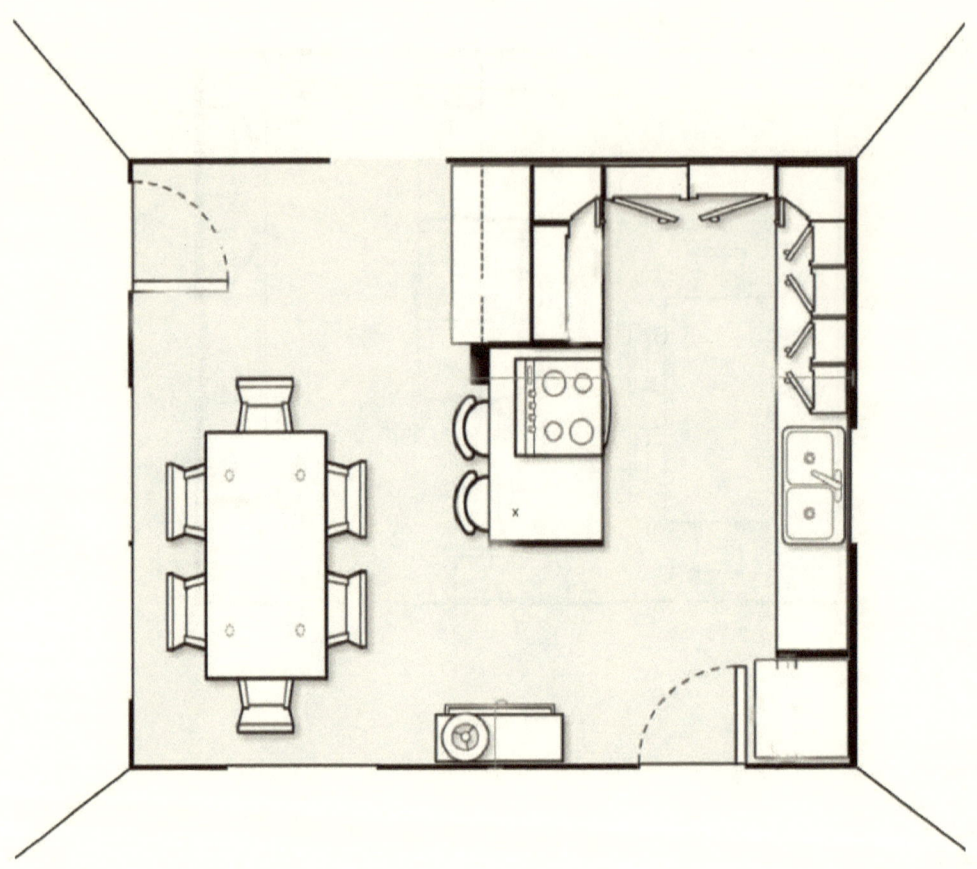

Starting with our
chosen vanishing
point we have
projected all four
corners of the room

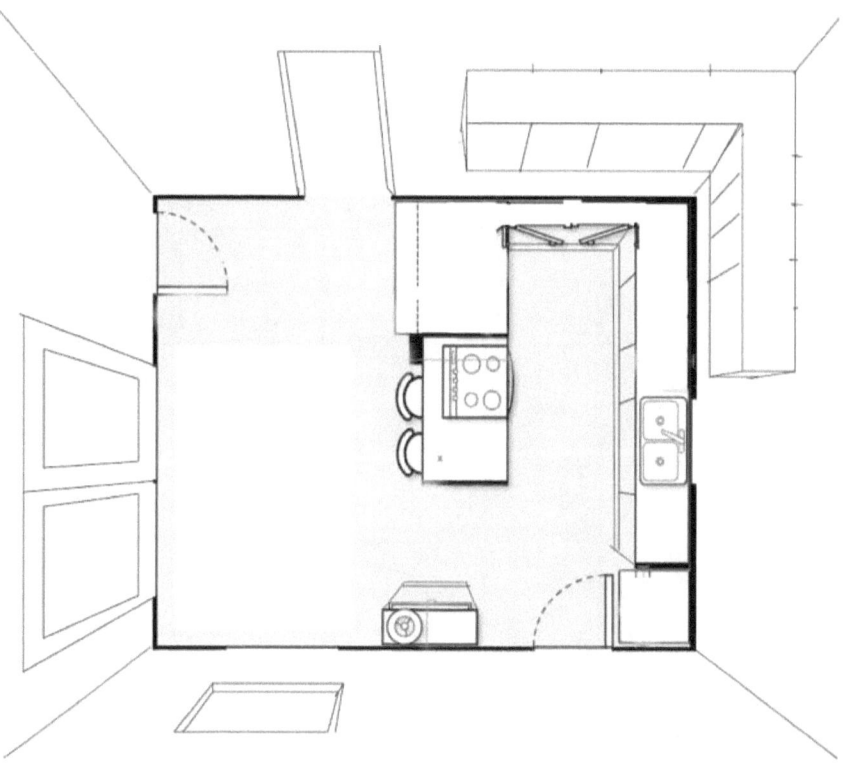

Deleted more
unwanted items
and continue with
carcassing and
room details

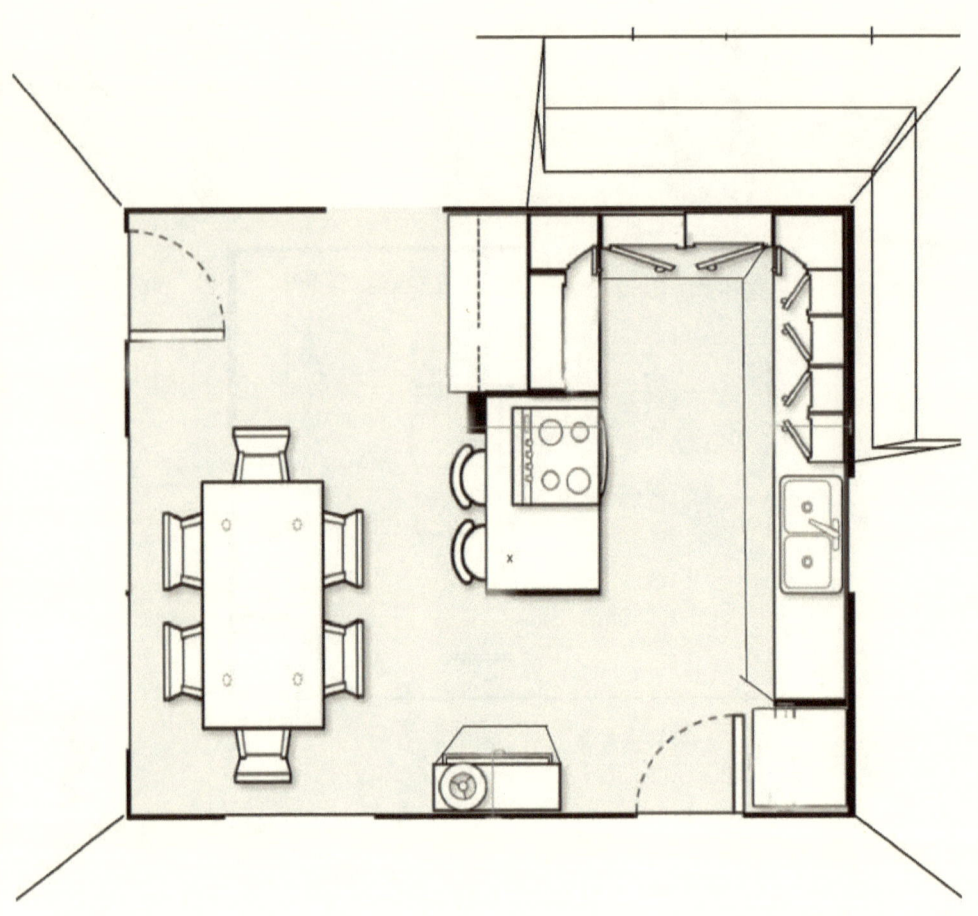

Now construct the
carcase outine
using the same
technique

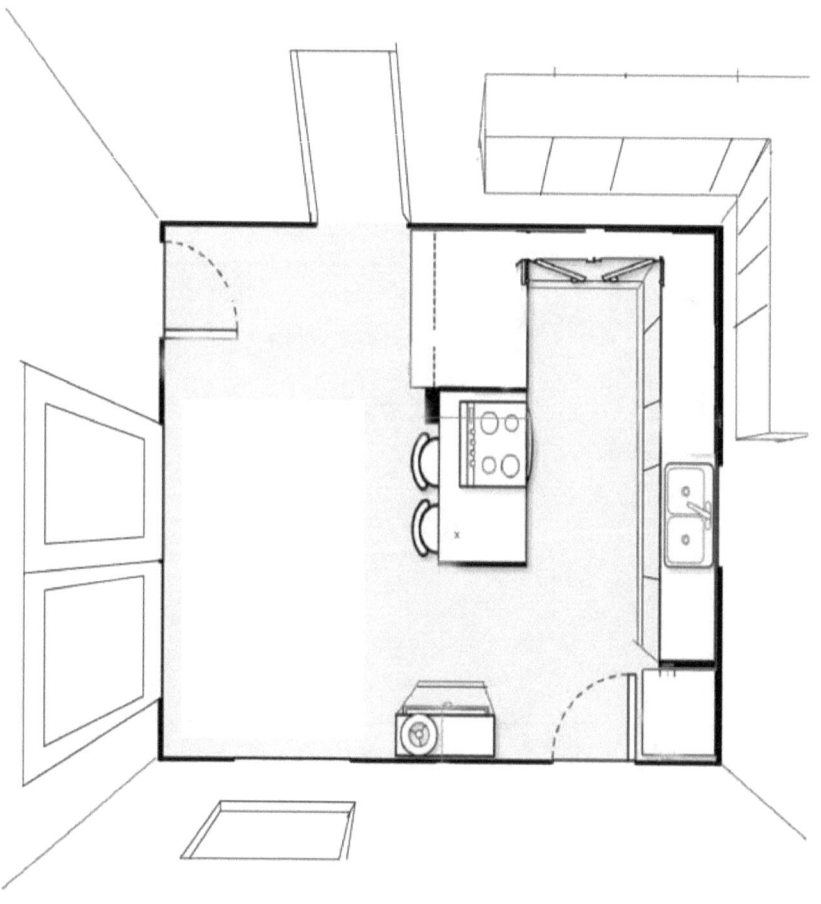

More room detail

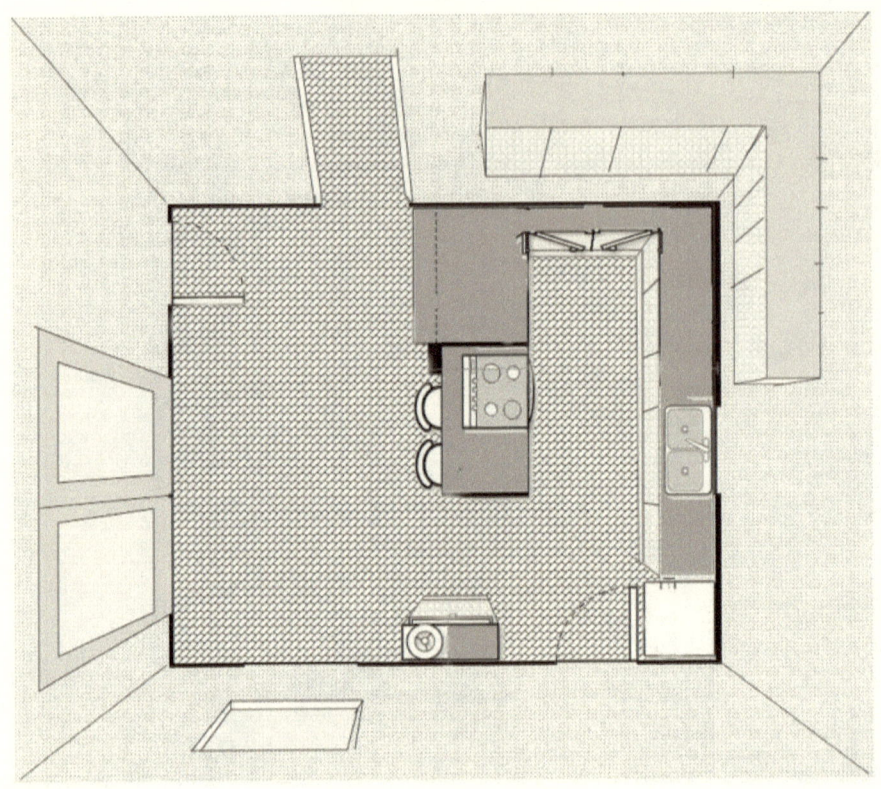

Continue with
detailing and ass
rendering.

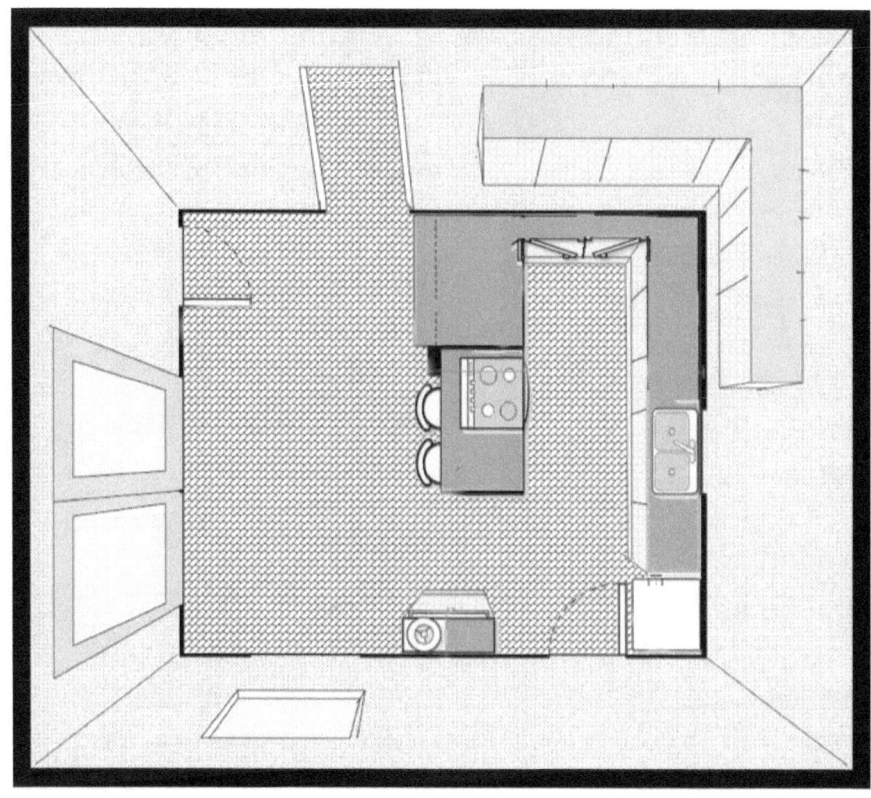

Possible finished
plan

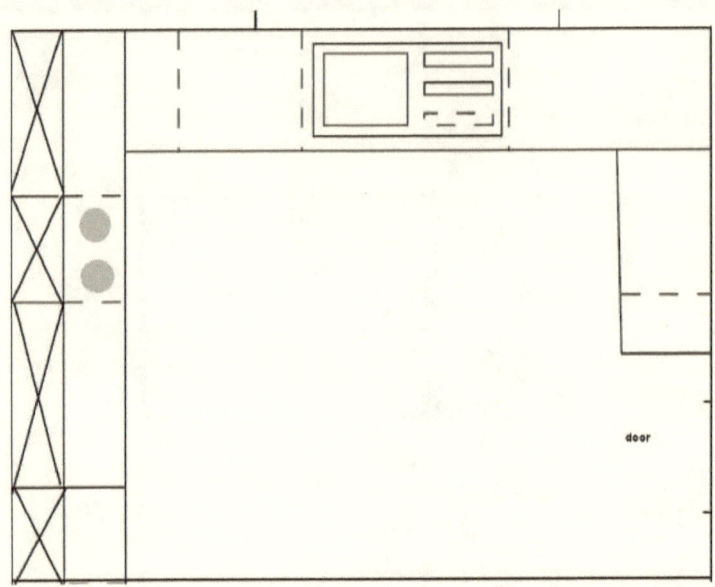

door

BIRD'S EYE FORMAL METHOD FROM SCRATCH

Start with your scale plan in very simple, basic format so you don't get too confused wti the liness espeically if you are using tracing paper. You may find however, that using a normal piece of paper you can trace the outlines and then just use the scale plan for reference as you develop.

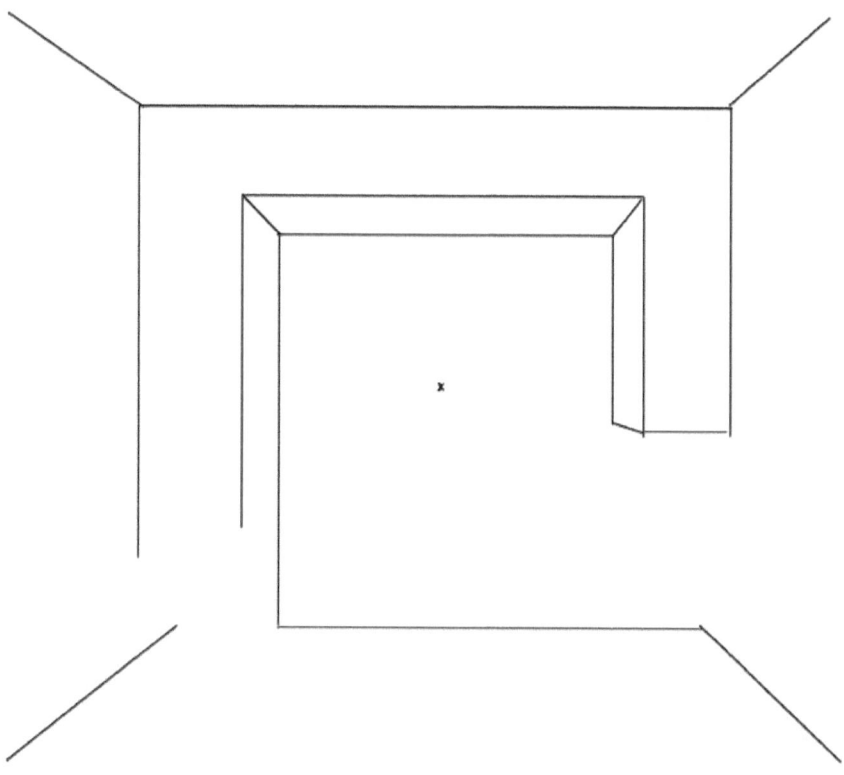

Locate your desired
vanishing point for
the best view and
project the wall
and the carcassing

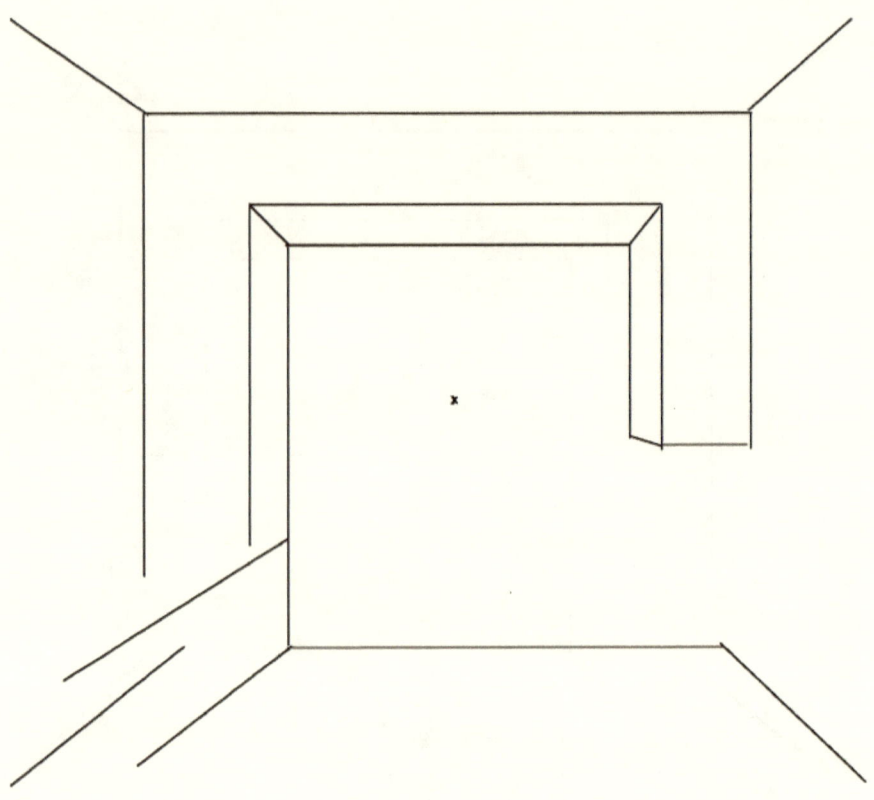

Continue with
profiling

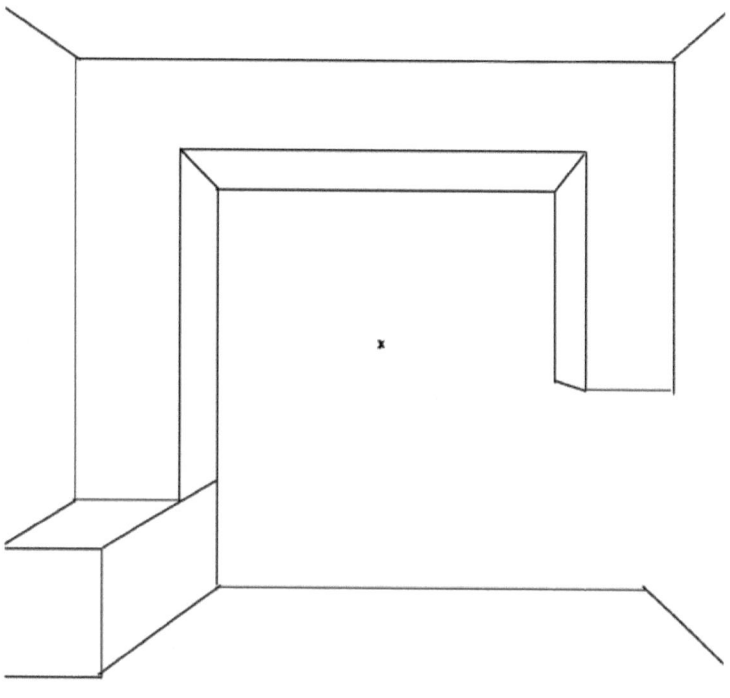

**Stzrt tidying and
detailing**

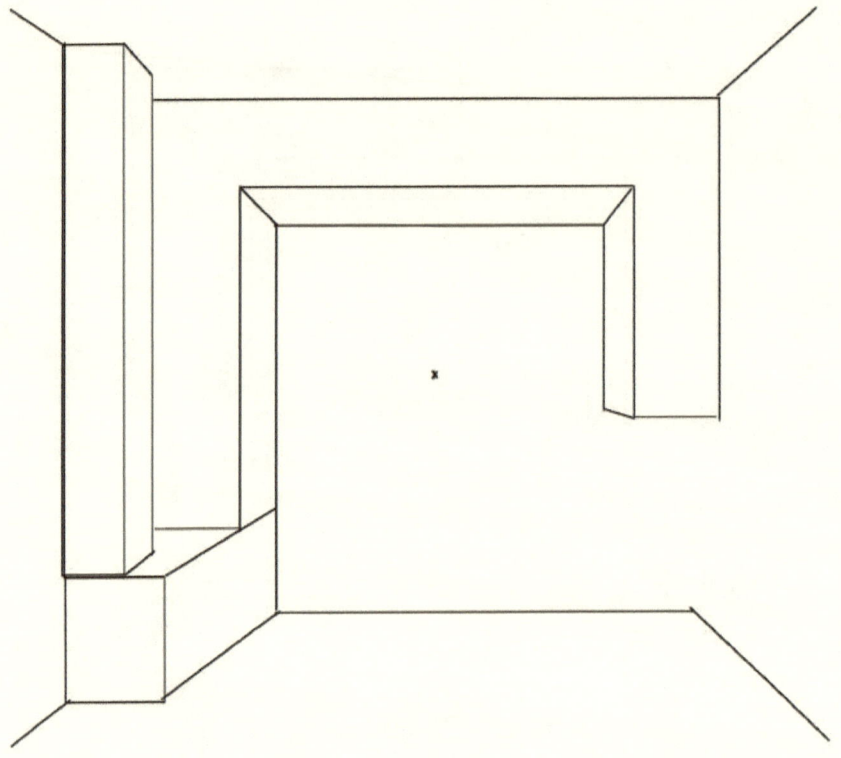

Complete carcssing

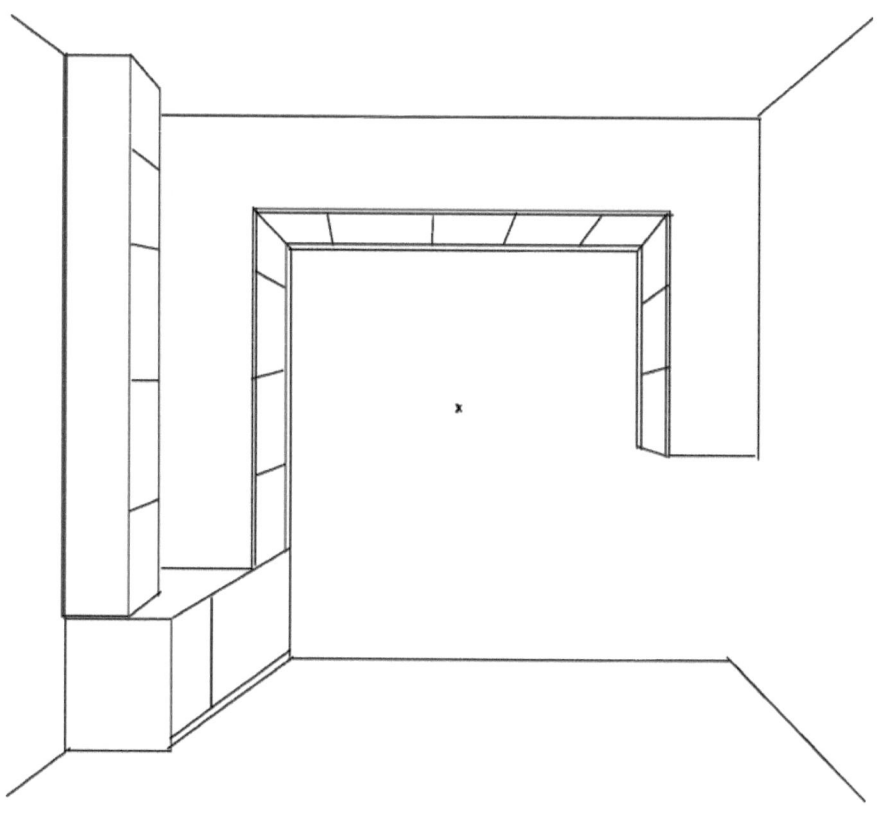

Continue with
carcasse detail

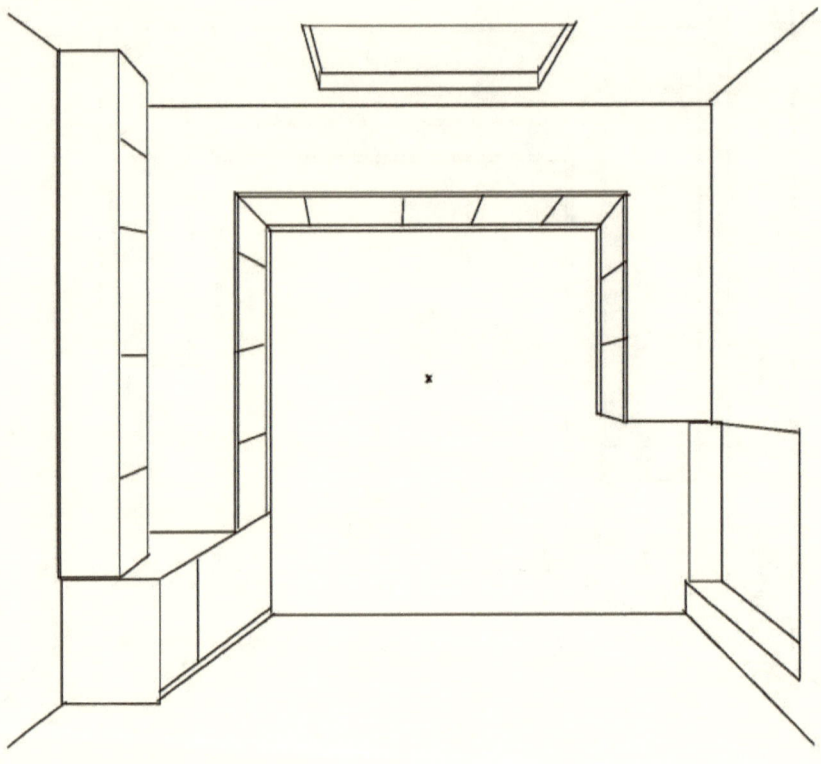

add architectural
details

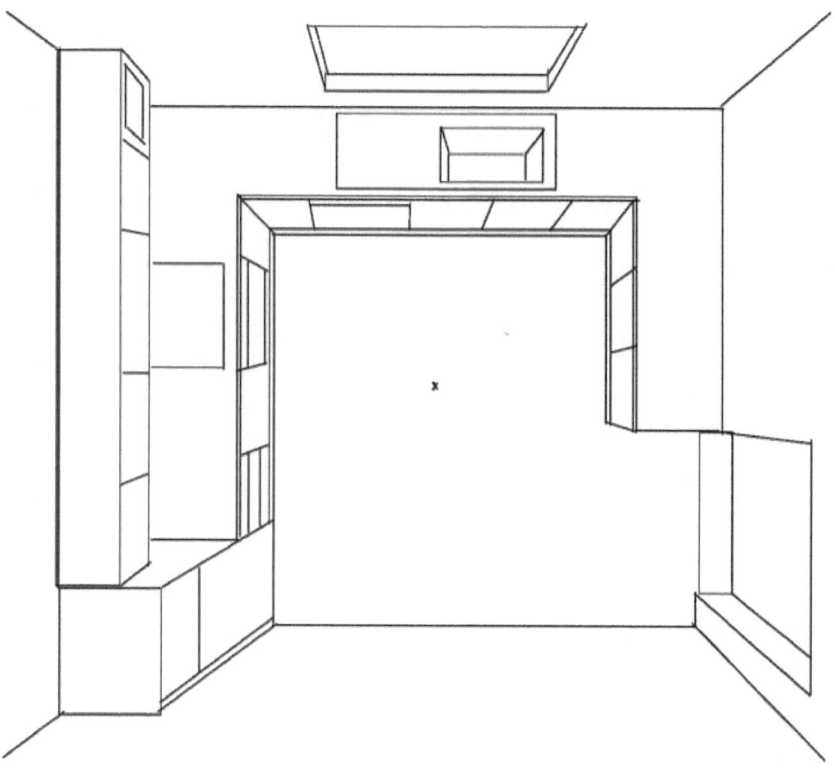

Continue detailing

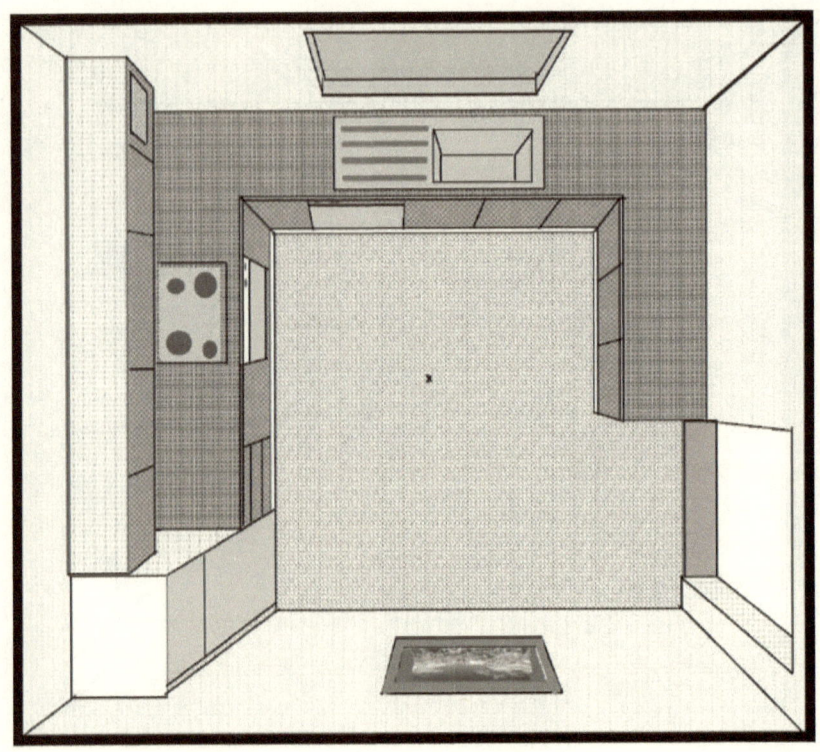

Complete detail,
border, rendering
as desired.

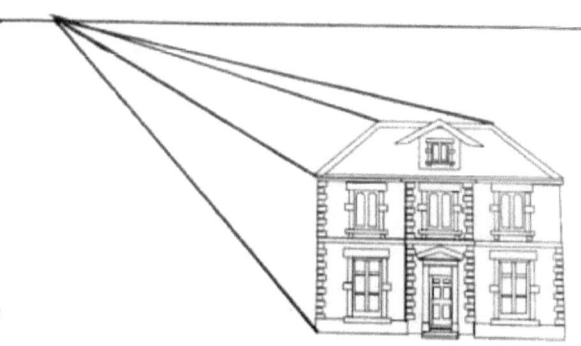

11

TRANSFORMING

This chapter is about taking a simple drawing - even a simple 3d drawing and transforming it into a 3d possibly even a startling transformation but with a minimum of time and effort.

Our fist example is the EXTERIOR 2 point drawing as shown above

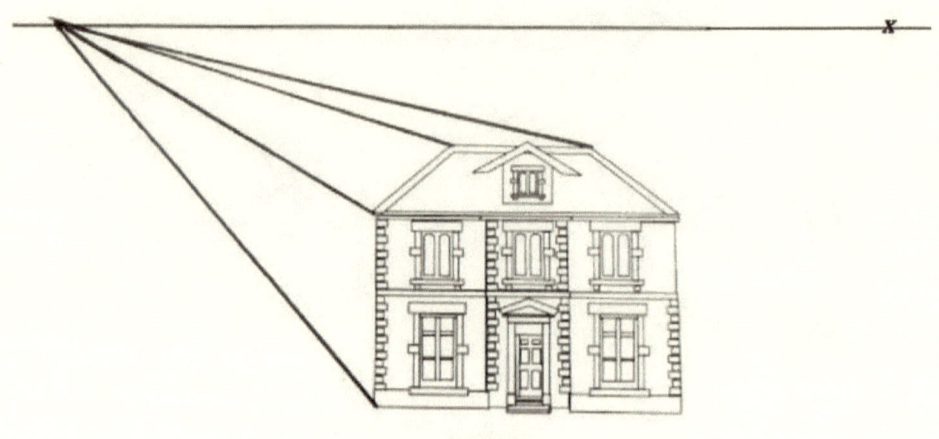

Firstly we take the
original drawing
and place a second
vanishing point on
the horizon line

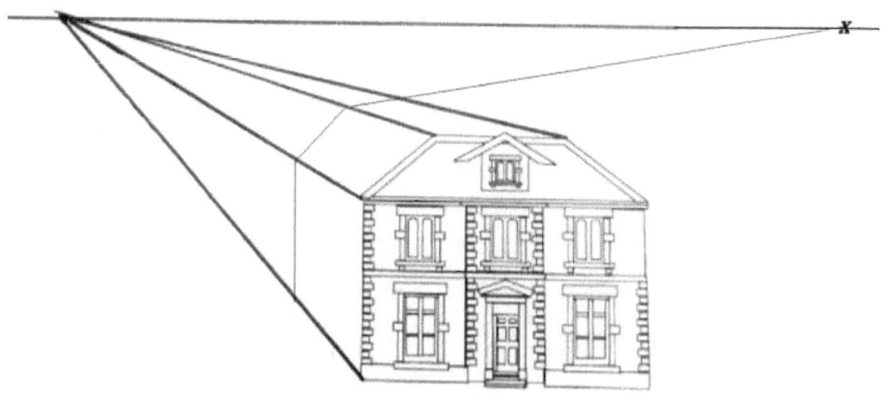

we then determine
the rear and side of
the building

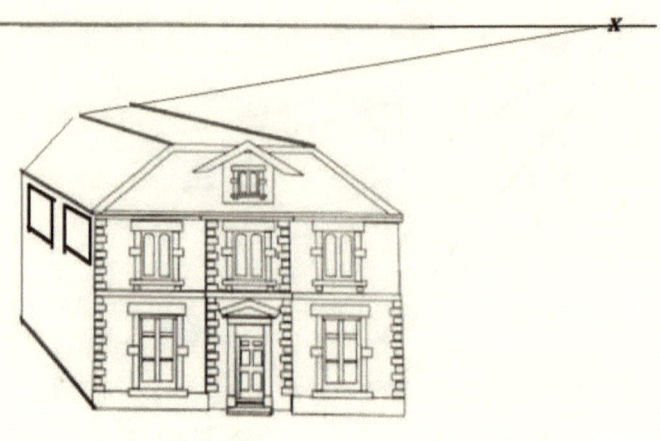

outline the building
and remove some
of the original
perspective lines

Next add a bit
more interest to the
side of the building

tidy the drawing

Unfortunately it
was a hand drawn
outline not drawn
accurately but still
makes an
acceptable
presentation

We can even add
some grounds and
if you wish more
details such as
plants, ponds etc.
Total time to this
stage 10 minutes

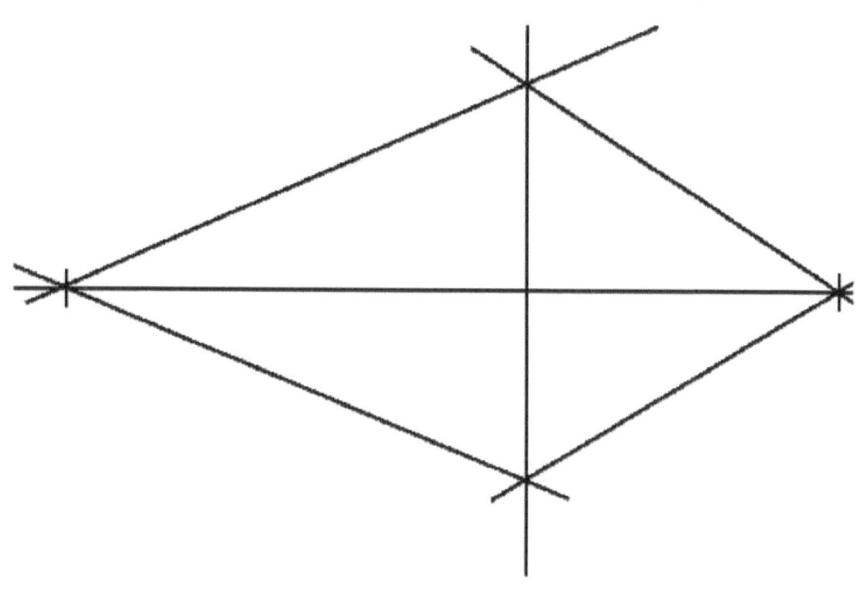

TRANSFORMING AN EXTERIOR 2 POINT PRESENTTION TO AN INTERIOR PRESENTATION

This exercise demonstrates the difference between exterior 2 point drawings and interior 2 point drawings and hopefully helps you to understand the effective differences

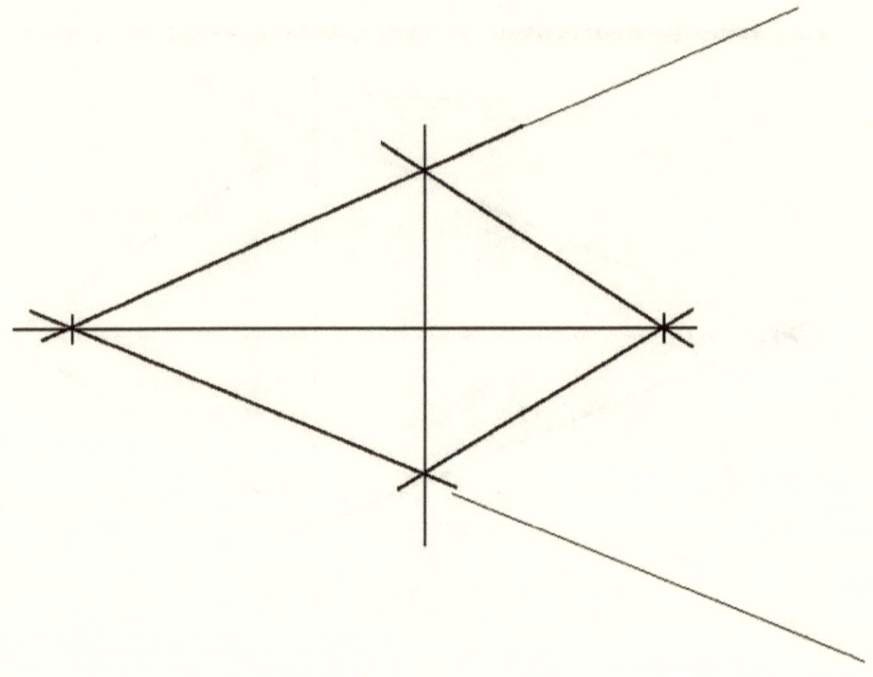

start by extending
the perspective
lines into the
opposite walls

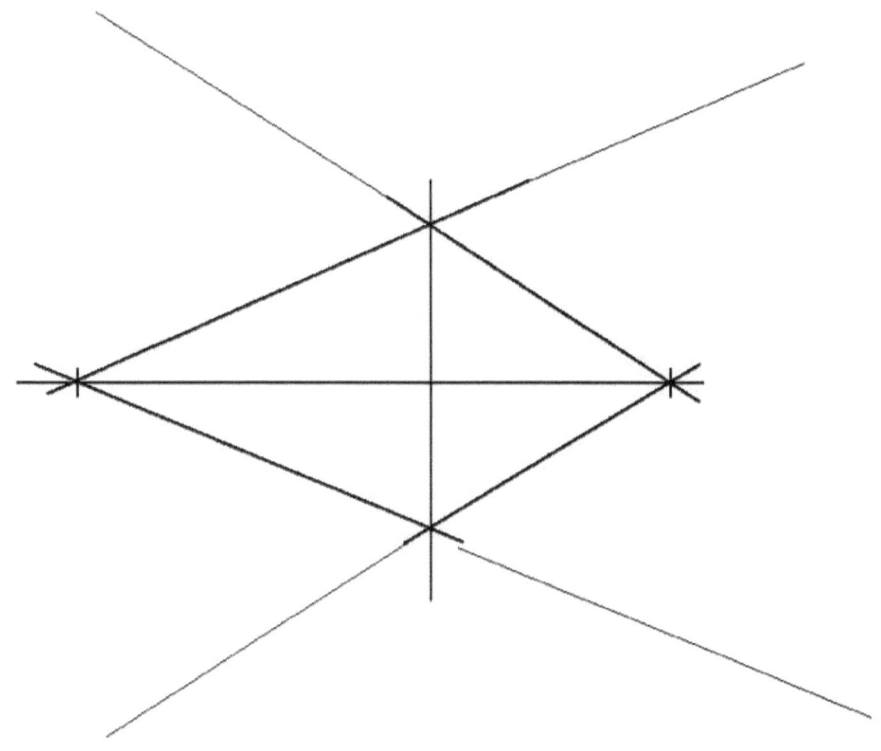

do the same both
sides

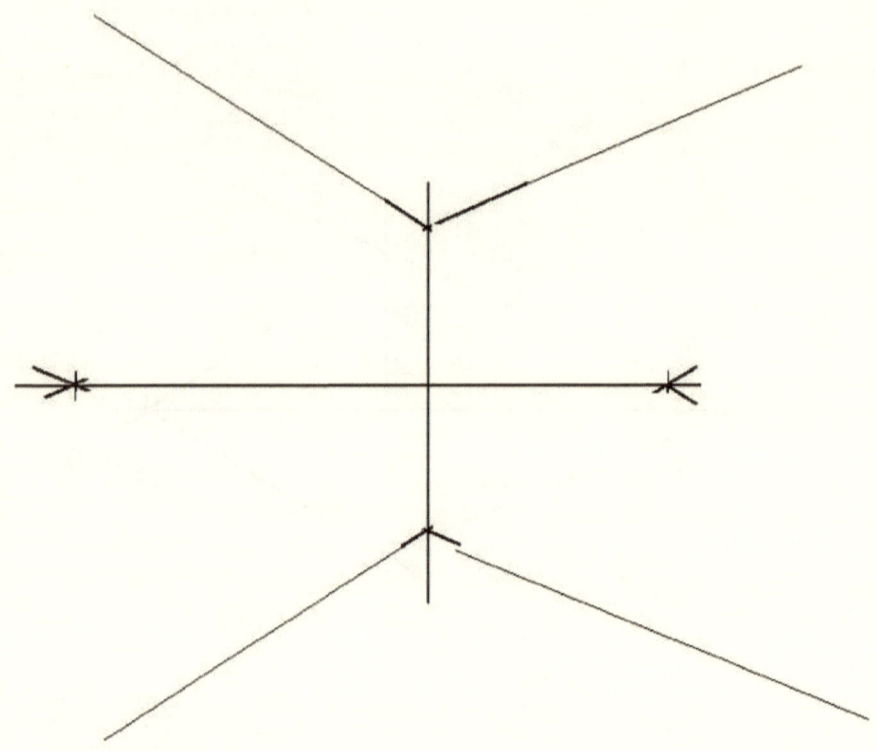

we now realize that
the vanishing points
are not far away
for effective
drawing. Interior
drawings are
obviously more
compact

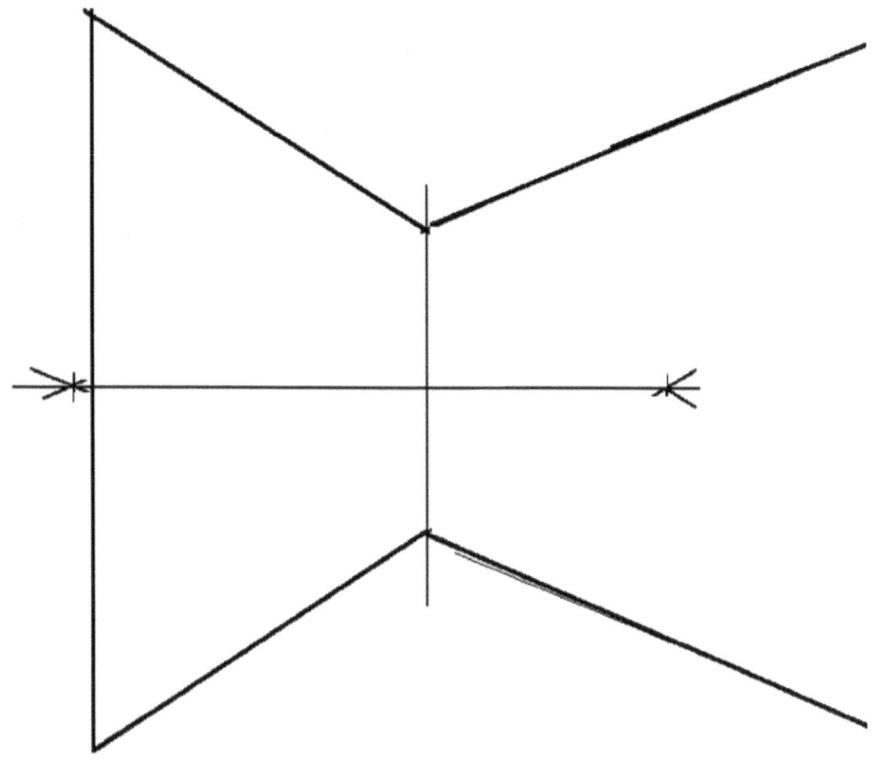

we have tidied up
the outline but still
need to work on
the VP

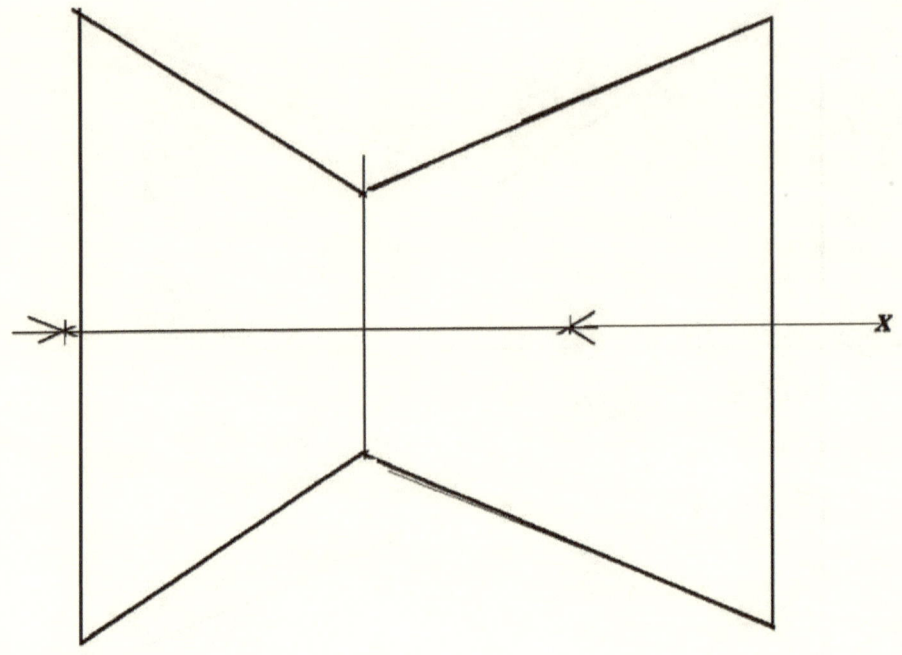

We have now
moved the RH VP
outside the room so
we can now begin
to construct our
room drawing. As
the VP has been
repositioned it will
be necessary to
redraw the LH
walls

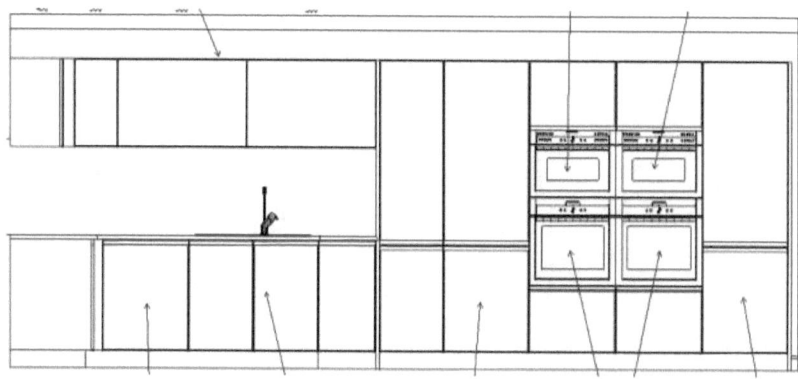

TRANSFORMING ELEVATIONS INTO 1 POINT

We are all used to drawing simple elevations both from a project execution viewpoint and for a sales presentation. Let's look and see how easy it is to transform such a drawing into an effective 3 d presentation.

You may also wish to look back at our Birds Eye exercise to see how easy it is to transform a simple scale plan to 3d.

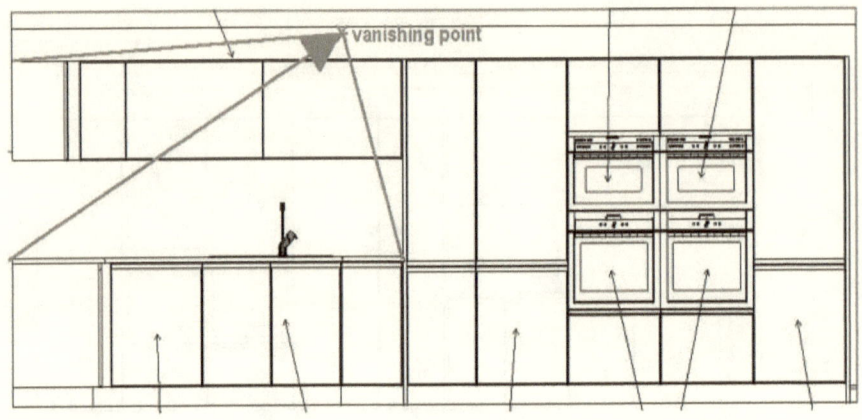

First choose a
suitable place for
the vanishing point

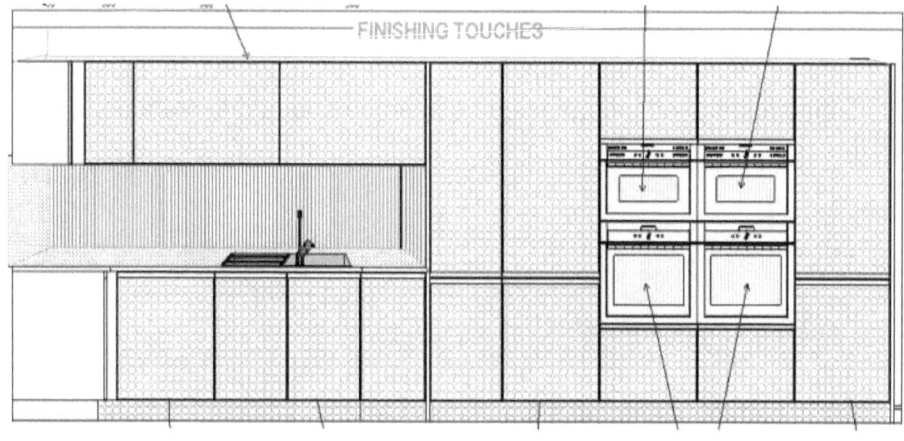

Make the drawing
come alive with
some 3d touches

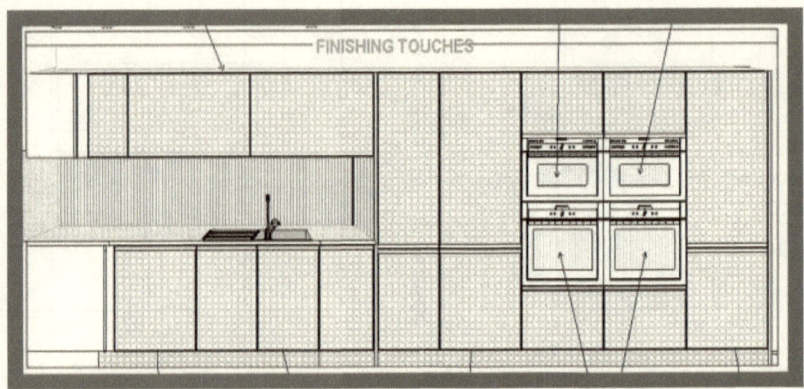

Enhance the
drawing with a
border

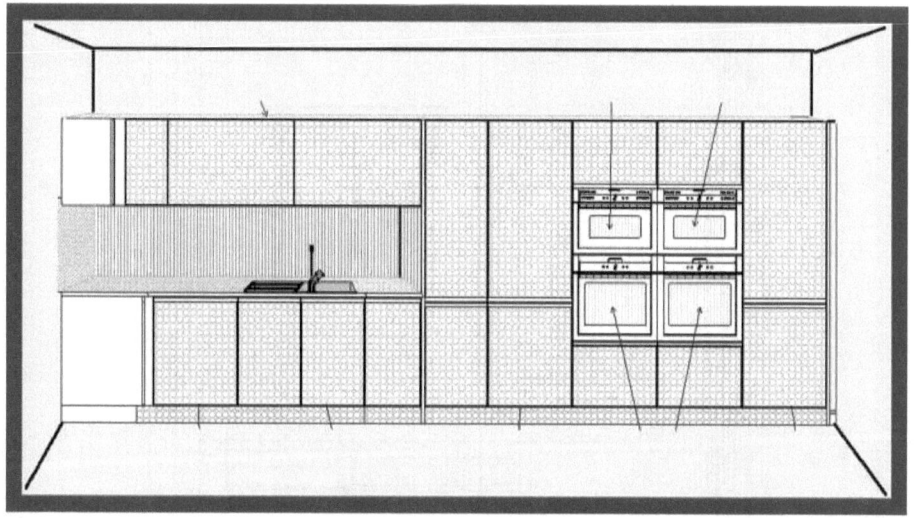

Even make the new
border into part of
the 3d room?

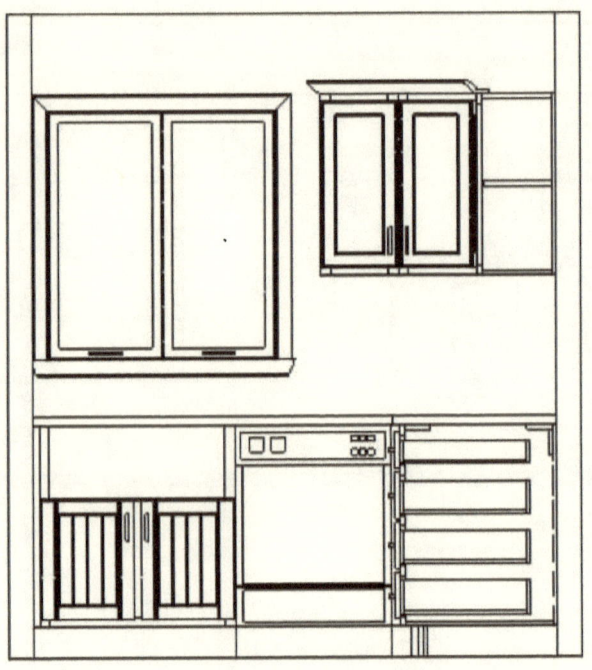

ELEVATION TO 1
POINT

This is nicely drawn elevation if a questionable plan, but it serves as a decent exercise from a drawing point of view.

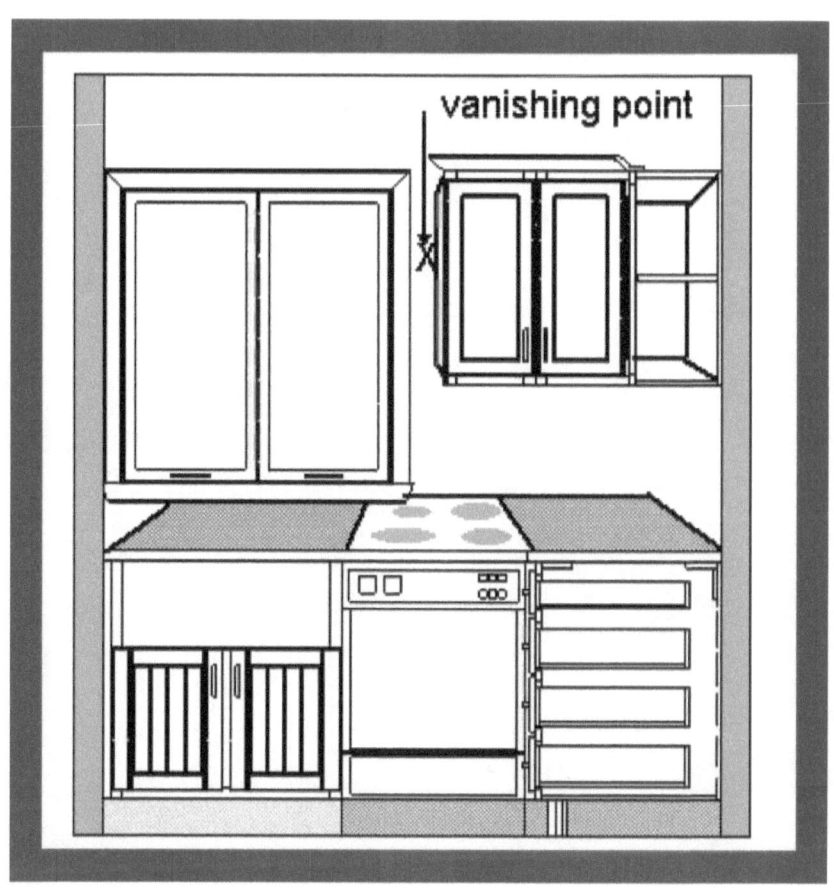

Looks good in 3d
but what a dodgy
hob.

LITTLE BOXES

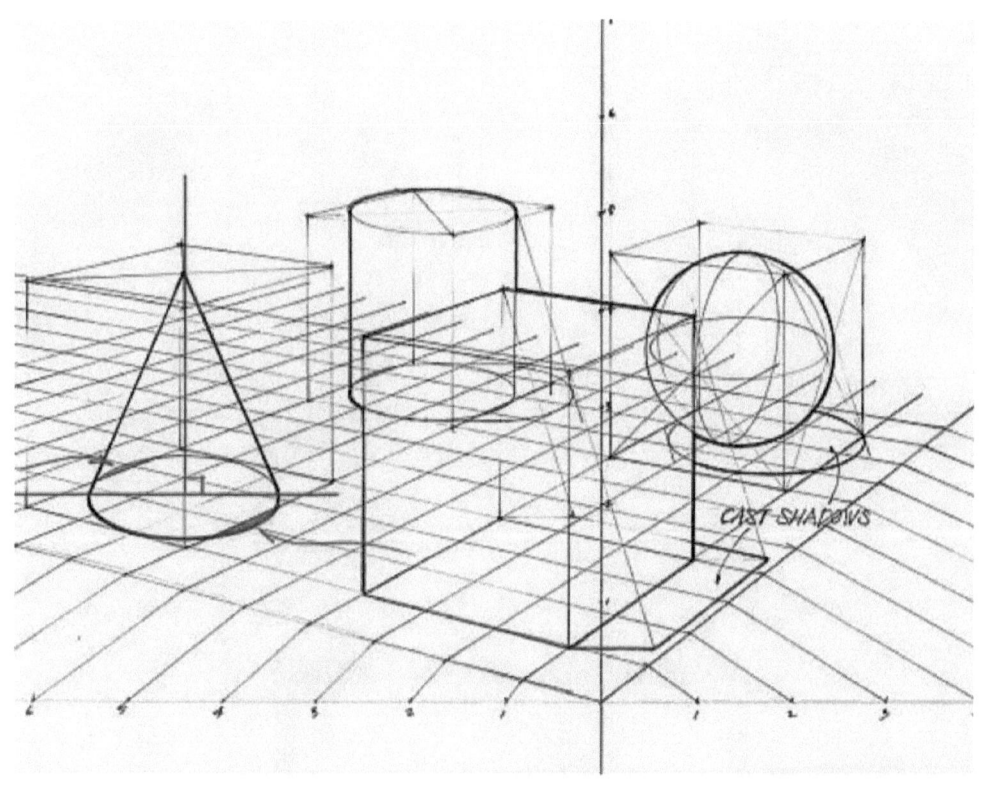

CAST SHADOWS

WHATEVER THE
SHAPE YOU ARE
SEEKING START
WITH A CUBE -
THEN SHAPE IT

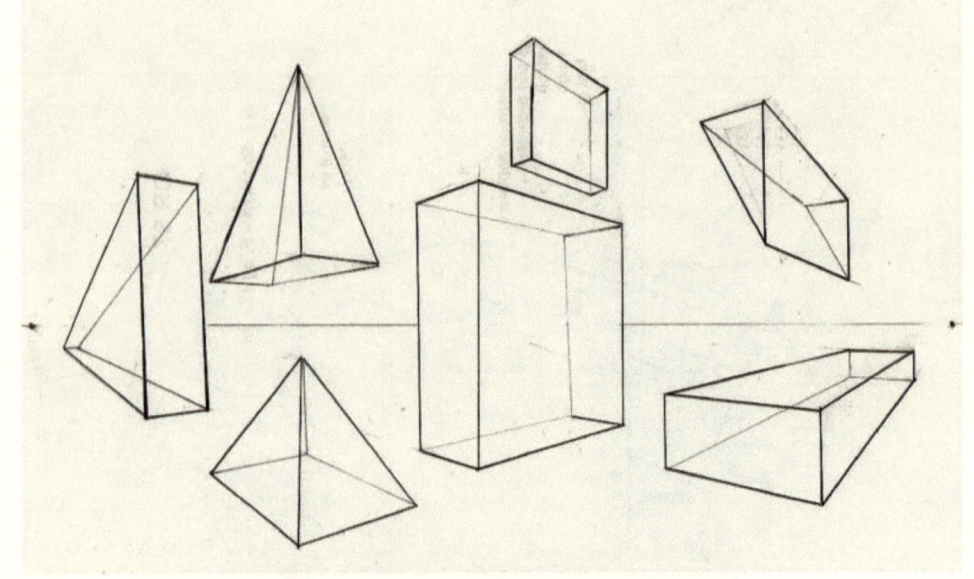

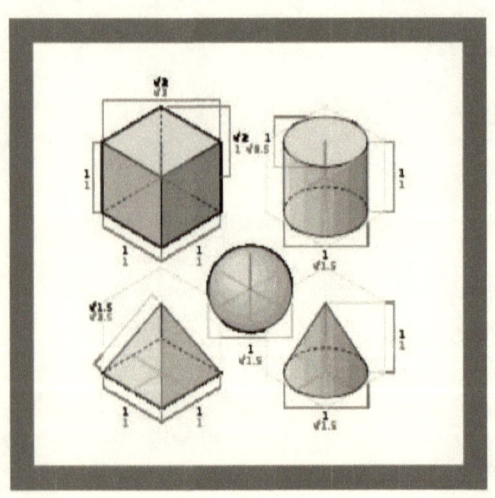

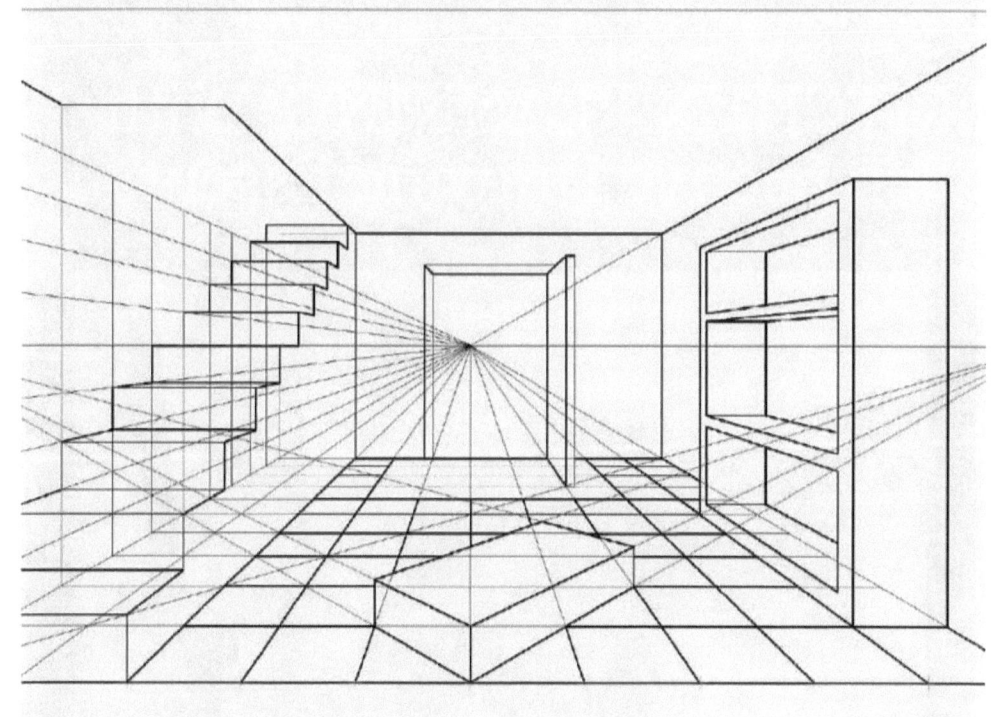

THIS IS ACTUALLY
A COMBINATION
OF 1 POINT AND
2 POINT -
interesting shapes

KITCHEN PLANNING With Perspective Drawing Essentials

Before you can plan a kitchen you need to know the layout and measurements of the room and all the architectural features of the room. You also need to know the location of the services and you need to understand the limitations of altering these services

This is a book specifically designed for the Paperback publication system. Monochrome has been chosen to allow the purchaser access to these advanced planning and drawing techbooks at a bargain price. The author has had an enormous amount of practical experience in planning, designing, installation, sales etc of all types of KBB projects from budget to extreme luxury. Couple this with nearly 40 years of training novices and professionals in the art of Kitchen planning plus the invention of the Perspective Ruler - an unbeatable package

CHAPTER 14

The Measure - Survey

This is a typical laser measuring device accurate to within 1.5cm & can measure up to 40 metres. This one costs under £100 which is not a lot considering the speed & accuracy of the device

You should also back this up with another method - always measure with at least 2 devices. For smaller measurements and for detailing service you will need a conventional measuring tape or measuring stick. the measuring stick is the most versatile but rather misunderstood in the UK. Anyone with a history of German kitchen design will be very familiar with these.

There are also some other measuring deices which are probably now a little superfluous such as the ultrasonic and the infra red devices. These did not have the accuracy and are prone to mishandling and errors. I think it is probably now time to dispose of these somewhat outdated items, but they are acceptable as a back up.

When using a traditional tape for measuring you need to remember that they have a floating end which can be used to hook around something or compress to measure directly from the face of an object or part of the room. For normal measurements there should be no reason for this kind of accuracy as you should build in flexibility into your plan. Even if your measurements are accurate the room is probably not square and this will throw out your plan by as much as 40-50 mm at some point.

GOLDEN RULE

Always build in flexibility.

There is possibly one area where you need to be utterly accurate and that is with expensive worktops. In most cases they cannot be successfully worked on site and they are extremely difficult to prepare and to cut so get it right the first time. In general terms the man made solid state surfaces can usually be worked afterwards to some degree - perhaps 2-3 cm. but some of the traditional solid surface materials such as marble and Granite or even slate do not really have any realistic flexibility. If you are fabricating stainless steel worktops you want them to fit - first time.

One of the most common errors in measurements are not providing the correct spaces for appliances. Built in appliances are usually stated as to the space they occupy and a 60cm built in dishwasher will fit into 60cm. But a 60cm freestanding washing machine will clearly require some 'wriggle room' and even other appliances will require some kind of extra space consideration. Maybe just for ventilation. refrigerators are clearly one of those important considerations as they will require some form of ventilation. Built in fridges should have ventilation built into their architecture. Freestanding fridges must have proper ventilation considerations. If you do not allow for these consideration you may find that the product will not maintain an accurate temperature and food which should be stored chilled may develop bacteria if it is not stored at the correct and constant temperature.

It is also necessary to provide ventilation for gas using appliances. There is also a consideration for kitchens where there are a lot of gas appliances. If in doubt ask a professional who knows how much air is required for these appliances to breathe. I have carried on a bit and I will repeat a lot of these points in the appliance sections but for now I hope you can realize the important of measuring quickly and accurately.

Clearly if you are in the customer's home you don't want to spend hours on the initial measure.. If you are also trying to provide a plan on the night and possibly even sell on the night. timing is a critical consideration.

Unless you are in an OTN environment it is usually best to do the most efficient measure possible and then provide your plan back at the ranch where you can ponder over any of the problems that might pop up.

This also gives you a chance to double check any queries you may have. Invite the buyer into the showroom to view the plan and the estimate.Always build in a few optional extra. Everyone has a budget no matter what they say. If you have a desirable extra show them the cost and sell them the advantages. This way you should be able to come out with the sale even if it is just a basic deal.

Floor Plans

The floor plan is the vital first stage of the Kitchen Planning. Firstly you need a working plan of the kitchen and services layout. It is vital to note all the key service positions plus the access to the main electric, water and draining positions

The more accurate the floor plan the more accurate your kitchen plan proposal and in particular the more practical that proposal will be.

Too many kitchen planners and designers try to place facilities where they are simply impractical. For example if you wanted to plan a kitchen with an island setting to incorporate a sink, how are you going to get the plumbing to it and more important how are you going to get the waste away. I have seen too many so called clever designers plan a kitchen in this way only to have to use a small bore pumping system to get the water away and sometimes even trying to use this for a waste disposal unit. The installation costs would be astronomical and the

on going servicing problems would give the householder many problems.

It is clearly attractive to plan an island for a hob but remember this is a major circuit with a large cable so you still need to get a new cable to this position. You might even consider a gas hob - even bigger problem and of course you need ventilation - How? Actually ventilation for a cooker hood in an island position is not necessarily that difficult but everything would ideally need to go in the ceiling so you would obviously need full access to the ceiling.

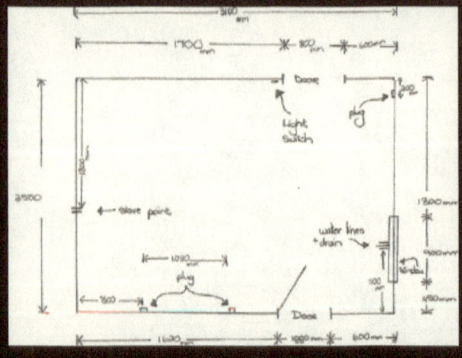

CHAPTER 15

Standard Notation

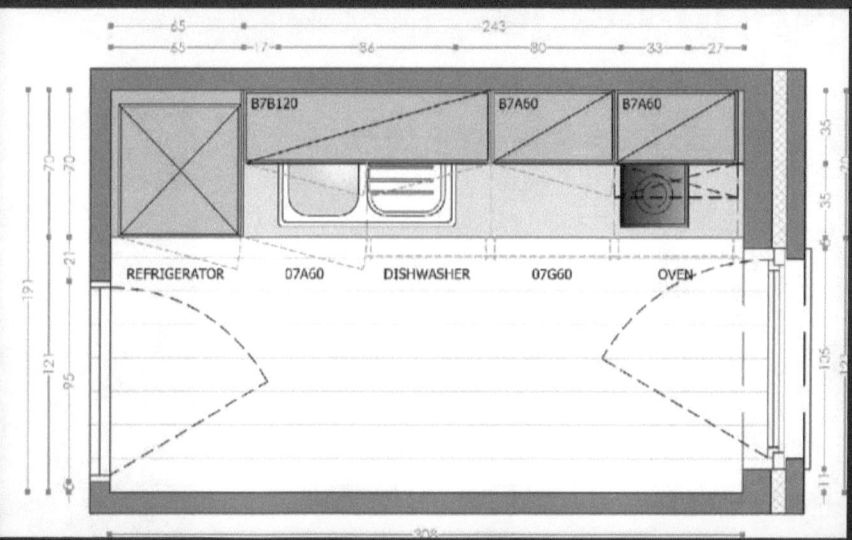

There is no point in providing a plan unless it can be read and understood by everyone including the installers.

See how the tall unit is crossed- correctly. The wall units are not crossed correctly, a half cross should denote the hinging but it is not oftenused these days useful to show the lines for base unit doors and hinging - also wall units.

Dimensions are fine but not necessary Appliances doors should be shown as drop down and dotted - as oven and

dishwasher. The small areas in front of the dishwasher and oven actually show drawer boxes which are obviously incorrect except unit 07g60 may very well have a drawer or be a drawer pack in which case multiple drawers should be shown. Best to number units with a legend looks tidier

CHAPTER 16

Drawing Techniques & Equipment

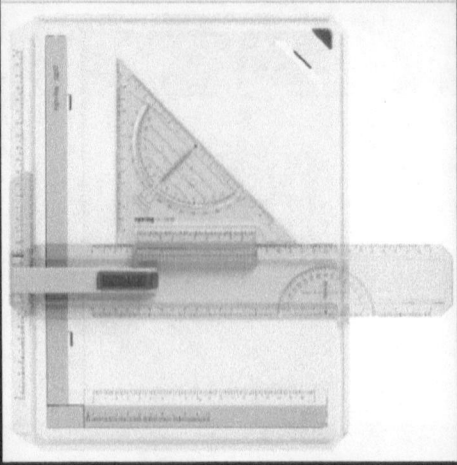

To draw correctly, accurately & easily use an A4 portable drawing board and set squares

•always draw with the board or square never freehand

•draw in pencil a proper pencil is best

•the parallel should be locked to draw

•use a 45° and 60/30° for all angles

•use a light touch so the drawing can be altered

•use a copier to add further detail and keep a master

•always draw by hand and then transfer to a computer if you are using one

•remember you will need a before and after plan showing all key features

CHAPTER 17

Planning -Ergonomics Anthropomentrics

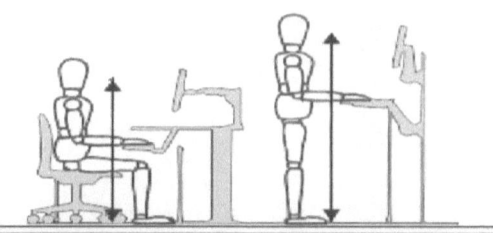

The study of people and their relationship with the environment around them.

When anthropometric data (measurements / statistics) is applied to a product, e.g. measurements of the hand are used to design the shape and size of a handle, this is ergonomics.

A well planned kitchen takes into account all the ergonomic and anthropometric considerations of modern planning but tempered to a reasonable extent to the customer's needs. Remember however, the more personal the kitchen the less salable to a 3rd party.

Anthropometrics is the comparative study of human body measurements and properties. Ergonomics is the science of making the work environment safer and more comfortable for workers using design and anthropometric data.

Perhaps these illustration can suggest to the planner that it is important to take into account the physical attributes of the end user. Clearly a 5 foot nothing housewife is not going to be very keen on 900 high wall units.

Similarly if there are a number of children in the house some or all of them may be working in the kitchen from time to time. For example if the sink is heavily used for dishwashing and in particular fresh vegetable preparation there may be a case for using either a continental style worktop height or a dropped zone in this area. If you are using a dropped sink zone then it would appear logical to adopt a dropped hob zone as well.

Electrics already have their requirements for accessibility of the height of switches and sockets but again there may be a case to take extra care when making extensive electric variations and installations to ensure that switching heights and socket positions are ideal for the household and not just for the house. You may have designed a wonderful lighting plan but if nobody can reach the switches it is wasted.

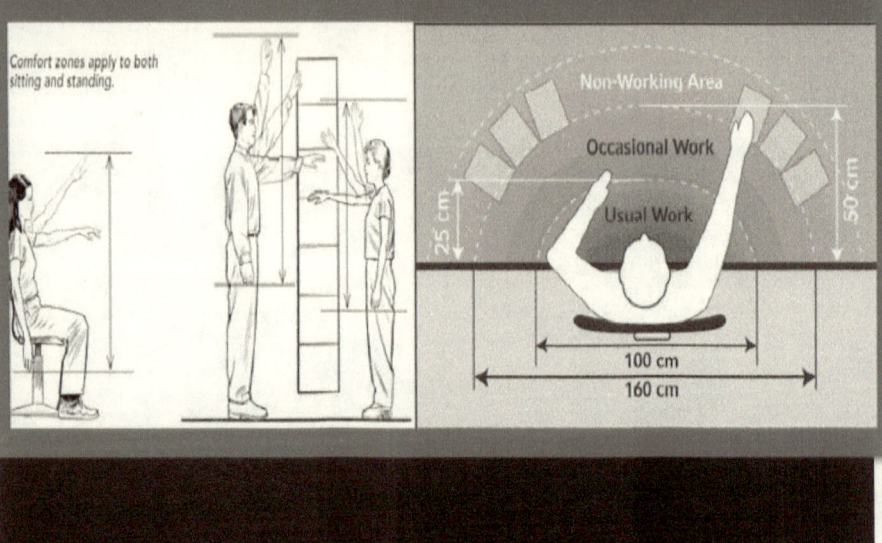

CHAPTER 18

Planning-Working Triangle

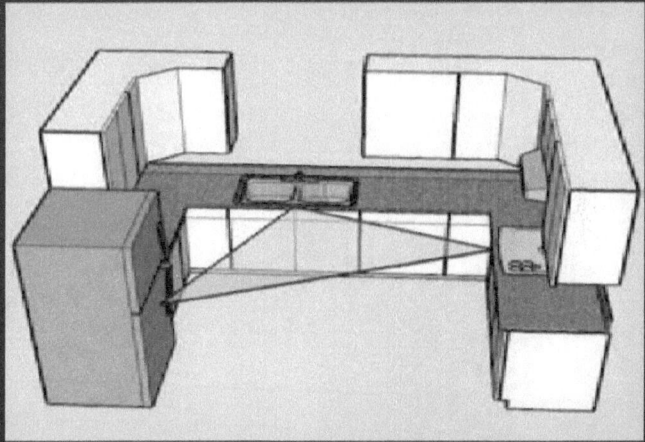

The working triangle goes back to various studies in the 1950"s and although somewhat dated it still have some relevance today particularly in basic compact kitchen design. It will have less relevance in the multi chef kitchen but still worth a consideration.

The simple principle is the concept of a measured space in which to work. The Triangle is measured between the 3 basic items in the kitchen - REFRIGERATOR - SINK - COOKER. The refrigerator represents the main access point for the PREPARATION area of the kitchen.

However it is clear that other consumables should be grouped near this area. The sink area represent the washing up or cleaning area of the kitchen. Clearly the DISHWASHER should now take pride of place in this area as does storage of related materials such as dishwashing power, rinse aid, dishwasher cleaner and the normal sink related products. The cooker probably needs a little more consideration. Basically the concept referred to an all in one stove but nowadays the oven can often be separate from the hob and of course every home now has a microwave. So there must be a consideration of all of these items and areas within the working triangle. If any one item is well outside the working triangle that must bring doubt as to the efficiency of the placement of these items. The working triangle traditionally has a minimum size of 3.6 metres and a maximum size of 6.6 metre. We would now encourage all planners to consider the size of the triangle when related to all the items within those traditional zones.

Particularly in very large kitchens we find the tall wall is commonly used. This was basically a German planning concept whereby the refrigerator and the Oven were both in tall housings or an oven housing placed next or near to a large refrigerator. We will look at this subject in a little more detail in our appliance considerations but tall walls are very questionable from a set down point of view. We will cover the essential rules for planning at the next stage but suffice to say oven set down space is absolutely critical to the safety aspect of a kitchen

and unless you have some set down space near the refrigerator this too and be a disappointing layout for the user.

REMEMBER THE KITCHEN WORKING TRIANGLE IS THE RELATIONSHIP BETWEEN

COOL - WET - HOT

Working Triangle minimum = 3.6m - maximum nominal 6.6m

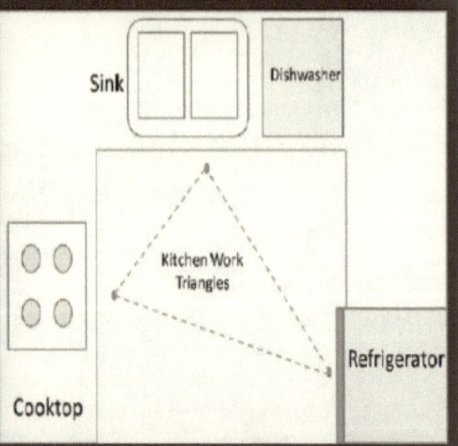

CHAPTER 19

Planning - General Considerations

What are the planning rules regarding ergonomics and anthropometrics. What are the planning rules regarding services and appliances. Are there any really rigid considerations that are peculiar to this area? Any restrictions as to service changes?

Have you forgotten anything?

What appliances does the customer want?

What sort of sink is required?

What is the best layout for the room?

What are the service preferences?

Is an eating area required?

Is there a budget?

Are there any existing appliances?

Are any appliances planned later?

What sort of style is required?

Can I duct the cooker hood to atmosphere?

Are appliance built in or feature or a combination of all these - especially the fridge?

The golden rules of kitchen planning. There are a number of rules that are quite simple and logical to follow

THE KEY RULES

300mm rule - plan for working space around hobs, cookers, refrigerators, cookers, ovens.

1200mm rule - ensure there is adequate space between facing base units

600mm rule - e.g. in a peninsular kitchen ensure there is a minimum of 600mm so that movement of appliances is not restricted - remember some appliances are 700mm or even larger - space accordingly

The 300 rule is our first one. this simply refers to 300mm being the optimum if not the minimum to use either side of a hob, or a sink, or up against a wall or around a hob or sink in an island unit. This is particularly critical when applied to heat producing appliances and particularly Gas hobs and cookers and especially Ovens next to refrigerators in either a built in situation or a built under.

IF AN OVEN IS NEXT TO A FRIDGE THE FRIDGE MAY NOT BE ABLE TO MAINTAIN TEMPERATURE.

We were on a planning course with Wickes when almost the entire hotel went down with food poising. We discovered the culprit. A commercial fan oven was right beside the main storage fridge. Salmonella developed because of the erratic heat.

IF YOU CANNOT FIND 300mm in some circumstances 100mm may be acceptable. For example an electric hob beside a tall house should be ok with 100mm but not a gas hob near a fridge housing. Also spacing appliances from a wall is vital

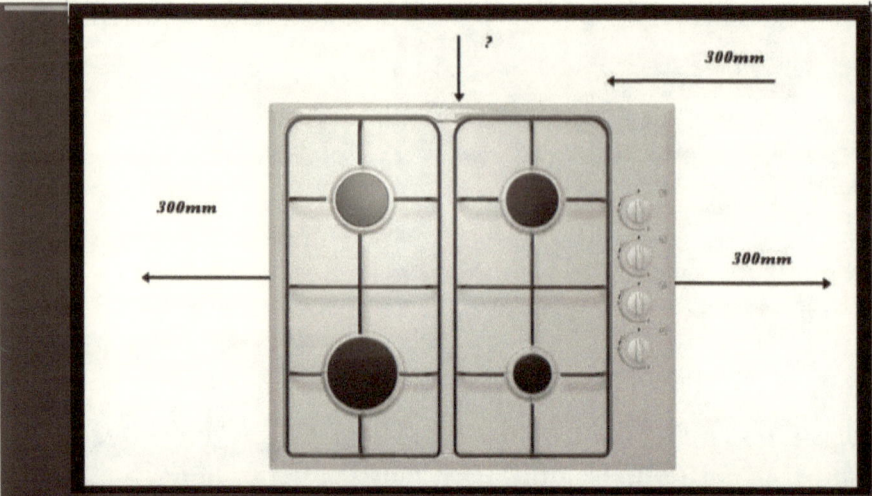

300MM RULE

All gas hobs should be spaced 300mm from - other appliances such as sinks - end of work tops, tall units-oven housings-wall. Electric hobs are similar with some flexibility

COOKER NEXT TO FRIDGE

There should be a minimum of 300mm separation of a cooker, oven, or hob from a fridge and especially a large side by side fridge. The fridge door should also open against the cooker.

COOKER AT THE END OF A RUN

A cooker or hob should never be at the end of a run and especially not in a traffic zone as the installation above. These are also very cramped kitchens.

Before

Before...

TALL UNIT IN MIDDLE OF A RUN

It is a simple rule of planning that you do not place a tall unit, such as this refrigerator in the middle of a run. Although it is 300mm from each corner it breaks up the usable worktop.

HOB AGAINST CORNER

There is insufficient space from the oven to the hob and the hob in this position is uncomfortable and could interfere with the worktop bolts and would contravene the worktop joint if moved.

CHAPTER 20

1200 Mm Rule

Facing units should have 1200mm space between. As you can clearly see this is not the case in the galley kitchen above

It is particularly important that if one working zone - in this case the cooker - faces another working zone - such as the sink in the illustration above, there must always be a minimum of 1200 mm separation for efficient working in the room.

Where two working zones do not conflict you may consider the 1000mm alternative but the door sizes must be carefully planned so they do not clash.

The only occasion where a small separation might be used is in a BACHELOR FLAT.

ISLAND 1200 RULE

American planning uses a lot of islands often where they are not suitable. The above example has two working zones conflicting - very poor planning

POORLY PLANNED ISLAND
The cooker is directly facing the island and with a drop down door would be severely compromised for comfort and safety

QUESTIONABLE ISLAND PLANNING

Although adequate space has been left in front of the cooker the space in front of the large 2 door fridge is inadequate. You would need to move the island just to position the fridge.

Check out the aga style range below. These often have plumbing either or both sides and produce a lot of heat which would be damaging to the worktops plus very uncomfortable seating opposite the cooker and too close to the sink.

CHAPTER 21

THE 600MM RULE

The is an absolute space rule from a health and safety viewpoint in that units at the end of a run or in the case of a peninsular construction - 600mm must be left as a minimum for the movement of traffic and appliances

Where we have larger appliance such as American appliances consideration must be given to these. Many U.S. appliances are 700 wide or deep and therefore this should be the minimum space. The regulation also takes into consideration the fact that in these situations there would be no doored units. If doored units were used there should be 600mm plus the door opening size.

CHAPTER 22

Kitchen Zones

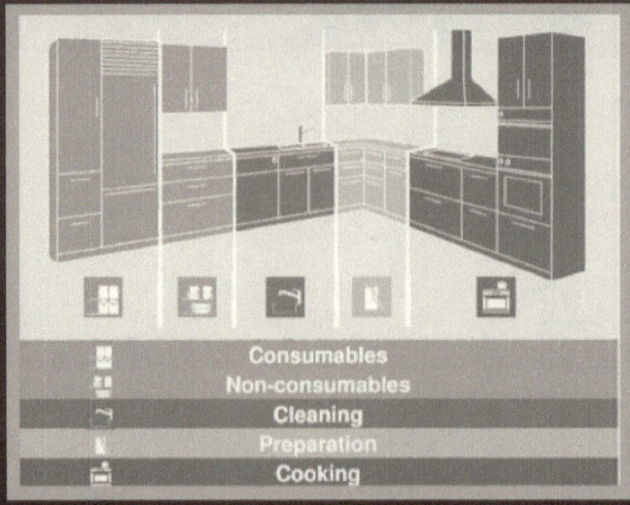

Consumables
Non-consumables
Cleaning
Preparation
Cooking

We have looked at the various planning requirements but there are other areas in the kitchens which we designate as Zones- preparation, storage, cool, wet, cooking, perishables, store cupboard, larder area, wine - perhaps you can think of more?

•Hot

•Cool

•Wet

•Preparation

•Cleaning

•Cooking Utensils

•China and cutlery

•Food storage

•Baking

•Serving

163

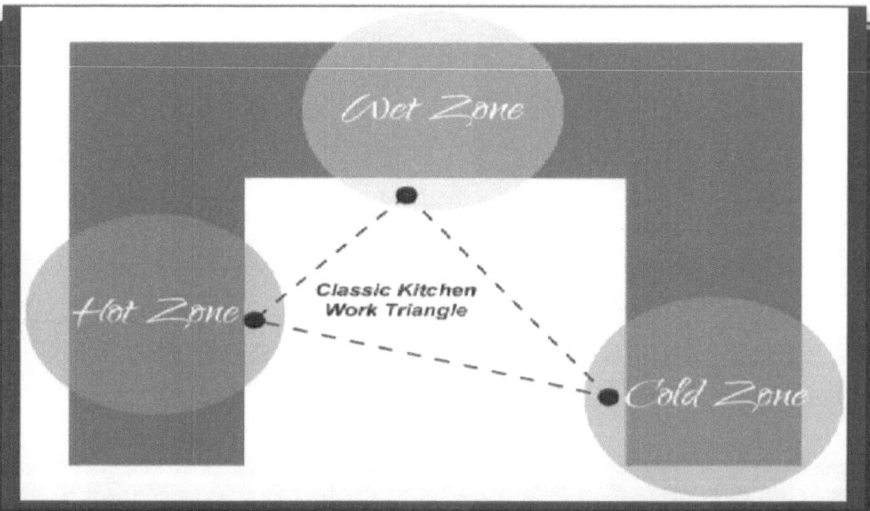

Wet Zone

Hot Zone

Cold Zone

Classic Kitchen
Work Triangle

CREATING THE ZONES
Arranging the kitchen into zones will create greater efficiency and user comfort

The kitchen zones can come in a variety of guises and many zones may be created by the Chef or the Sous Chef. For example the Sous chef might favour a microwave over for his/her main work and an Induction hob for hob top cooking. Clearly the preparation zone should be near these two facilities. For example the Sous Chef might also favour a multi function Food Mixer for his/her main dishes. As these tend to be quite large items and often with a considerable amount of accessories you may need to set aside quite a bit of storage in addition to worktop space. With the availability of 45cm dishwashers there is now clearly a case for providing the sous chef with his/her own dishwasher station. I am sure many of you

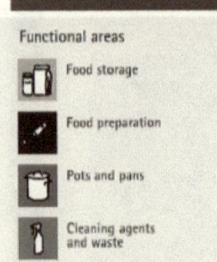

Functional areas

Food storage

Food preparation

Pots and pans

Cleaning agents
and waste

China and cutlery

THE IMPORTANCE OF ZONES
Not everyone will require the same zones and double chef kitchens will need extra zones such as baking

will already have found how difficult it is for two chefs to share the same dishwashers, especially with large mixing bowls.

Similarly with an induction hob there are many pans that cannot be used and will require separate storage and easy access to the sous chef. The sous chef

might also evolve a requirement for certain cooking dishes for the microwave station. Two chefs can easily get on each other's nerves

CHAPTER 23

TWO CHEF KITCHEN

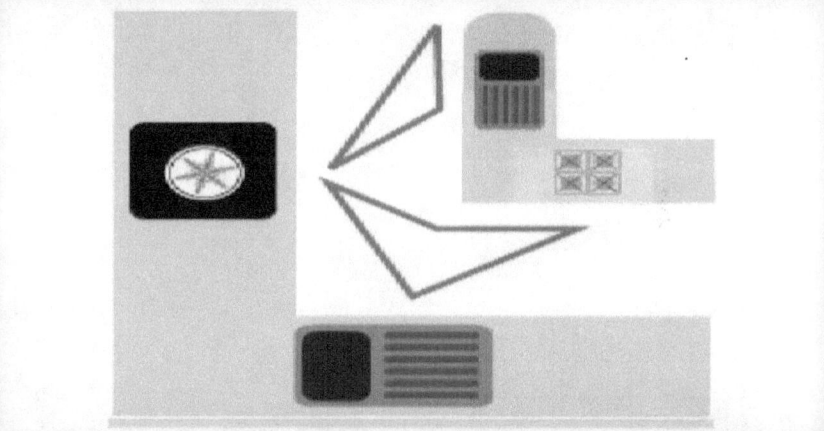

the Double working Triangle

Double Working Triangle

To make this sort of kitchen work with two chefs it must be of a quite considerable size and almost certainly will require an Island.

We will usually expect one chef to be the main chef and the other is the sous chef. the main chef will have the main triangle centred around a large sink and dishwasher, large fridge and full cooking area. The sous chef will usually share the large fridge but will have his/her own hob area - possibly specialised and almost certainly a 2 burner induction. And will usually have a smaller sink on the island which can be used for prep and cleaning.

The sous chef will usually be delegated about 1 metre of worktop space as a minimum and probably will have only one or two small gadgets. The sous chef will probably work in a 2.5 m triangle.

When we first introduced the concept of a double working triangle back in the 1980's a lot of delegates scoffed at the idea. However, today, as we know, many families have two chefs working in the same kitchen and not just as an alternative. When creating a large family meal for guests this can involve a number of dishes and some of these will be specialist dishes that Dad or one of the kids may be trying to perfect. they will want to be in complete control of their area of the kitchen and the appliances they need.

It is also very important that the sous chef does not get in the way of the main chef and can carry our his/her tasks with complete independence but still co-ordinated for the final result.

It is also quite probable that the sous chef will also be working on solus meals but will want to use their own dishes and appliances.

They say that kitchens are now 30% smaller than the 60"s but they have not considered some of these big country homes and barn conversions where the kitchens are quite enormous and can easily accommodate this kind of concept.

This sort of kitchen will almost certainly incorporate a large ice n water fridge or possibly even a his and hers fridge. Our last kitchen had just such a twin two door Liebherr fridge arrangement

As the sous chef will probably be working with the microwave this will need siting away from the main oven and there will be a hob on the perimeter and a small hob on the island

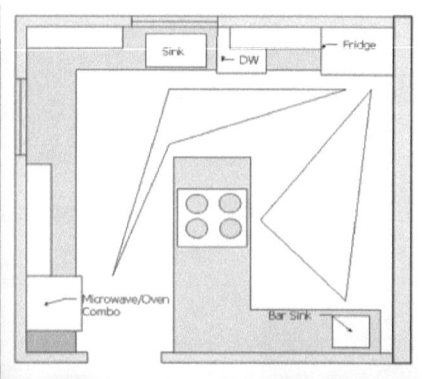

This is one of the biggest topics in planning a large kitchen in a large house with a modern house-husband who takes interes in his home and family. Many husbands or male partners have now developed a good cooking sense and will be keen to take over the kitchen on many occasions. Equally the female partner/ wife will probably resent his presence in the kitchen and certainly resent any intrusion into here kitchen working zones and areas.

It is therefore exceptionally important to provide dedicated facilities as much as possible. Certainly a sink, microwave and possibly a second oven would be of primary consideration, but there is also a case to incorporate a second, perhaps small fridge for the second chef use only and possibly even a second dishwasher.

Everyone gets their own ideas as to how they load these items so it will save many a dispute if everyone controls their own area. Indeed if you have a very large house a completely-separate adoining kitchen would be a real bonus. Unfortunately the chances of that are maybe 100 to 1

I have always emphasised the important of using the best possible and most appropriate appliances. No good having a large modern family and a 5 cu ft fridge or a 45cm dishwasher for a big household - possibly, however as a second dishwasher?

CHAPTER 24

Media Centre

Every kitchen requires a media centre of some sort if only for entertainment but much better with a full computer facility for both entertainment and information. Maybe even to order the groceries on line?

The media centre concept for the kitchen has gone way beyond the little TV in the corner perhaps with a built in dvd. Even themore sophisticated 4 in one flip down sets do not inspire the more modern households.

People are now getting used to bigger and bigger tv and bigger and better pictures. These larger screens have also come into the monitor market so it is possible to link a computer to an HD ready large screen 32" monitor or bigger. If you have got an 85" giant viewscreen in

This is not only a three door ice 'n water fridge it also provides TV, DVD, CD and has a host of computer functions. - I want one!

the living room it is unlikely you will be satisfied with a 10" flip down when you go into the kitchen.

As they have now twinned these entertainment centres to high quality and yet compact sound systems the whole market is open either for the ambitious product supplier or more probably a high quality bespoke kitchen designer with some quality fabricating equipment and/or skillful installers. With the modern solid surface materials there is no reason why an imaginative designer could not come up with something not only elegant but imminently usable as well. What better than to sit in the kitchen while the food is being prepared and doing your days work at the same time.

There are increasingly a wide range of media products that can be used in the kitchen but now is the time to make the widest possible interpretation of the products and usage.

In larger households and particularly an American household a great deal of time is spent in the kitchen which may even have a family room attached.

It is clear therefore that an entertainment centre is probably not only attractive but essential. And what about the toddlers? They will also need entertainment while mum does the chores (or maybe even a house dad?)

Clearly a computer will have an air of necessity in a busy kitchen such as this. The cook of the house will certainly want to access his/her recipes on the com-

This is a fully fledged media centre and can have a fully functioning computer such as an Apple 27" cinema screen and using a wireless keyboard you can sit at the breakfast bar and enjoy a whole media experience.

puter and perhaps even cook along with their favourite food show?

There certainly are a plethora of choices with the various wifi facilities available using an all in one computer such as an Apple with a built in or wall hung option of a computer of whatever sort and a monitor perhaps interlinking with a tablet. The options are virtually limitless and the range of costs similarly. It just takes a little understanding on the planners part.

CHAPTER 25

Kitchen Layouts

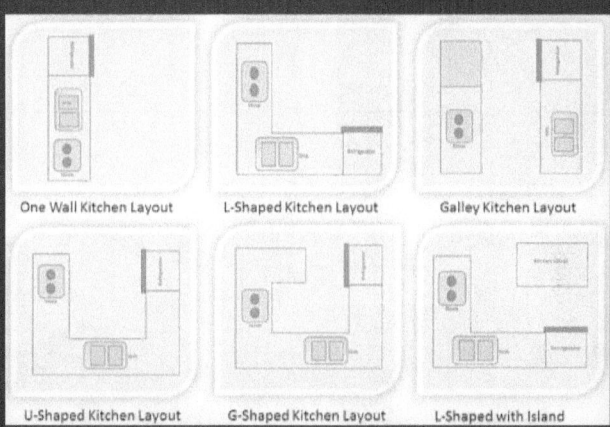

One Wall Kitchen Layout   L-Shaped Kitchen Layout   Galley Kitchen Layout

U-Shaped Kitchen Layout   G-Shaped Kitchen Layout   L-Shaped with Island

Most kitchens fall into a pattern of layouts similar to those shown here. All layouts even the 'one wall" or more commonly called an 'in line' kitchen must follow the safety and planning rules. In this sort of compact kitchen it will almost certainly require compact appliances and sink choices.

I recall attending our first Planit computer planing course in the 1980"s, This was early days for computer planning and the chief lecturer who eventually became a colleague as we took over the outside training, made a comment about how he was actually a kitchen planner himself and he was able to use the computer for planning all types of kitchens except for the circular kitchen as in an oast house for example (Planit were based in Kent) In fact producing a com-

KITCHEN LAYOUTS
standard kitchen layouts
shown here with ar
working triangle

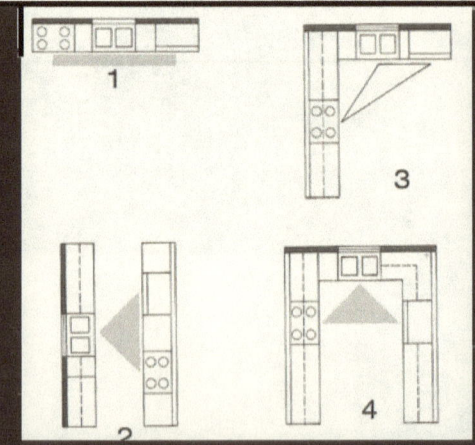

layout for this sort of kitchen is possible with almost any computer system. Just go to the auto-plan facility and change the actual units as required for appliances etc. They tend to plan simple 1000mm units in this mode but it is very quick and simple. In the final analysis the room will dictate the layout. I would however, comment that in the circular kitchen an island might have been a logical choice.

Any standard kitchen layout benefits from the simple fact that the three major zone in a kitchen - hot - cool - wet each need their own working area and ideally their own wall if possible.

CHAPTER 26

APPLIANCES

Kitchen planners often seem to believe that the furniture is the most important part of the kitchen. Frankly that is not true. If you look at the prices of appliances you can see that these are the most important. An Aga can cost over £5,000. Even a big fridge can cost over two grand.

APPLIANCES

WHAT TO LOOK FOR

•choose the best size

•45 or 60cm is standard now

FULL SIZE DISHWASHERS
Although the standard size is 60cm
there are many different basket
configurations with some of the
top German machines holding up
to 25% more than the more basic
varieties

•50cm may still be available

•table top is an option for a small kitchen

•built in as opposed to built under is possible

•always go for the best you can afford

•a dishwasher could be used 6 or 7 times a day

•look for the quality of the stainless steel

•look for the quality of the baskets

•a top level cutlery basket is the best

•always use the built in softener

•always use a quality detergent - test it

•use a cleaner regularly

I started selling dishwashers early in the 1960's, almost when I first started work. Dishwashers were actually introduced pre war but they were very crude. The older dishwashers were often top loading because of door sealing problem - very crude and not very convenient. You soon learn to recognise quality in a dishwasher. Quality stainless steel 18/8 looks and feels so much better than the cheap material used in the cheapest or even cheaper dishwashers. Look at the quality of the baskets - a

Miele dishwasher clearly has a much superior basket coating. We used to have two floors in our appliance showroom Downstairs they would sell the cheap Italian dishwashers. We refused to sell that rubbish and we only had quality - mostly German dishwashers at least 2 -3 times the price. Even in volume we sold twice as many as they did downstairs.

I was in the appliance trade for nearly 20 years before I started on my kitchen career so I developed a huge understanding of all sorts of appliances. We used to have regular meetings with Alfred Sorkin of the ERT and we would contribute numerous articles on electrical items - kitchen appliances and built in appliances were one of our forte and dishwashers in particular was a favourite topic. We tried to get the UK manufacturers to get their game in order - The old Swanmaid dishwasher was built like a tank but it was so crude it was laughable - I actually passed my Swanmaid engineer course with one of the highest ever scores - it was frankly a waste of time. Within about 2 years the Germans wiped the floor with their products.

When I started my kitchen career dishwashers were still in their infancy. We had purchased a dishwasher early on when the modern ones came through so we had been using dishwashers for at least 10 years before selling kitchens. We had grown used to the enormous benefits of a dishwasher. The typical comment was in response to the question "do you have DISHWASHER?" reply 'yes - the old man"

there was still a lot of apathy and resistance so I developed the challenge. Buy a dishwasher for your new fitted kitchen and if you want to return it for a full refund and a free unit in place of the dishwasher there will be no charge. NOT ONE PERSON EVER TOOK ME UP ON THE CHALLENGE.

In late years during the 90's when we were training hundreds upon hundreds of kitchen sales staff there was still resistance about selling dishwashers. Very few of the delegates had one or even had used one at home. It was hard work convincing the delegates of the value of the dishwasher. Cleanliness, storing the dirty dishes until washing is needed and actually more energy efficient than hand washing.

Today something like 90% of modern kitchens are sold with a dishwasher

CHAPTER 27

Washing Machines

In reality they are probably best considered as not built in or integrated but they are readily available and still readily available as integrated versions.

Perhaps for a Yuppy kitchen where the washing machine would be little used and would not want to be seen there might be some justification.

For a family kitchen with the machine being used a number of times a day it is questionable. It would also nowadays be common to have a laundry room. If there isn't one perhaps it would be best to build one.

FEATURE APPLIANCES

For hard working households feature appliances are the best value - you can get matching sets of dishwsher, washing machine, refrigerator maybe even cooking?

The washing machine is the hardest working appliance in the home after the dishwasher. Some machines are lucky to last 2-3 years and literally fall to pieces. Again always buy quality but a Miele washing machine costs around £1k in freestanding format. Feature appliances are always a way around the problem, stainless steel, orange, red. Get some matching fridges and dishwasher and you have a very presentable set.

CHAPTER 28

Sinks And Taps

The correct choice of sink and tap is crucial to the end result

What to look for

•Coloured sink can lose their looks early

•stainless steel comes in varying quality

•multi bowl sinks are best for large kitchens

•make sure the plumbing is well executed

•pull out taps have a wearable hose

•taps with external springs need cleaning

•boiling water taps have a safety issue

•waste disposals may not be allowed

•waste disposals need perfect plumbing

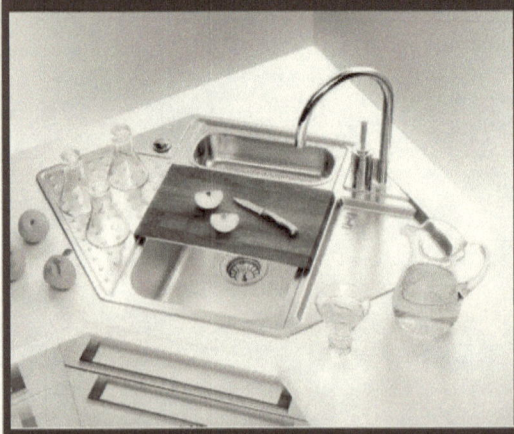
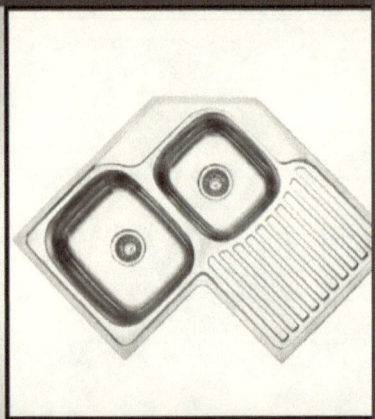

CORNER SINKS

The 45° sink is very practical the linear corner sink is frankly, not

•don't move the sink away from the drain

•check where the actual gully is before moving

•svp's can be very intolerant

•the quality of a tap is vastly important

Proper corner sinks are made for those elegant corner solutions found in Continental kitchens. Although we have been showing delegates how to use corner solutions it has not been taken up to the extent that it should have in UK kitchens. there is a lot of resistance to the old fashioned corner solutions which literally cut off the corner of the room.

This lead to a great deal of dissatisfaction from the buyer and much negative feedback to the seller. -however the corner sink arrangement is still very worthwhile in compact continental style kitchens. It is important from the plumbing viewpoint that you use a full size unit made for the corner and not just a unit turned to the corner unless you know your fitters well. The L shape corner sink is frankly used only by planners who don't have a great deal of experience and probably don't have a full corner unit in their range or have little idea how to execute proper corner solutions.

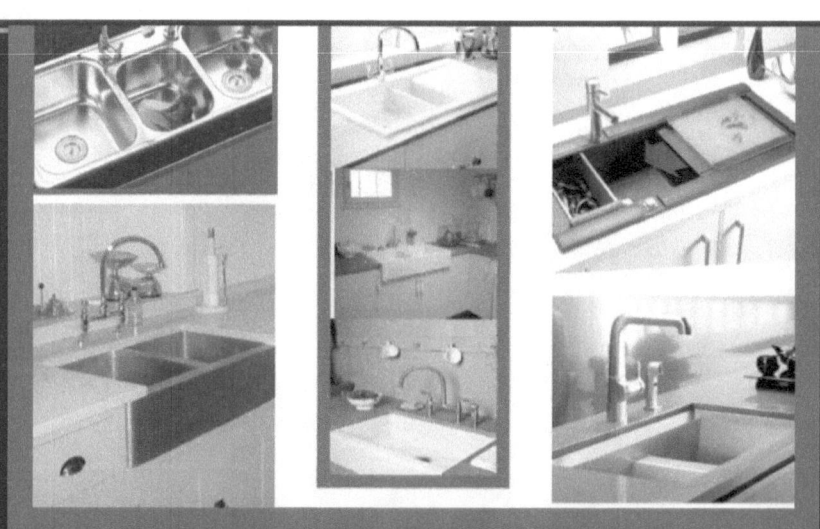

The only really practical sink is probably a 1.5 bowl stainless steel high quality sink but customers also want fashion. However this must be tempered by a little practicality - would you really want to clean a copper sink? ceramic sinks are nice but without a tap ledge?

It is certainly not ergonomically or anthropometrically sensible.

The modular sink is perhaps a thing of the past but it is well represented in the under-mount sink market for use with solid surface materials. In this guise it is probably an elegant choice but in the old traditional format - usually a round bowl and drainer - it is more of a fashion symbol than an efficient working sink.

The main problem in a conventional laminated worktop is the lack of a tap ledge and if installed without a drainer it is a dis-

aster. There are drainers for all sizes and shapes of modular sinks - everyone needs a drainer. If you imagine that the installation of a dishwasher precludes the need for a drainer you are bonkers. In a solid surface material worktop you can make the surface into a grooved drainer - not necessarily all that efficient but it does serve the purpose unless you drown the top.

The other big trouble with conventional worktops is that they blow if not properly sealed. I know hundreds of very good plumbers who never seal worktops properly or make only a token gesture. In the early days of German kitchens using top quality Duropal or Resopal worktops we were rewarded with dozens of blown tops. As these tops are higher density than conventional tops they expand more dramatically. EVERY WORKTOP MUST BE SEALED. Not having a tap ledge makes it even more unnecessarily vulnerable to water ingress.

ALWAYS USE A DRAINER AND A TAP LEDGE

Modular drainer   Modular Square drainer

Mod sink inc tap ledge   Modular sink

CHAPTER 29

Plumbing Placements

The only realy convenient place for a washing machine is in a laundry room - if not you need careful planning & plumbing.

This layout looks OK? The rule of thumb is to place the washing machine and dishwasher eithr side of the sink buto hang on a minute. One of the reasons for the rule is to have the plumbing all contained within the sink base - including the isolation valves. In this layout that is not possible. Indeed the plumbing is getting very messy and very stretched. Amateurish We also need to reconise the structural

problems. By placing the machines at the end we have had to introduce end panels which are not very attractive and structurally are not all that sound without a lot of work. Also we need to consider that a dishwasher is usually loaded from the drainer. Pointing in the opposite direction here.

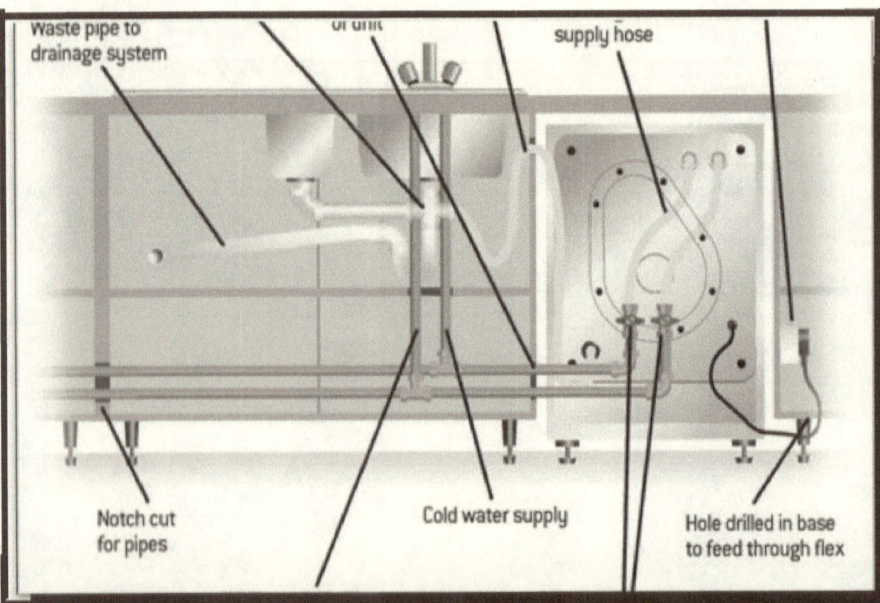

Waste pipe to drainage system

or unit

supply hose

Notch cut for pipes

Cold water supply

Hole drilled in base to feed through flex

LOOKS A GOOD LAYOUT?

On face value this looks like a professional layout. But let's analyse

We can see where the waste pipe exits the sink base probably to a yard gully straight out the back. But why so far away? The drain hose is shown going into the sink waste but very high? Most washing machines have a cut out only at the base. It is always best to use a stand-pipe for a washing machine due to the very high flow waste and water consumption. The minimal standpipe could be compromised here.

Isolation valves and water connections to the rear of the washing machine? Stop valves should always be visible and accessible without moving the washing machine. What would a little old lady of 85 do?

Socket next to the machine. Extra work and unnecessary violation of the adjacent unit. Always use a socket more conveniently sited with a control switch above the worktop. Why cut the plug off the machine and drill a hole in the base?

Seems a lot of work for a negative result

This doen;'s look a bd layout. Can we find any faults. Sure we can

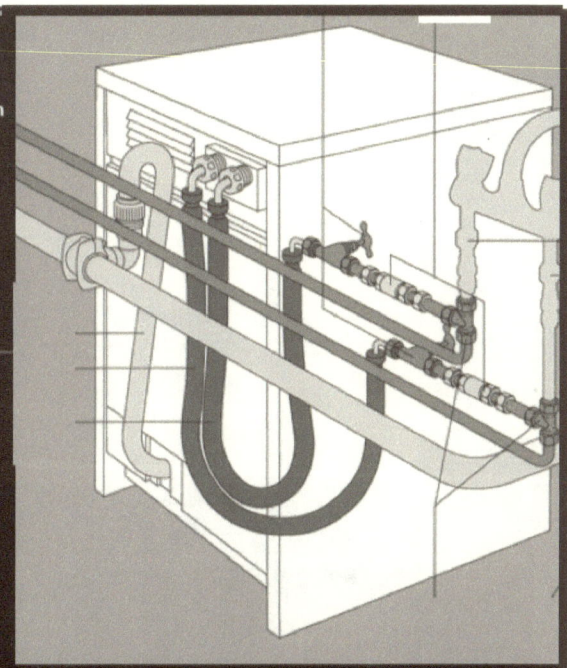

The use of stop cocks is perhaps a little questionable in this day and age. Generally service valves are more convenient and not so ugly.

The waste combination with the sink is very shallow and almost certainly will be overcome by the washing machne flow at some point. It would also probably bubble up into the sink every time the washing machine pumps out. Even in a laundry room this would not be much of a recommendation.

standpipe would join directlyinto the yard gully without branching with the sink or at the very least join with the sink waste at the lowest point possible.

Tthe worst offence is the mini stand pipe behind the washing machine. Even with a 42mm waste this would cause the machine to stick out quite a bit. The standpipe is anyway far too small. A proper

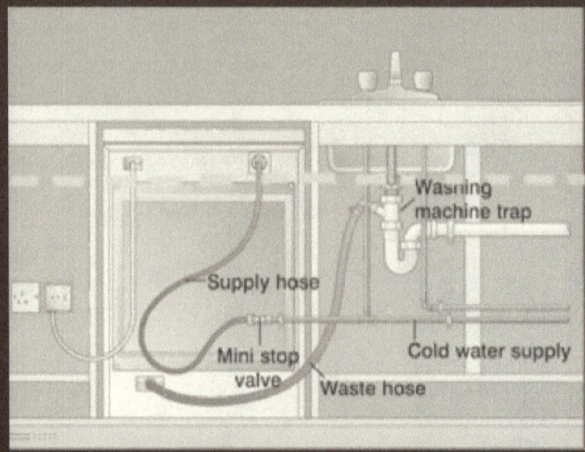

DISHWASHER CONNECTION

ALL IN ALL NOT TOO BAD AND NICE AND CLOSE TO THE SINK

This shows a connection using a diy washing machine trap. Not a problem as a dishwasher uses very little water would never compromise such a waste connection. But a stop valve behined the dishwasher is frankly ridiculous.

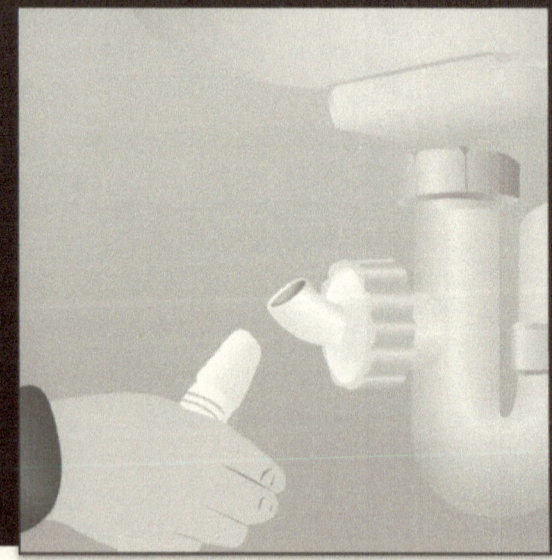

CORRECT DISHWASHER WASHING MACHINE PLACEMENT?
A modern appliance intensive kitchen. Looks a good layout?

Washing machine and dishwasher either side of the sink. Hopefully the plumbing all nice and neatly in the sink base with a high flow standpipe for the washing machine.

The dishwasher is even correctly positioned under the draining board.

But one of the problems is with the fridge. Although these is a kind of working triangle there really isn't any preparation area as such. Plus there is only an end panel between the washer and the fridge. As we know, end panels are not great structure.

Worst still the dishwasher is right near the corner possibly not even with a proper corner post. the dishwasher door would barely miss the door handles and most probably would hit them without modifying the handles

Although we are diverging from our main topic we must comment on the non use of standard notation. Solid lines are lines you can see. This shows the worktop being cut to pieces. Always use dotted lines below worktops.

So how do we accommodate the dishwasher in this configuration? would a customer in 22014 really buy an expensive kitchen - probbly 10k plus without a dishwasher. If so the sales skills of this designer need to be questioned.

Everything is quite well positioned and the kitchen offers an excellent working triangle but the dishwasher needs to go under the draining board. I would initially explore what could be offered in the way of a laundry room. It is often not that difficult to achieve even without planning permission. But if we are to leave the building intact and incorporate the dishwasher within the main kitchen layout we need to consider the possibili-

ties. The simplest would be to reduce the sink base and revert to a standard corner layoug and place the dishwasher to the left of the sink unit. The only criticism here is that you would be left with a second rate corner base. Linear corner units are not that efficient.

This room is big enough, however, for a 45° solution. You may also consider placing the washing machine - probably an existing one in the corner behind a furniture door. Very easy to do and aesthetically a huge benefit.

I once asked one of our DIY store delegates, who was a kitchen planner os som eyears experience, why he planned like this. His reply? " I think it looks good"!! I couldn't ever see the logic of that statement.

Whatever way you look at this stupid configuration it is inelegant, impractical and frankly USELESS!

•The kitchen structure is compromised

•

•The plumbing is compromised

•

•The performance is compromised

•

It is total waste of time

As I hope we have realized by now the plumbing cannot possibly be arranged to be efficient and inevitably there is going to be some if not a lot of plumbing behind the machines thereby ruining the line of the kitchen. You would almost certainly end up using extension hoses both inlet and outlet. More to leak, more to go wrong. More difficult to fit.

A WASTE OF TIME!!

NEVER DO THIS!

Here we have a perfect practical layout. Works well, doesn't look too bad. Everything is in a proper, efficient, working position.

The designer seems to have found a good, practical solution for all the problems and the installation seems as efficient as possible. Even the beam has been addressed quite well.

The only criticism would be that it is perhaps over simplistic and the towel rail space in the corner is quite material intensive without being attractive.

When you offer a simple solution like this it is always worth offering additional bits to jazz it up. You may just lose the deal to another designer with a rubbish plan but a bit of pzzaz.

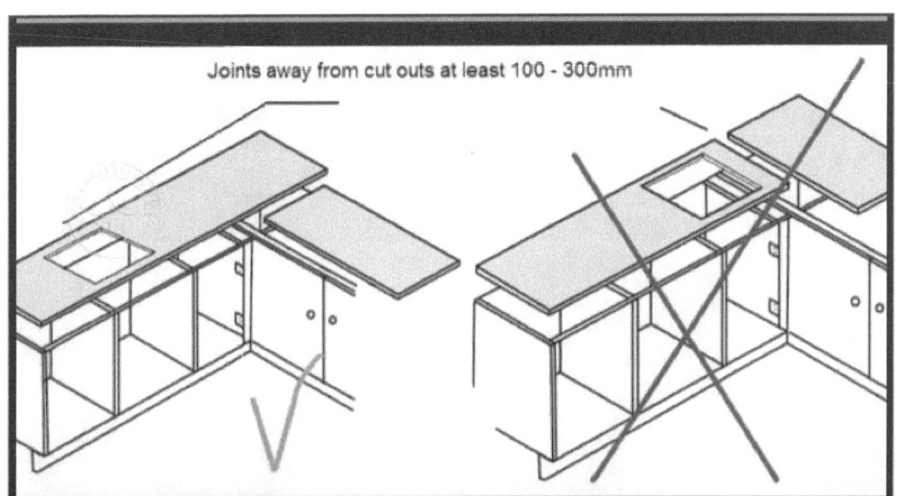

Joints away from cut outs at least 100 - 300mm

WORKTOP CUTTING
ALWAYS PLACE WORKTOP JOINTS AWAY FROM CUT OUTS. THE TWIN DISHWASHER LAYOUT IS GREAT BUT REMEMBER THE PLUMBING AND THE STRUCTURE.

CHAPTER 30

Waste Systems

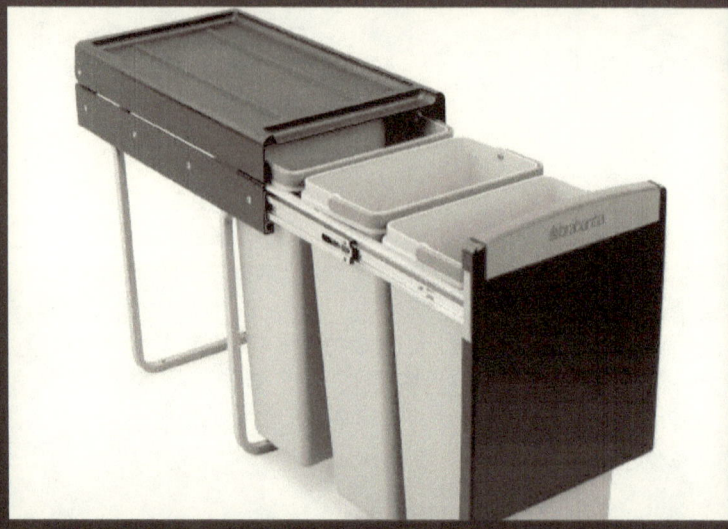

This is the age of recycling and built in recycling bins are in.

What to note

*all kinds of kitchen waste bins

*they don't need to be built in

*food waste is a particular problem

*waste disposal units may not be practical

*waste compactors may have their problems

*some sewers just cannot take WDU

*some local councils will not accept heavy bins

*councils make money from recycling

Waste bins come in probably more shapes, sizes, colours and uses than almost any other product you will buy or fit in a kitchen. We particularly like these big recycling multi bins. Frankly we have gone off the idea of waste bins in the sink unit as they are usually too small to be very practical. Although I don't mind emptying a bin once a day I would object to emptying the darn thing many times a day.

I have to confess that I have fitted hundreds of not thousands of built in swing out bins in the past but I think we need to move on a bit now..

Waste disposal units have never really been that popular in the UK. We were selling quite large quantities of W.D.U. in the 1970's and were on of the main agents for the main UK WDU distributors and manufacturers. A lot of the British suppliers favoured batch feed. i.e. you fill the unit with food waste, Fit the lid and run it for a preset period and then rinse the sludge away. A bit tedious. Most people prefer continuous feed but there are obvious safety problems and it is best not to use with young children around.

There is a big concern with plumbing. If your waste is straight to gully then OK but if it is indirect it can block and it will get expensive.. If you don't have a mains sewer system don't fit one.

There is anyway concern over the condition of UK sewers as many are very old and frankly cannot stand any real volume of the sort of sludge that would come from an entire estate of houses fitted with waste disposal units. There is actually a survey underway at present to analyse the problems this might cause. It is also worth thinking about the recycling of food wastes as this is increasingly being used as fuel. If you flush it down the waste pipe that energy is lost.

Then there is a waste compactor.. As far as I am aware these are all US products but I have seen some European models modified for Integrated use. As integrated is a dying breed I believe most people would be quite happy with a feature appliance such as the stainless steel model only about 400mm wide.

We didn't sell that many but at the price they are a premium sell anyway. Having had one since the mid 1970's I had good reason to appreciate them and a lot of reason to hate them. It is a hell of a job getting the compacted bag out. Some models now have an easy open bing area but it is not quite as simple as they make out. When we first came to the West Midlands and they reduced the garbage collection to bi weekly we had a big row with the local council and told them we had to buy a waste compactor. They retorted by not collecting at all because it was too heavy. We won in the end but we had to keep the weight down. Eventually we got used to recycling. So the issue is not yet settled.

CHAPTER 31

REFRIGERATION

What do most people dream of? How much space do you need?

What type of Frdge do you want

•American 3 door

•German quality fridge freezer

•cheap larger fridge

•stainless steel exterior

•brushed metal exterior

•separate freezer in the kitchen

•separate freezer in the garage

•Smeg style retro fridge

•side by side built under

•integrated or decor frame

•matching feature appliance

The US style 3 door ice and water fridges have dominated the 'market for' charts for some time, the American market has never really taken to integrated appliances and a great deal of their

Feature appliances started big time in the 1990;s and are still going strong. Check out the idea with the customer - they may very well be taken by the colours availalbe

built in appliances were developed many years ago before there was any rationalisation. All americans tend to think imperial measurements. But integrating this sort of fridge is not possible except in some clumsy fashion. A few were made with decor frames so decor panels could be used on some but most of these fridges are FEATURE FRIDGES - in other words they want to be seen, not covered. Also remember that products this size need lots of ventilation so do not cover without this consideration. If you place a unit above make sure there is plenty of space at the back to breathe

The other consideration and the reason why we rejected the idea some years ago is the ice and water facility. I am sure more and more buyers will not use tap water except for cooking. then why would you use tap water for your ice and ice water. There have been well documented warnings about using ice cubes in hotels. Unless you are very sure of the place you are staying you should never use ice cubes except in minute portions.

As we would never drink tap water anywhere we would never plumb in one of these fridges without a water purification system. Not a water softening system which may also be desirable but a water purification system. The costs of this would be probably more than the fridge.

The major market for built in refrigeration is still the large tall fridges These are available in all shapes and sizes and some of these have variable use compartments so you can choose it to be a freezer or a fridge. Never try to integrate a customer's existing appliance. It will never work for long it isn't designed for the purpose. At best you will get varying temperatures. At worst you could inflict the family with food poisoning.

When planning for this kind of appliance it is always worth recommending a quality product. A quality kitchen has a life of around 20 years or even more. A budget appliance has a life of 5 years or so. A quality appliance has a life of maybe 10-15 years but will still need replacing during the life of the kitchen.

Will you be able to get another product of the same size for your plan or design. Always think about the versatility of the space you are planning.

Another pitfall is the tall wall. Traditional German design often planned for tall units along one wall with the fridge and the oven. Clearly this is not good planning unless the products can breathe and you have set down space especially near the oven. Clearly however a fridge also requires set down or woking space immediately adjacent. Don't just make the kitchen pretty make it work as well.

Although the arrangement shown here looks tidy it is basically a disaster. The poor old fridge is going to suffer breathing anyway as there is no obvious ventilation and sited directly beside the oven means that there must be a considerable amount of transmitted hear and of course there will be heat spillage every time the oven or the fridge is opened. In this particular example with the freezer on the side next to the oven means that it is virtually impossible for the freezer to be able to maintain it's temperature. This will result in food deterioration in as little as a week instead of the 6-12 months aimed for.

The furniture arrangement is also clearly in doubt. What has happened to the base corner line. We can only assume that it is lost. Although there is some worktop to set down from the oven it is also under pressure from the door of the tall unit which opens directly over the worktop. This also appears to be a solid surface worktop as it has undermount sinks. Solid surface worktops actually have a very limited heat resistance - actually worse than a quality laminate top. Anything coming directly out of the oven could mean a ruined top. At the very least the top should have some stainless strips set in the to to ensure no hot pans can be set directly on to the top.

This customer probably paid in excess of £10,000 for this kitchen - they didn't get a bargain.

And so to complete our fridge considerations let's look at some other ideas. First of all the huge 20 cu foot or bigger commercial fridges require a whole different consideration. They are designed for precision temperature maintenance but they are very unforgiving and need exemplary ventilation. If you ever get stuck with designing one of these give it plenty of space and plenty of ventilation.

The next one along is a quite unusual very slim fridge. You can, of course get 200 or 300mm wine fridge but this is a conventional fridge around 400mm wide - not easy to find but very useful.

The other items are the popular built under 600mm modular fridge or freezer or combo. Usually in built under or integrated version. You should also be able to get decor panels version but these are not so popular as before and decor panels may not be easy to get hold of in many kitchen designs.

For mostg people who have considered the pros and cons of the various choices the tall fridge is probably the best buy. You can build them in or integrate with supreme ease and if you buy a really good quality product such as a Liebherr or similar you will get a product which works well and lasts for many years.

If anyone has ever designed a Jewish kitchen with the milky and meaty areas you will also know the benefit of having two of these in a kitchen with a configuration to suit the family.

The only weakness I have ever found in these products is the shelving and the baskets. These can be surprisingly flimsy and it would be nice to see some more robust designs.

As with all these choices FROST FREE is always the best possible choice but even more critical with regards to ventilation. If the ventilation is not right the frost free won't work In

non frost free fridges any excessive frosting is almost due to poor ventilation or settings.

Defrosting fridges is one of the most boring jobs on earth.

CHAPTER 32

COOKING

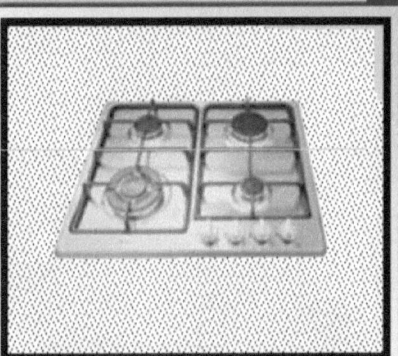

Probably the biggest subject in the kitchen

Points to Note

- What are the current facilities

- is the customer keeping the same format

- Is the customer changing from gas

- if so is there a full cooker circuit

- are the oven and hob on the same wall

- if not can we extend/move the circuit

- does the customer required mixed

- do we have both services

- if gas is it in the right position

- if not can it be moved

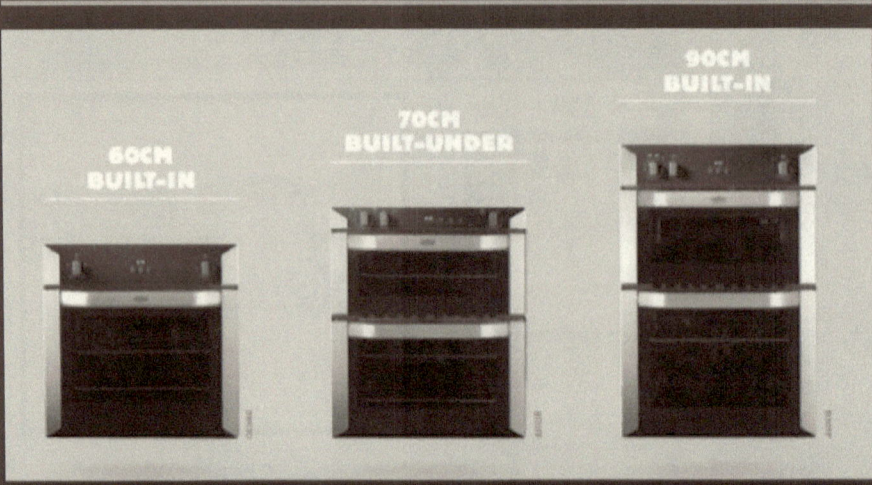

60CM BUILT-IN

70CM BUILT-UNDER

90CM BUILT-IN

COOKING AND COOKERS AND HOBS

Although the 700 mm oven is shown as built under it can also be used as a built in although with a standard 900 aperture you wold need a 200 filler.

can we provide proper ventilation in the beginning ovens and cookers were all imperial sizes and then the Continentals invaded. So they became more or less a standard size. We used to harangue the UK manufacturers for their 21" models which were growing increasingly out of date. Eventually they either confirmed or went by the wayside.

The market was dominated by Neff, Bosch, Aeg and other German manufacturers. Nowadays the Eastern Europeans are in on the act and even the Japanese.

The choice of cooking products is a huge subject and one that needs to be resolved before

the planning takes place. It is likely you will want to resite the appliances, especially in the bigger kitchens. But is that possible? I remember going on site to sort out a planning mess when we have had to channel the floor to move the gas pipe or run a 6mm electric cable across the room - not a good idea and very expensive.

If the budget is tight leave the appliances as is.

The Kitchen market i actually smaller than the appliance market. Many kitchen planners ignore the fact that the buyer is quite likely to spend more money on appliances than on the entire kitchen. Often the planner will try to go for the lowest common appliance denominator and completely lose sight of the customer's needs and aspirations. In the early days of B &

Q kitchens they sold mostly Bernstein rubbish and would put a £199 oven and hob package into the equation to finish it off. A waste of time. Only when Spring Ram came on the scene and the appliance manufacturers took more interest did they start to understand what planning quality appliances means. They still don't have a complete idea of what they are doing but they have improvide a hell of a lot since the 1980's. Planners are often actually afraid of the price - even more so than the customer. Our message was always plan for good appliances and leave the option is open for even more sophisticated appliances which you can sell as add ons. Once they have chosen the kitchen you can then spend some time upgrading the appliance choices.

The freestanding cooker was and is an excellent value for money choice. You can buy a high quality product and end up spending a lot less than ovens, hobs, housings, installation etc. In Scandinavia this is still the favourite option. When the kitchen Division of Electrolux first came to the Uk I made a big point of saying their brochure was not in keeping with UK market. Virtually all the featured kitchens had freestanding cookers - at that time the kitchen market was almost all about built ins. They failed in their attempt to enter the market. But the market changes.

The choice of hobs or burners on your cooker is many and various. In the old days we had electric or gas and most of the electric cookers were spiral radiant elements. American cookers stil have these elements but UK cookers are no

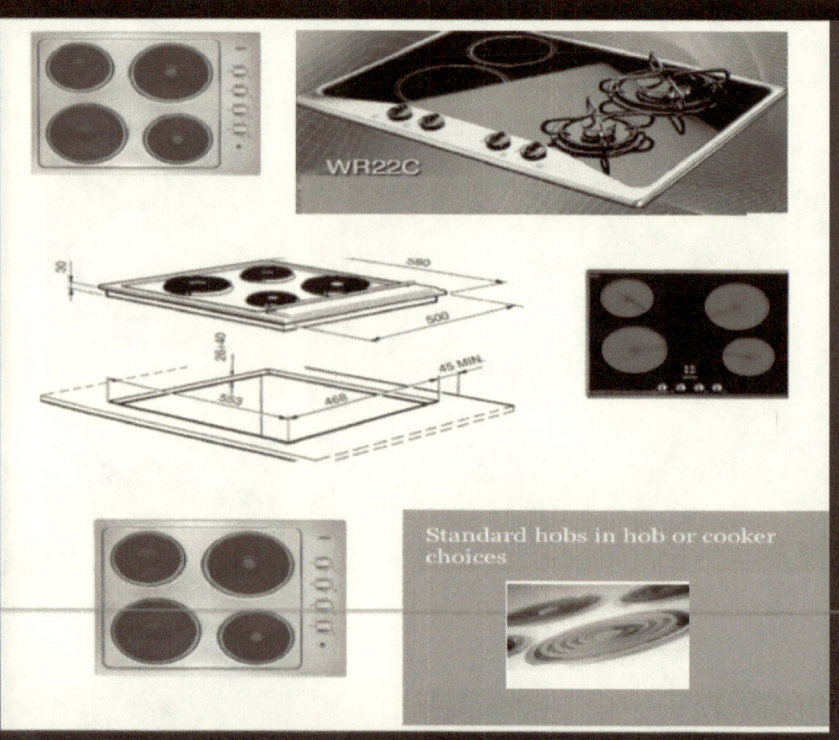

WR22C

Standard hobs in hob or cooker choices

longer using them and use the solid plates. There was a lot of resistance in the old days but we just told the customer it was like a radiant but with the gaps filled in. It was also flat all of the time and the radiant rings were never flat. The resistance faded.

Ceramic hobs came in a little later but they tended to tarnish very easily and were some-what difficult to clean. They are much better now but still not perfect. It is also true to say that the burners on ceramic hobs are often just crude wire spirals - not impressive. I would also question some of the current touch control

you are paying a fair bit for the product - BUY QUALITY.

You can get mixed gas and electric hobs and cookers with standard elements or ceramic ele-ments. However as a gas hob gets pretty mank looking very quickly I would question spendin a lot of money on this sort of hob. I would als question the wisdom of using any gas in a mod ern expensive kitchen. it may suit your cookin style but it won't stay looking expensive for long. We used to convert at least 50% to elec-tric in the old days and with modern styles of cooking probably more.

cheap - as little as £30. It hasn't yet affected the induction hob market but they are now much more compact than previous. In many cases they do fit within the worktop or at least very nearly..

Induction hobs are the one single reason why you should be able to convert at least 70-80% of customers to electric,. They are as responsive as gas, quicker than gas, much more energy efficient than gas and incredibly cleaner. As with all cooking appliancesBUY QUALITY and especially with something as high tech as an induction hob.

A good quality hob should last 15-20 years. A gas hob only looks good for about a year and then it is very sad. You can get most of the variants of style in the induction. THIS IS THE FUTURE

Domino hob s have been around for years. Always sold well in Germany, Always struggled over here. Available in , electric solid plates, electric ceramic, electric induction, gas, deep fat fryers, realistic barbecue grilles even sinks to match.

They are the designers choice and can make a really stunning array but they will take up quite a bit of space but they lend themselves superbly to the multi chef kitchen which requires different hob stations.

One thing to remember is that they need ventilation. Often a downdraught counter top venti-lator is the answer but these can be expensive and difficult to duct out.

However, for really dedicated designers they are probably the ultimate choice and receive enormous customer satisfaction.

To finish off this look at cooking we should also consider the two extremes of built in ovens.

There are number of 90cm wide by 600 high ovens but some are a bit of a cheek and only put a control panel either side to make use of the width. A well designed oven would have a drop down door the full width of the oven and consequently a 50% larger oven than normal. Using two of these in a special tall unit would create a stunning display.

At the other end of the scale you can now also get small fan overs 600 wide by 450 high.

These can create useful built under overs or built in single or double or built in to a tall unit with a working height to suit the smaller chef and perhaps even the normal chef?

In a really compact city centre kitchen where space is an expensive premium use the 45 high oven with 45 wide appliances to create a lot of work in a very small space.

CHAPTER 33

The Range

These are the customer's choices not the designers and are not designer friendly

Check out these points

•They might have plumbing either side taking up a lot of space

•they need a lot of ventilation

•they need a lot of respect for excessive heat

•the heat can also produce an overly hot kitchen

•because of the plumbing and the heat you need to be very careful with the furniture.

•you cannot bring a worktop too close to the range or the top can be damaged

•can be used with matching feature products in the same colours

•they are incredibly heavy

CHAPTER 34

WORKTOPS

This is a rather large subject which is changing as we speak. Many of us are still stuck with laminate tops and not always high density worktops. A few of us regularly sell solid surface tops but there are limitations even with this. Granite and marble abound.

We recommend always choose the best the budget can handle

We have been selling and fitting laminate worktops for something like 70 years. The early formica worktops were mainly commercial quality and as such lasted for many years. Then came the German postformed worktops followed very soon by cheap locally produced tops. Laminate tops were badly fitted and badly jointed in the early days and many still are. Metal jointing strips were cheap and practical but not pretty. The best fitters could mitre a top properly and soon the mitring jigs were quite cheap so it is common.

The big problem is sealing. Cut outs are not sealed properly, joints are not sealing properly but the worst is the sealing above a dishwasher. Most German tops now have edge sealing but even the best fitters still forget to seal the to just above the dishwasher which is then deluged with steam on a daily basis and stats to blow after only about 1 year. A complete waste. If a quality laminate top is fitted well it will last many years. Fitted badly and it might not last the year out.

Ceramic worktops are a relative newcomer and generally come from those countries that specialise in ceramic sinks. they are extremely practical but generally of set sizes and anything bespoke would be very very expensive.

Glass worktops are becoming very popular and can be fabricated in a huge range of colours and made to literally any shape and are as elegant as any solid surface worktop.

Clearly they are glass and are fragile so care is needed

Solid surface worktop shave been around for many years now and have got a lot better but they are still not as durable as marble or granite but much easier to install and much easier to use with designer flair.

The latest integral sinks also now have a stainless steel base to reduce the enormous wear in the earlier versions with completely moulded sinks. At anything up to £1000 a metre you need something that will last.

They certainly have the lasting ability there is nothing much stronger than granite Marble can stain so be very careful but is still much more resilient than solid surface.

We have shown here a very elegant corner sink solution executed in granite

Stainless steel is a great idea but with heavy duty kitchen life it can become battered and scratched. Choose wisely. It is of course the most practical and hygienic surface.

There are many kitchen specialists offering solid wood worktops. Some of the hardwoods may be ok but they all need treating not just when installed but on a regular basis and they can harbour germs unlike solid surface or the other types of tops.

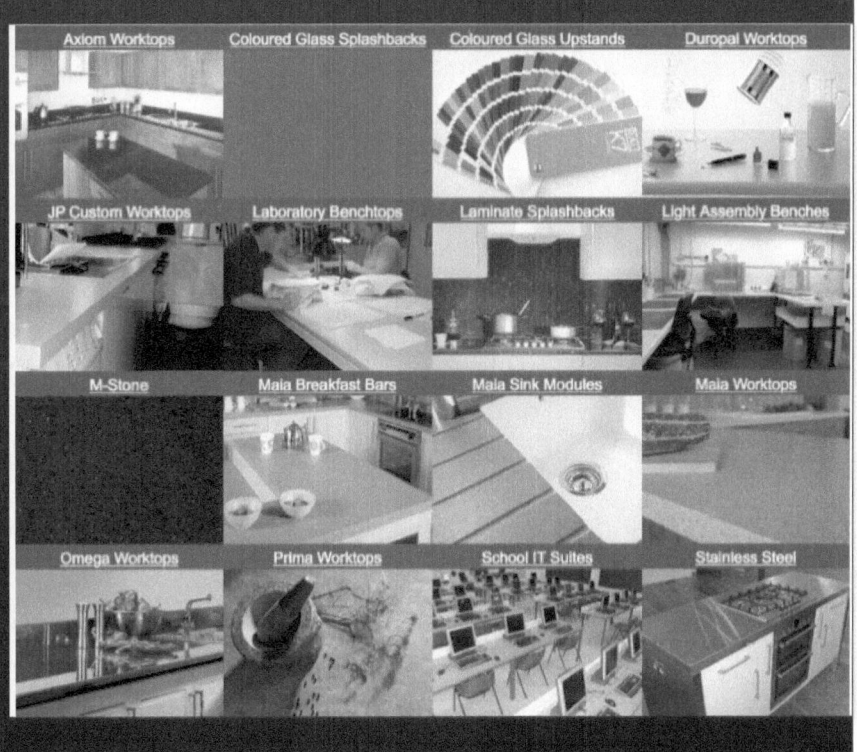

CHAPTER 35

UNITS - Cabinetry

The design and construction has changed little over the last 30 years or more. As then the best kitchens are still German made using German components. In particular Blum and Hettich have probably, the best reputations.

Types of Units	Timber
·MFC	·RIGID
·MFC HD	·RIGID - glued
·MDF	·FLATPACK
·MDF HD	·UNASSEMBLED
·Solid Surface	·COMPONENT

There are a number of
German companies in
this market but none
better than
Kessebohmer. Good
bonus sale.

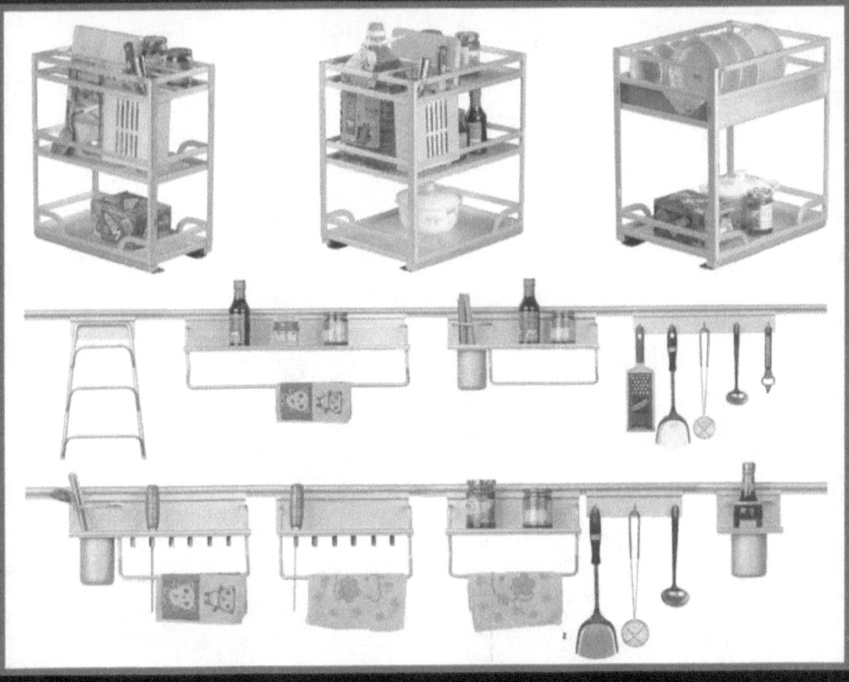

CHAPTER 36

The Mezzanine Solution

Corners are always a problem in a kitchen and linear corners are not efficient or attractive. The linear hob in the left illustration is unattractive and impractical. The 45° solution on the right is wasteful .

A linear corner is not workable either psychologically or practically. The ergonomics of a corner are quite simply unworkable for the normal homo sapien. You feel uncomfortable unless you are working against flat worktop. Try standing at the V of the corner - it feels naturally weird and uncomfortable. The L shape sink shave the same problem . They are just not natural. The hob in this illustration not only looks ridiculous it has been cut right over a worktop joint - not a clever thing to do.

The German kitchen planners and installers very early decided that a 45° solution is the best for a working corner and
set down the sizes necessary to accommodate a standard solution . Unfortunately
they didn't take it far enough and most solutions involved cutting off the corner
with a false wall - what a waste you could
bury your grandmother there.

I hope you can see in these examples th
the 45° corners are much more attractive
and actually release the corner space to b
a real working space. But wasting all tha
room?? There are occasionally excuses fo
doing this possibly because there is a chi
ney in the corner or a large flu. But for n
reason?

The other problem with the 45 corner is
the worktop. Early worktops were only
available in set sizes so to find a top to fi
the entire corner is difficult and expensive. At best you might just manage it ou
of a Duropal 1000mm double round and
in most cases you would have to source a
1200 double round to do the job effi-
ciently. Very expensive

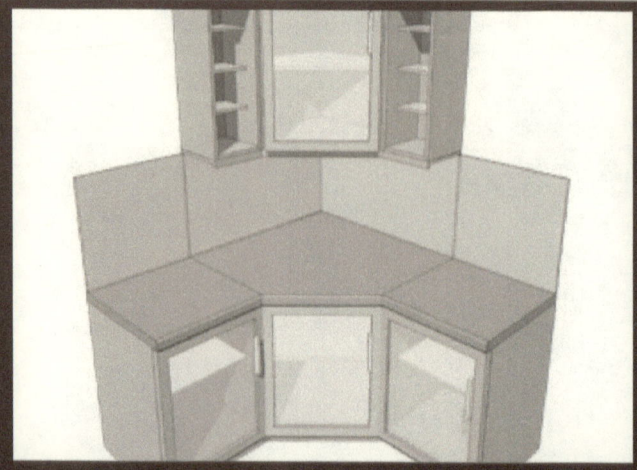

SPECIAL CARCASSES AND WORKTOPS

The standard size full corner base unit is fitted for a 400mm door but for practical purposes any size could be made but the larger doors would need a bigger carcasse

The other problem is the unit used for the corner. In the case of an appliance that is no problem and the extra space can be very useful to accommodate the services. A dishwasher or a washing machine needs plumbing so that will be taken up by the extra space.

Clearly the most efficient use of the 45° corner is for an appliance but any 45° corner significantly enhances the design and means that you have smaller linear worktop sections. This is a big bonus for handling especially with the heavier tops

such as granite and marble. I think you will agree that the 45 is a hands down winner but we still have the worktop problem.

So how can we make this more efficient and better positive feedback.

The idea of the mezzanine shelf started to germinate early on but it was when we were funding our own showrooms - mostly on a shoestring - we realized there must be a better way and so the mezzanine shelf or top was born.

THE MEZZANINE SHELF
A SIMPLE - ELEGANT AND VERY PRACTICAL SOLUTION

Quite simply the idea was to use only standard 600mm worktops which are readily and cheaply available. That means the mezzanine shelf is a separate small piece placed usually around plinth height at the read of the corner solution. You can even use the sink cut out on many occasions with a separate edging material such as wood edge.

The result is very attractive but also more welcoming than the expensive over-size top. As the mezzanine is higher than the surround worktops anything placed on it is more accessible even behind a hob.

This solution can be executed in all worktop materials and is a real money saver and yet is a much more exciting solution thn the alternatives. Just have a look at some of these various worktop solutions including tiled areas.

We have presented this solution over many years but I have to say that with the DIY stores we used to have a lot of apathy towards even such an obvious benefit.

THE DESIGNER MEZZANINE

This could be an appliance or just a working corner. Perhaps even with an illuminated perspex of toughened glass panel in the front of the mezzanine

Strangely we had much more success with the Dutch and the mezzanine solution appeared very early in many kitchens planned in the Netherlands.

We have also used the same method to create linear worktop extensions and have used this in conjunction with duplex tops to avoid complicated jointing. In a corner you can use different heights for the corner than the adjacent tops and therefore only butt joints.

Check out this versatile corner solution but note here that we have proposed a glass fronted mezzanine which could then have a stunning lighting effect as shown in the mock up here.

For standard corner base units with 45° doors it is possible to get the carousels with a completely circular profile instead of the V cut for L shape corner base units

CHAPTER 37

SERVICES

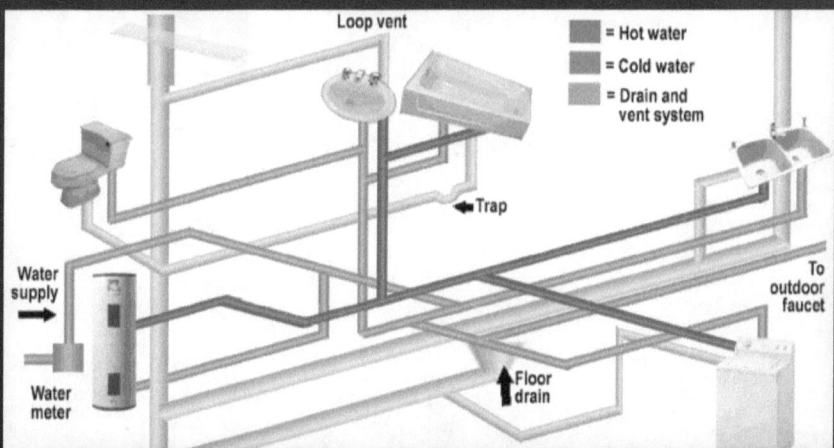

This has long been a problem area. Most delegates don't want to know but to be an efficient designer you have to know at least the basics. I would urge you to at least get to grips with the essentials of DIY services.

Points to Note

•Where is the gas meter

•is it a smart meter

•where is the main gas supply in the kitchen

•is the customer retaining or installing any gas appliances in the kitchen

•is the boiler in the kitchen

•is the boiler being replaced

•can the boiler be furniture fitted

**Take care,
Be Gas Safe.**

SERVICES
What do we need to know about gas?

•do we have a leaflet for the boiler

•what are the ventilation requires

•is the boiler outlet anywhere near the cooker hood extraction

Gas is nasty stuff. `Produces enormous amounts of wasted heat and the user tends to have it blasting away at top heat no matter what they are doing. This also makes it very hard work for your dishwasher so can lead to customer remorse if they cannot clean their dishes properly.

Still think yourself lucky you will hardly ever find a gas refrigerator any longer.

The mains points you need to look at are the meters and the boiler.s Deal with the meters by encouraging the customer to have a SMART METER which is a once only job and never needs reading again and hopefully you can resite the meter outside the kitchen and so solve your planning problem. If not make sure the meter is very accessible as the meter reader will never bother to scramble around a cupboard to read the meter.

Smart meters should be recommended for all new installations

In the case of the boiler most boilers can be housed but watch for the manufacturer's recommendation - get a leaflet.

In the old days we used to encounter big old fashioned meters gas and electric in the corner cupboard or other very unhelpful positions.

Many a time we have boxed them in only to be harangued by the meter read because he couldn't read it.

Frankly you should not get involved and you should automatically ask the customer to get smart meters installed. The energy companies now recommend this and it is often FREE. Once the meters are moved they should be outside the kitchen and often in the outside cupboard. Access is still required for any possible maintenance or upgrading but other than that it will not interfere with your kitchen design.

If the customer gets any resistance from the energy company have a word yourself. Sometimes they will acquiesce when they realize it is hampering a major job.

If you really have to box them in, do so in the largest unit you can accommodate in your design and make sure they are readily accessible as sooner or later they will have to be moved and replaced with smart meters. Just think of the money the energy company saves by not using meter readers.

Placing boilers in a cupboard is a confusing problem. Many opinions will say that if it is a room sealed boiler it doesn't matter. But in most cases it does. You need space for heat and for access/servicing. If you enclose the boiler and the servicing company can't get access you will be in major trouble.

This is the General Guidelines

The amount of ventilation required will vary depending on if your boiler has an open flue, a balanced flue or a room sealed flue. Ventilation requirements vary vastly so if i were you i would contact the boiler manufacturer and ask their advice or go on the internet and source the information. All boilers have a GC number. Gas Council number. This is a seven digit number that is displayed on the data badge on the inside casing of the boiler. This is the models exact make. With this information you can go online and source the ventilation requirements for your boiler. Older boilers will require HIGH AND LOW VENTILATION. NON CLOSABLE AND NON FLY SCREENED WITH MINIMUM HOLE SIZES OF 5MM PER HOLE. Most people don`t realise that if a boiler overheats in a cupboard and burns a house down that ignorance might affect your house insurance. Lastly ,new condensing boilers normally don`t need ventilation requirements as they run cool BUT WILL REQUIRE AROUD 5MM ON THE SIDES AND AROUND 150 MM TOP AND BOTTOM FOR SERVICING

Regs for Calor gas or oil are very similar.

ELECTRICS

As with all services only qualified and registered fitters should do the work

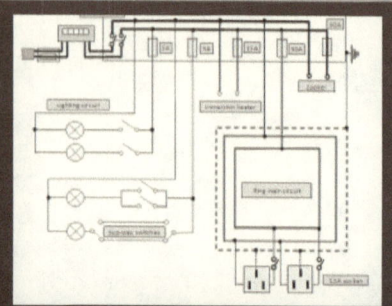

Points to Note

•If major rewiring is necessary it is best to install a dedicated ring main for the kitchen

•if you are mounting a hob and/or an oven make sure the cooker circuit is at hand or can be resited.

•You can route the cables via the furniture but make sure it is ducted or covered

•small appliances are not too energy greedy but even kettles are 3kw these days.

•Plan for plenty of sockets there is usually no restriction depending on floor space

•You should not fix switches and sockets to the fabric of the kitchen units unless it is a separately regulated circuit i.e for a waste disposal.

•

electric
safe

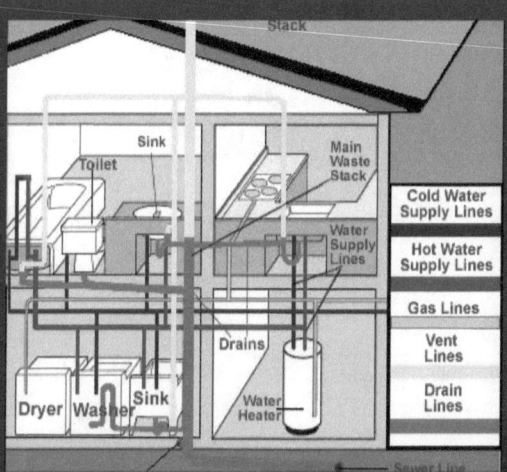

Stack

Sink

Toilet

Main
Waste
Stack

Cold Water
Supply Lines

Water
Supply
Lines

Hot Water
Supply Lines

Gas Lines

Drains

Vent
Lines

Dryer Washer Sink

Water
Heater

Drain
Lines

Sewer Line

PLUMBING

Kitchen plumbing is fairly simple - don't complicate it

•

•Important Points

•If you have a washing machine and a dishwasher in the kitchen put them either side of the sink never side by side.

•don't use extension hoses unless essential

•note the position of the stop tap- if it is within the kitchen area make sure it is accessible and make sure it works

•check the waste run - make sure it is efficient for both the washing machine and dishwasher. The nearer the gully or the svp the better.

•don't plan for cheap plastic Y adaptors. If the customer cannot afford a proper plumbing job they probably cannot afford your kitchen.

•American ice and water fridges need plumbing

CHAPTER 38

VENTILATION

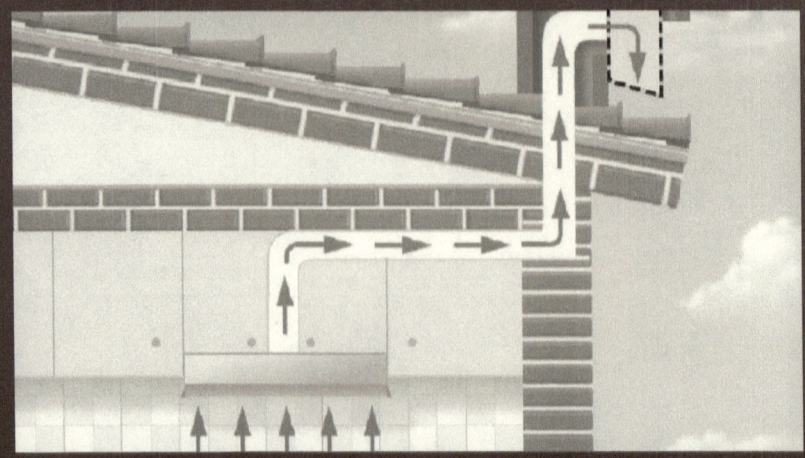

It is very amateurish to design a kitchen without ventilation - and it must be ducted not recirculating. Omit it and the kitchen will quickly deteriorate.

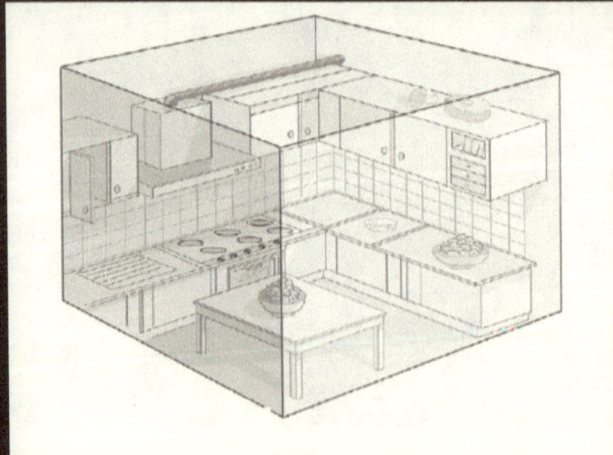

CHAPTER 39

LIGHTING

What a subject you could probably write a whole new book about kitchen lighting. Suffice to say it is one of the most important aspects of any Kitchen. This very pretty kitchen seems well lit but there is no worktop lighting?? Remember led is king

Remember a kitchen needs to b e hygienic and lights do tend to collect the muck.

Downlighters are now a bit passe but by using the new LED replacement bulbs there may still be place??

Worktop lighting is clearly the most important lighting feature in a kitchen - you need to see clearly where you are working and perhaps reading recipes?

CHAPTER 40

DESIGN - BESPOKE

This section requires a real dedicated designer who has the ability to visualize a design study but even more importantly must be able to execute the project. It is pointless designing a dream that no one can create. Design can be traditional or modern

The definition of design is rather tenuous but essentially it is using your chosen product in a more imaginative and innovative way and probably adding to or modifying the basic units to provide a more attractive and hopefully efficient end user experience.

What design isn't is to offer arty farty creations that frankly don't work but may look ok. To be brutally frank thE kitchen on the next page works on an aesthetic level but as a practical working kitchen it is a joke. The tall wall is simply unworkable and the fridge would struggle to keep it's temperature. There is very little usable worktop space for the ovens or the fridge.

For such an expensive kitchen there appears to be no preparation area unless that was the intention of the island and its small circular bowl. But the little bowl in a not too convenient position needs a bit of rethinking. But it is very pretty and with some re-thinking on the tall wall I am sure that it would make both a stunning looking kitchen and a quality working kitchen.

41

KITCHENS & APPLIANCES OF YESTERYEAR   (1950 STYLE)

In the early days of built in kitchens the continentals forged ahead quite early. The Brits and the Yanks still produced some reasonable products but it was the German manufacturers leading the charge towards quality and standardised product.s In the UK the standard oven size was 21". In the States the standard size was more like 27". Both sizes were very difficult to accommodate in modern metric units. The Yanks still tend to use the odd sizes but the Continentals have moved to a 700mm size which is closer to the American Idea. By the time the Brits caught up with the size issue most British companies were dead or dying.

This is a 1950 built in oven - doen't look too bad but modern chefs will miss the drop down door but probbly be happier with the analogue timer.

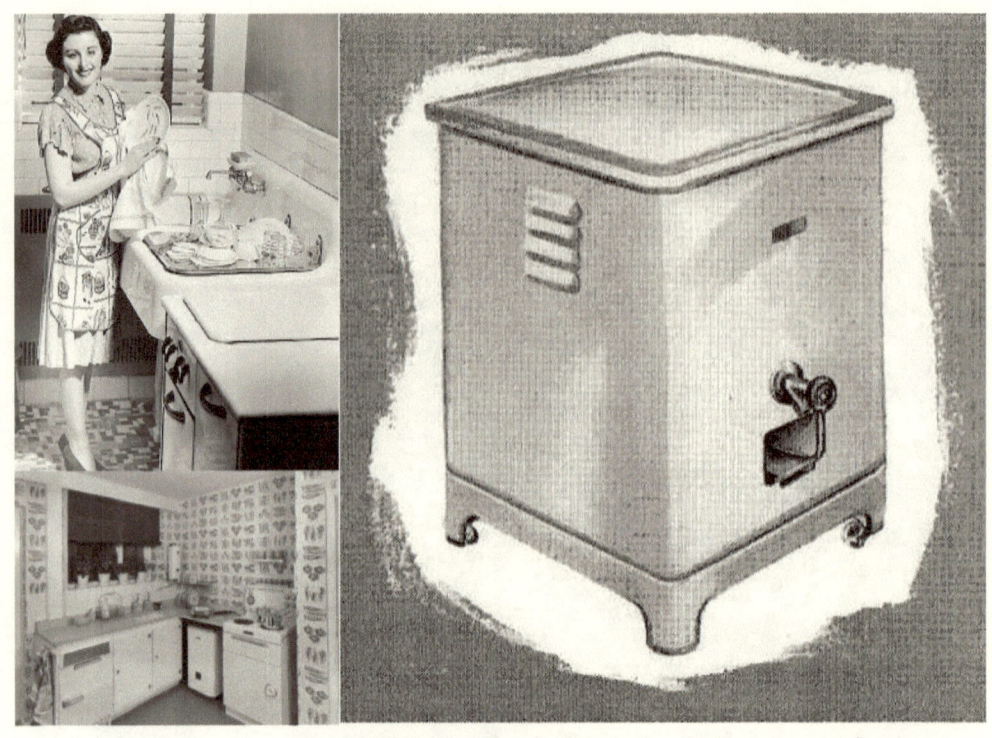

21. Gas-heated Washing Copper with vitreous enamel outer casing, tinned copper pan, chronium plated draw-off tap. 19″ square, 26½″ high.

An amusing little montage of 1950's appliances. Top left the dishwasher of the day - Mum with her cast iron kohler sink. Below a typical kitchen of the day, although fitted was beginning to make headway.

The washing machine is left over from a bygone era - thank god but they were easy and cheap to repair.

Do you remember the
Bauknecht mini kitchens
of the 60"s and 70's.
This is a predecessr - a
bit strange and doesn't
bit the mini tag very
well

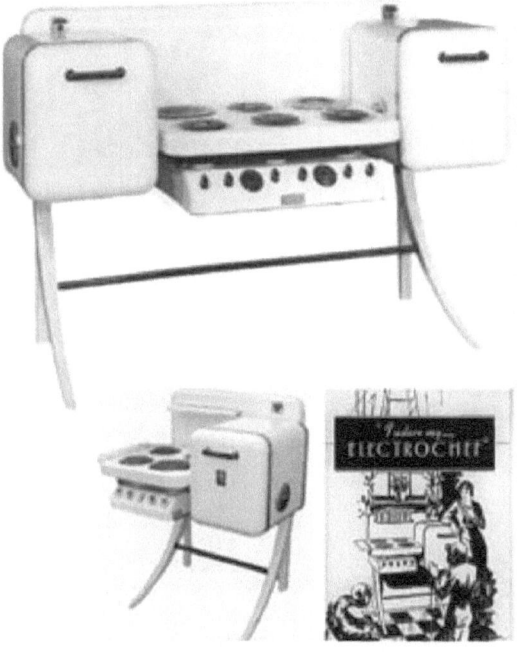

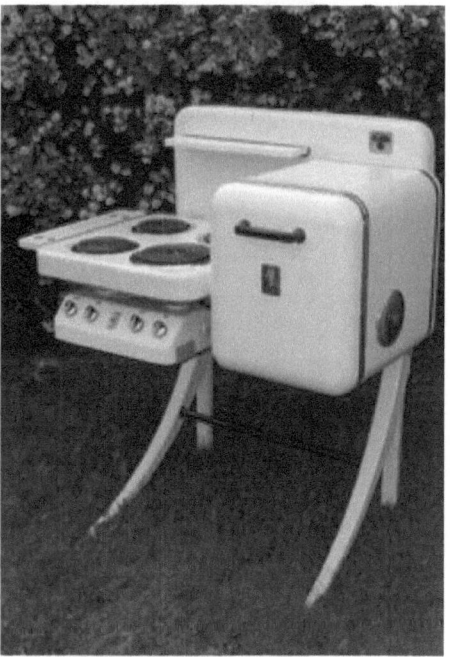

We have some weird products on this page mostly not 1950's but the slim top loading mchine was very popular a few years later.

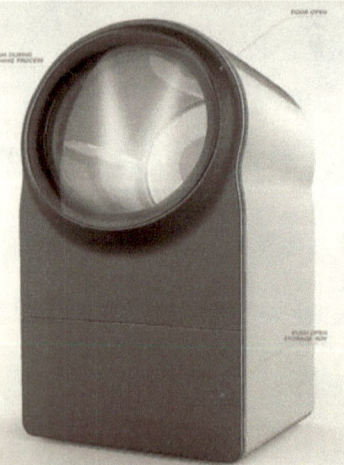

On the following page we have the rather wonderful Westinghouse auto washer which we

bought in 1954- very stylish. Dad bought it for Xmas from Patti-
sons and we sat and watched it thrpough a complete cycle.
Better than TV - we sat enthralled.

This shows a couple of
typical 1950's kitchens -
depressing isn't it.

The kitchen below is a better example of a 1950's kitchen and the one on the right is what 1950 thought a future kitchen would be.

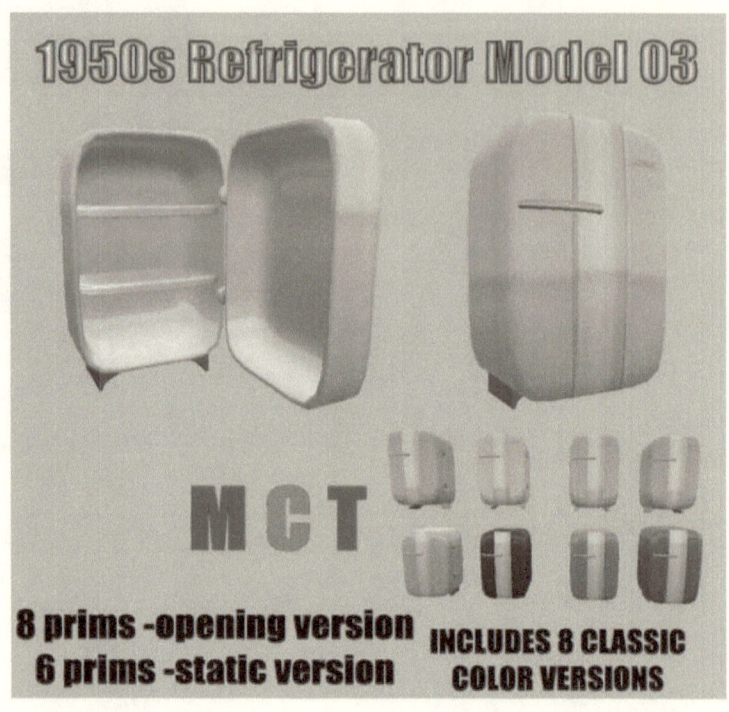

I don't think you can describe these refrigerators as anything but weird.

On the next page we have an image of a 1950 wood kitchen. Not to bad under the circum-

stances especially with the limited range of refrigeration.

But on the following page we have a 1950 media centre. Amazingly prophetic.